Disappearing Object Phenomenon

ALSO BY TONY JINKS

*An Introduction to the Psychology of
Paranormal Belief and Experience*
(McFarland, 2012)

Disappearing Object Phenomenon
An Investigation
TONY JINKS

McFarland & Company, Inc., Publishers
Jefferson, North Carolina

LIBRARY OF CONGRESS CATALOGUING DATA ARE AVAILABLE

Names: Jinks, Tony, 1970– author.
Title: Disappearing object phenomenon : an investigation / Tony Jinks.
Description: Jefferson, North Carolina : McFarland & Company, Inc., Publishers, 2016. | Includes bibliographical references and index.
Identifiers: LCCN 2016041155 | ISBN 9780786498604 (softcover : acid free paper) ∞
Subjects: LCSH: Parapsychology.
Classification: LCC BF1031 .J559 2016 | DDC 130—dc23
LC record available at https://lccn.loc.gov/2016041155

BRITISH LIBRARY CATALOGUING DATA ARE AVAILABLE

ISBN (print) 978-0-7864-9860-4
ISBN (ebook) 978-1-4766-2451-8

© 2016 Tony Jinks. All rights reserved

No part of this book may be reproduced or transmitted in any form or by any means, electronic or mechanical, including photocopying or recording, or by any information storage and retrieval system, without permission in writing from the publisher.

Front cover images © 2016 iStock

Printed in the United States of America

*McFarland & Company, Inc., Publishers
Box 611, Jefferson, North Carolina 28640
www.mcfarlandpub.com*

For my family

Table of Contents

Introduction   1

Part I

1: Jottles Are More Than Disappearing Objects   7
2: A Typology of Jottles   14
3: Additional Features Applicable to All Jottles   29

Part II

4: How Prevalent Is the Phenomenon?   35
5: Collating Case Studies—Finding the Common Threads   71
6: Thinking Skeptically About Jottles   76

Part III

7: A New Approach   97
8: External Agents   124
9: Human-Centered Causes   141
10: What Are Jottles? (In My Opinion, at Least)   157

Chapter Notes   167
Bibliography   175
Index   181

Introduction

> Whenever a set of unusual circumstances is presented it is in the nature of the human mind to analyze it until a rational pattern is encountered at some level.—Jacques Vallée, *Dimensions*, p. 164

Early one evening in August 2008, Kate left work and drove across town to her modest two-bedroom suburban home where she lived alone. Pulling into the driveway, she switched off the car's ignition and extracted the key—one of many on an overloaded key ring. Fumbling through the set as she walked the few short steps to the porch, she found the front door key and inserted it in the lock. As the door swung open the sound of a ringing phone drifted up the corridor. *That's Michael about tonight,* she thought as she dropped her handbag and charged down the hall in the hope of taking the call before it stopped ringing. She got to the phone just in time, and spent the next few minutes making arrangements for later that evening. With plans finalized, Kate returned to the porch to fetch her bag and keys. The bag was where it had fallen, but the keys were no longer hanging from the doorknob. Kate's mind was blank. She *knew* she'd used the keys to enter the house and was quite certain she'd left them in the lock. Even if they had been left dangling from the lock, surely they wouldn't have been stolen, would they? The street was empty, and the bag was left untouched. These questions raced through Kate's mind as she retraced her steps to the car, although she knew the keys couldn't be anywhere along the front walk. Having no luck exploring the driveway, she returned to the house and examined every inch of the garden beds around the porch, as well as inside the door, under the hallway rug and behind nearby furniture. Nothing. Out of sheer frustration (and her date now cancelled), Kate spent the remainder of the night turning the rest of the house upside down looking for her keys, but they were nowhere to be found.

A few years later, and in a distant city, Mark and Courtney were curled up on the sofa in their sparse but tidy living room, watching television. During a commercial break Courtney raced to the kitchen to get a snack, giving Mark the opportunity to switch channels. Apprehensively, he used the TV remote control resting on a nearby cushion to find better viewing, then returned the control to its original position. As he expected, Courtney complained loudly upon her return about Mark's choice of show, so reluctantly that he reached for the control once more—but it was no longer there. Curiously, he looked down at the cushion, then behind the cushion, then under the cushion. Dragging himself up from the sofa, he jiggled his clothes in the expectation that the control would fall to the floor, having been tangled up in his shirt or trousers. Nothing hit the floor. With Courtney's help, Mark physically removed all the cushions and shook them vigorously, but to no avail. He and Courtney then used their hands to feel around any crevice that might hide a large black plastic object. Exasperated, Mark turned the sofa upside down on the off chance the remote had somehow worked its way underneath. Still no luck. To the amusement of Courtney, Mark expanded the search area and spent the next thirty minutes crawling on his hands and knees in an increasingly desperate attempt to locate the missing item. Finally he gave up and came to the uncomfortable conclusion that the TV remote had literally vanished from the face of the earth.[1]

These two stories are examples of the *Disappearing Object Phenomenon (DOP)*, also labelled *Just One of Those Things ("JOTT" or "jottle")* by paranormal writer and researcher Mary Rose Barrington.[2] Both expressions suit the events reported by Kate and Mark. However, I prefer the second phrase because it captures the essence of a mysterious disappearance—it's *just one of those things* that occurs now and then and life goes on as usual. In deference to Barrington's pioneering work I'll appropriate her versatile neologism "jottle" to describe situations where objects behave in the fashion of Kate's keys or Mark's remote control.

Type "jottle" (or "DOP") into an Internet search engine and a list of Web pages will pop up on the screen. These are usually a minor component of much larger sites exploring various weird and wonderful paranormal occurrences.[3] Jottles are therefore considered a paranormal subject in the fashion of flying saucers, ghosts and psychic powers. Michael Thalbourne, in his book *A Glossary of Terms Used in Parapsychology*, suggests paranormal events are *miraculous*,[4] and this word certainly fits Kate and Mark's experiences.

Then again, jottles *aren't* like flying saucers, ghosts and psychic powers. After all, everyone is familiar with alien abductions—in a Western context at least. This doesn't mean you necessarily believe abductions are real. Indeed, you might be militantly skeptical—but you're at least mindful that UFOs allegedly originate from "outer space" and abductees claim they've been kidnapped by small grey aliens with big black wraparound eyes. You're also aware that many people profess to have witnessed the residual image of someone who is now dead (a ghost), and that there are individuals who swear they were once thinking about a long-lost friend seconds before that friend phoned them—a purported example of psychic precognition.

Jottles are different because this is one of those obscure paranormal topics people are either vaguely familiar with or they've never heard about it *at all*. For most, to learn about jottles is to experience them personally, and since these *experients*[5] don't possess existing knowledge of the phenomenon they will embark on a maddening search to find out if anyone else has lost objects in similar circumstances. Their first port of call is—naturally—the Internet. With regard to object disappearances, there are sites which list "classic" stories like Kate and Mark's, although there's no serious attempt to separate "good" (high information) cases from "bad" cases. Nevertheless, experients might find comfort in reading the tales of others and conclude that they're not alone in being targeted. Of course, experients also want to know *why* their keys or remote control mysteriously disappeared. So alongside the haphazard assemblage of strange cases a variety of *explanations* exist for disappearing objects. Perhaps a poltergeist lurks in the experient's house, or maybe fairy-folk are playing tricks on them? Alternatively, there might have been a distortion in space and time—something to do with "wormholes" or "parallel universes"—where these objects are transported, never to be seen again. After a few minutes of perusing these enjoyable (but ultimately unhelpful) solutions the experients might add their own stories to the blog, and then forget their "disappearances" ever happened.

This makes jottles very different from more popular paranormal topics, where believers vastly outnumber actual experients. For instance, lots of people believe in UFOs without claiming to have actually *seen* one. However, it's unlikely people will believe in the reality of jottles unless one of their possessions has disappeared in mysterious circumstances. That doesn't answer the question of whether jottles are real. Surfing around the Internet, it's very difficult to find valid research of the phenomenon, either supportive or critical. There aren't any books on the subject, and scientific articles are very rare—even in publications such as the

Journal of Parapsychology or the *Journal of the Society of Psychical Research*. One exception is a short write-up of a jottle study day that took place in London back in 2003.[6] Some very clever and qualified people participated in the discussion, but the findings were inconclusive and there hasn't been much formal interest in the topic since then.

Why Aren't Jottles a Popular Subject?

I'm not really sure why jottles aren't more popular with those who *haven't* experienced them, although two interrelated possibilities spring to mind. First, stories of disappearing objects aren't as viscerally shocking as tales of scary nonhuman entities. Contemporary paranormal subjects like "Black Eyes Kids" and "Shadow People" are what *really* interest paranormal devotees, not vanishing car keys. There's also a sense of pointlessness about a jottle, and the surrounding circumstances are so mundane it's hard to take them seriously.

The second related reason for why jottles haven't achieved the attention they deserve is that they are so *ordinary*, hence there's a justifiable suspicion that they are perfectly explainable. Jottles aren't paranormal—they're nothing more than a misinterpretation of something that happens to everyone at one time or another: losing things. And objects do go missing in quite extraordinary circumstances. For example, consider the case of Tucker and the missing wedding ring. A story from late June 2014 tells how a dog owned by Lois Matykowski of Stevens Point, Wisconsin, stole a popsicle and ate the whole thing, stick included. Two days later, Tucker vomited all over the house carpet. Mixed in with the dog's "puke" was Lois's wedding ring that had been lost for five years. Apparently some digestive quirk allowed the recently swallowed popsicle stick to dislodge the ring from inside the dog's alimentary canal where it had been hiding for all those years (after he'd eaten it, of course). Five years previously, the loss of the ring had caused great angst, with Lois searching her house from top to bottom. In a news article she expresses how devastated she was when she first discovered she'd lost the ring and adding, "How do you replace something like that? Not only the value of the ring but just the emotional ties too."[7]

On the surface, Tucker's enlightening story doesn't have much in common with Kate's missing keys or Mark's missing remote control. Neither Kate nor Mark owned a large pet like Tucker who could swallow a bunch of keys or an eight-inch TV control. Kate was petless, and Mark and Courtney possessed two goldfish. However, that's not the point; there could *still* be hidden, "Tucker-like" variables acting in both households that rationally explain the disappearances. Look hard enough and the reason for the missing keys and remote control will become apparent. In Kate's case, the explanation is perfectly human: someone was hiding around the side of her house, playing a trick or taking the opportunity to steal an unattended set of keys that would assist in a later robbery. With regard to Mark's TV remote, the likely solution is much closer to home. It's feasible that Courtney took the control because she was sick of Mark's selfish domination of the TV and decided "enough was enough."

And even if there's no easily discernible explanation for a mysterious disappearance, we can always turn to *psychology* and the many theories associated with the capriciousness of memory. Perhaps Kate and Mark were tired or emotionally stressed or distracted and these transitory states distorted their recollection of where they last placed the lost objects (conveniently ignoring the fact they might never find the object again). The point is, people all over the world lose things all the time, although most never interpret their loss as paranormal, let alone slightly strange. It's only when the experient unnecessarily projects a sense of mystery onto the disappearance that their appraisal becomes distorted. They might reconstruct a convincing memory of where the missing object was last placed—keys in the door or a remote control on the lap, when in fact such a memory is far from accurate. That seems a no-nonsense theory for jottles. Case closed. End of book.

Is it? In fairness, stories of disappearing objects often contain details that can't so easily be dismissed. For that reason I'm going to persevere, as a problem like jottles won't be solved until we have a good understanding of what that problem is in the first place. I can guarantee that those who reject jottles out of hand haven't considered them in sufficient detail. That consideration starts now.

Investigating Jottles

Let's accept that jottles are—or at least *could be*—paranormal. When it comes to exploring paranormal topics, there are three questions that need to be answered and I've borrowed these from the comprehensive book *An Introduction to Parapsychology*.[8] First, is the phenomenon we're interested in *ontologically real* (i.e., authentic)? Keys and remote controls obviously go missing around the home all the time—that's real. The question is, do they go missing for paranormal reasons? Second, assuming jottles are legitimately paranormal, is it possible to determine what *causes* the phenomenon?

The third question is *phenomenological*—how does it personally feel to experience a mysterious disappearance? On the surface this last question doesn't seem helpful in understanding whether jottles are authentic or what causes them. However, appreciating the experient's perspective might generate hypotheses about the processes underlying a disappearance. If something you own mysteriously vanishes, you might have good reason for attributing the loss to a mischievous spirit residing in your house. With little else to go on, maybe such a bizarre suggestion is worth further examination.

Using these three points as guidance, this book sets out to investigate the credibility of "objects behaving badly." And before I start, let me make it clear that as I write this I have absolutely no idea what my concluding remarks will be. It might turn out that jottles have a sensible explanation, in which case I will wind up the book with a psychological exposé of why they are mere misrepresentations of everyday "lost-and-found" events. On the other hand, if the evidence suggests that jottles are credible, then I'll make a serious attempt to come up with some ideas how and why they're caused—naturally with the help of experients' own explanations. That means getting tangled up in theories of the paranormal, which will be no easy task. Whatever the outcome, I do know that an investigation of jottles starts with an appreciation of the *subsequent events* that occurred in the lives of Kate and Mark.

PART I

1

Jottles Are More Than Disappearing Objects

As you might suspect, I've been deliberately holding back some information. There's more to Kate and Mark's stories than the simple disappearance of a set of keys and a TV remote. If they were objects that simply vanished it's unlikely Kate or Mark would have recalled enough detail to tell me these tales years later. Instead, both their jottle stories have a memorable second act. I'll start with Mark, for reasons that will shortly become apparent.

Mark (The Story Continues)

Mark never found his missing remote control. It was truly gone for good, so he purchased a generic replacement later that week and quickly forgot he'd ever misplaced the original item. One afternoon about three months after the first TV remote control was lost he was again watching television in the same room and on the same couch. This time Courtney was out visiting, and he was alone in the house with the new control by his side. He made a quick foray to the bathroom and returned to find everything was where it should be except the control, which was missing. With a sinking feeling, Mark realized he had a problem. Something was stealing his remote controls! Deep down he knew that searching for the new remote was pointless, yet he still tore the room apart to look for it because he found it hard to accept he was the target of something "paranormal." Of course he never found the second remote, and he refused to tell Courtney what had happened when she returned home that evening.

Within a week a third control was acquired, and this one lasted another few months until it went missing from the living room overnight. Mark distinctly remembers placing it in a cradle next to the TV before turning off the lights and heading for the upstairs bedroom. Following the disappearance of the second control he was particularly vigilant with this third one, constantly making a mental note of where he placed it each time he finished using it. The next morning he was the first one out of bed and he wandered downstairs to find remote control number three absent from the cradle. All the external house doors were locked and no alarm had been triggered during the night. Nothing else was missing around the house, and the goldfish certainly weren't to blame. From that moment, and much to Courtney's annoyance, Mark decided that remote controls were overrated and unnecessary pieces of technology. Indeed, the process of getting up and physically changing the volume and channels on the television was good for cardiovascular health (his tongue-in-cheek rationalization). As of the writing of this book, no further possessions belonging to Mark or Courtney have gone missing, and they still reside in the same house.

Clearly, to take the idea of "mysteriously disappearing objects" seriously we first have to trust the honesty of Mark's story. It was personally related to me in great detail, and I have no reason to doubt him. Mark certainly doesn't crave publicity or outwardly exhibit a style of narcissistic personality that encourages lying. Mark isn't even his real name.[1] A skeptic might dismiss his tale as fantasy or an outright fabrication to trick gullible people like me. And yet, in order to maintain a consistent position on the subject, the same skeptic would also need to dismiss the next case, and the one after that, and the hundreds more that are equally unspectacular but puzzling nonetheless. They can dismiss the lot if they want to (and probably would); however, I think that says more about *them* than it does about the people who suffer from jottles.

So, putting aside any immediate rationalizations of Mark's experiences—such as sleepwalking, or poor memory, or outright hoax—let's consider the most salient elements of his story. First, his jottles are *recurrent*, which enhances credibility compared with a "one-off" disappearance. Second, the objects being jottled are of the same *variety*, suggesting the phenomenon isn't random. Third, the events center on Mark rather than Courtney, so we might term Mark the *jottle agent*.

Kate (The Story Continues)

Kate is also an agent, since she was on her own when her jottle occurred (assuming there wasn't someone hiding around the side of her house playing tricks). However, what happened to Kate next *wasn't* a recurrent disappearance. After she spent a few days sporadically searching, Kate's annoyance dissipated and she accepted her keys were lost for good. That wasn't to say she was content with this loss. It was demoralizing because the car key was the only one she possessed. She was forced to organize a replacement, which was stupidly expensive, and arrange for other keys to be cut for the front and back doors, the garage, the mailbox and the office. Armed with a new set, she made sure she looked after them with particular care from that moment onward.

As far as I know, Kate hasn't lost these new keys. However, there's a twist. You see, Kate was only renting her modest two-bedroom suburban house and within the year had secured a far better job in another city to the north. Changing towns meant settling down, so she bought an apartment closer to the town center and renovated it fully. Her new job was satisfying, but the hours were long, so she often came home late and tired. One evening she returned to the apartment as usual and placed her keys—the new ones—in a hallway drawer. She then moved on to the bedroom, where she found her keys—the original set—lying on her bed. Kate says she stayed outwardly calm, but she felt nauseous and giddy. She knew there'd been no visitors to the apartment since she'd left for work that morning, and of course she couldn't blame a dog like Tucker for eating the keys and regurgitating them a year later in the new location.

So what can we make of Kate's expanded narrative? Well, it's obvious that jottles don't solely involve permanently disappearing objects like Mark's TV remote control. That's another reason why I'm using the term "jottle" rather than "DOP," since the disappearing object phenomenon doesn't refer to situations where objects *reappear*. In addition, the reappearance occurred in an entirely different location than the original place of loss, and the time delay between the initial disappearance and eventual reappearance was substantial (although we don't know yet if a period of a year is typical). Most disturbing was the location of the old key set—on the bed. This furnishes the reappearance with more personal significance than if it were simply discovered *returned* to the lock of the front door of Kate's original house.

While there are substantial differences between Kate and Mark's jottle stories, they are both intrinsically linked. Each involves the mysterious disappearance of a non-sentient object small enough to hold in the palm of the hand. They both also appear focused on an individual as the agent and occur in or around a home environment. That said, there's no point trying to force a single explanation onto either case at this stage, as there's no evidence that a recurrent object *disappearance* and a time-delayed object *reappearance* share the same underlying cause.

A New Tale from Martin

Things get more perplexing when we consider this new jottle story from Martin. A mature-aged university student, Martin experienced an object *appearing* from nowhere. This time I'll relate the story in Martin's own words (edited for ease of reading). He sought me out after hearing a talk I'd given on the subject of "objects behaving badly":

> A couple of years ago I was at home in the kitchen doing some cooking. According to the recipe I needed an egg, and I knew I had a carton of eggs in the fridge. But when I looked there were no eggs. Whoever used them last put the carton back knowing it was empty, so I was pretty annoyed with that. There were definitely no eggs in the carton. I just didn't have the energy to go out and get another carton from the shops, so I gave up that recipe and found another one that used ingredients I already had but no eggs. The strange thing was, I went to throw the empty carton in the bin and found there was an egg in it after all! I knew there can't have been an egg, but I sort of brushed it off as too weird and went ahead with cooking the original recipe using the egg I'd found. In fact, I'd forgotten all about it until you just asked for a story. I guess that egg was behaving badly?

Martin's story is about an *appearing* object, which becomes a third variety of jottle distinct from Mark's disappearing TV remotes and Kate's reappearing keys.

Giving Jottles the "Hynek Treatment"

Now that disappearances, appearances and reappearances have been identified, it becomes clear that an investigation of jottles cannot simply involve the arbitrary recounting of weird experiences, followed by claims of how poltergeists, fairies and time-warps might be responsible. There needs to be a more scientific approach to the topic. In this task I'm assisted by, of all things, investigations into UFOs. Back in the early 1970s, astronomy professor J. Allen Hynek wrote his first book on flying saucers. These objects had been wandering the skies for 25 years—at least in public awareness—and Hynek was not pleased with the approach of earlier authors who had cashed in on a very popular subject.[2] Of these amateur books, he wrote in his preface, "They regale the reader with one UFO story after another, each more spectacular than the other, but little space is devoted to documentation and to evaluation. What were the full circumstances surrounding the reported event? How reliable and how consistent were the reporters (all too often it is a lone reporter) of the event? And how were the UFO accounts selected? Most often one finds random accounts, disjointed and told in journalese (7)."[3] This statement could equally be applied to the current treatment of jottles as a paranormal phenomenon. Hynek goes further when he discusses the importance of seeking patterns in a *database* of UFO cases:

> The problem central to this treatise is whether there exists, in the considerable body of data on reported UFOs, any "genuinely new empirical observations" calling for "new explanation schemes." Very little ought to—or could—be said about what those new explanations schemes might be before a thorough examination of the data has been undertaken; this would be truly putting the cart before the horse. In such a controversial subject, which so frequently has triggered highly emotional reactions, examination of the data must come first; only then may we arrive at any judgment about new empirical observations. Indulging in explanation schemes before we know what there is to be explained is an arm-chair luxury [50].[4]

Apart from his reference to "highly emotional reactions," which are without doubt more intense for flying saucers than jottles, this statement fits perfectly the study of disappearing, appearing and reappearing objects. Jottles therefore deserve "the Hynek treatment." Nonetheless, this doesn't have to be in the form of a strict research thesis bogged down with tables of numbers and statistical outputs. Such a treatment might be scientifically respectable (or only *slightly* respectable, considering the topic), but the result would be dull to read and would lack serious consideration of *all* the possible causes. Instead, I will take a more balanced approach to investigating jottles, transcribing interesting stories in full to retain the human element but at the same time methodically scrutinizing hundreds of cases as a *whole* (the database) in the hope of identifying relevant features and patterns inherent to the phenomenon. Concluding judgments about what jottles *are* will be linked directly to these newly discovered patterns (should they exist), and no potential explanation will be too kooky for me to consider.

If the thought of data analysis is unappealing, don't be concerned. This book is merely an introductory exploration of jottles, and as such the analysis will be deliberately superficial. I'd prefer to achieve a global understanding of the characteristics of jottles rather than get caught up in the nitty-gritty details associated with complicated mathematical outputs (most of which don't make much practical sense to me anyway). Hard studies of the phenomenon might come in time. For now, we simply need excavate the barely touched landscape of jottles to see what's hidden beneath.

The Stories to Include and the Stories to Leave Out

Before this excavation begins, I need to place certain constraints on what stories are included in a "Hynek-style" database. First, I'll only use tales referring to inanimate objects. That's perhaps a little unfair, as there are plenty of cases of humans allegedly disappearing (or appearing or even reappearing). Naturally, these often involve individuals you would *expect* to disappear, either because they're flying over the Atlantic in a small aircraft and are never seen again (no surprise) or they have a shady history and plenty of enemies. On the other hand, there are tales involving missing people that do seem vaguely jottle-like. One such story is the historical case of 65[5]-year-old James Tedford. In early December 1949, Tedford was travelling in a bus from St. Albans to Bennington, Vermont, after visiting his estranged wife. He was seen to reboard the bus after a brief stop at Burlington, but he never got off at the Bennington veteran's home where he lived.[6] As the story goes, multiple people saw him sleeping in his seat, wearing an army overcoat and cap. However, somewhere between stops he apparently disappeared, with his luggage still on the bus and a timetable left on his seat. The popular conception is that he vanished into thin air while on the bus, but like many missing person stories there's a gap between when he was last seen and when he was reported missing a week or so later. Regarding Tedford's disappearance, there's enough evidence to suggest he didn't "dematerialize," even though no trace of him was ever found. Then again, six people did go missing in the same area over a five-year period,[7] giving rise to the mystery of the "Bennington Triangle."

Is there any connection between Tedford's disappearance and Mark's vanishing remote control? Or might Tedford have turned up somewhere else a year later at some other location, like Kate's keys, but was never identified? The answer might actually be "yes" for both questions, and for this reason I'll reconsider disappearing (and appearing and reappearing) people later in the book. But for now let's keep things simple and focus solely on the strange behavior of nonliving objects.

The second constraint is that for a story to be considered a "true" jottle, the experient must believe they've encountered something that *cannot* be explained rationally. Whether that belief is legitimate or not is unimportant at this stage and is something an analysis of the database can potentially determine. What is important is to avoid any disappearance, appearance or reappearance tale that the storyteller *knows* deep down is perfectly understandable. One example is the ubiquitous story of the sock that disappears

1: Jottles Are More Than Disappearing Objects 13

from the washing machine at the local laundromat. Although an urban myth, socks do regularly vanish—and of course most people implicitly understand this event isn't a jottle. The sock has found its way into a crevice in (or under) the machine or has ended up in someone else's laundry pile. Another easily rationalized example involves the cell phone or handbag discovered lost from an unlocked car parked overnight on a downtown street. These cannot be classed as jottles if the experients accept that their possessions were stolen by a thief. There's also the situation where we search our house for something we haven't seen in many years (e.g., a book or a tool) and find it *isn't* in the place where we think it should be. Naturally we accept this incident for what it is—a misplaced object, although some people *might* interpret the loss as "paranormal" and if they do their tale will be included in the database. If it transpires that such banal stories (and the associated judgment) comprise the bulk of the collection, then we've strong evidence to suggest that jottles are a perfectly explainable phenomenon after all.

The third constraint is that only firsthand accounts will be considered. There might be plenty of interesting historical jottles from decades or centuries past, but these usually won't possess the necessary detail to allow a valid analysis to be performed. The fourth and final constraint is centered on *where* the stories originate. In order to collect accurate, firsthand accounts, all the cases in this book (including Kate, Mark and Martin) necessarily derive from English-speaking Australia and New Zealand. That's simply because the research was conducted in Australia (with some help from a few New Zealand experients). Nonetheless, this isn't a limitation, as content-wise these Antipodean tales are—in my opinion—indistinguishable from stories emanating from the United States, Canada and the United Kingdom (and various European and South American countries also). That makes jottles a truly worldwide phenomenon.

2
A Typology of Jottles

Now that the constraints are in place the next step is to categorize the story database, and that requires a *typology*, or a set of labels classifying jottle *type*. Luckily, Mary Rose Barrington has already done the hard work for us and created six elegant terms to match the different manifestations of jottles—some of which we haven't met yet. I'll work through these terms now one at a time.

The first "type" of jottle is a *flyaway*. That's where an object inexplicably disappears from a specific location and is never seen again—like Mark's missing remote control(s). Then there's a *walkabout*, which involves an object found missing from one location and reappearing in a location different from the first—that is, the object literally "goes walkabout." You will notice that matches Kate's experience with her keys.

A new type of jottle is a *comeback*, when an object mysteriously disappears from a specific location then reappears at the *same* location after a varying period of time. That could range from minutes to years!

Barrington's fourth jottle is also novel—a *turn-up*. This is where a familiar (e.g., owned) object is discovered, or "turns up," in an unexpected location. On the other hand, a *windfall* involves the unforeseen appearance of an object that is *not* familiar to the experient. This label best suits my story of Martin's egg. Finally, there is a *trade-in*, which is a combination of a flyaway and a windfall. It involves a trade, or a swap, of one object for a different object.

Of course, there might be overlap among the various "types"—and beware, this gets complicated! For instance, a comeback might be closely related to a walkabout since they both involve reappearing objects. Alternatively, a flyaway might simply be a comeback or a walkabout that hasn't reappeared yet. A turn-up might even be the same as a walkabout, but the original loss wasn't noticed by the experient! Regardless of these small complications, Barrington's six labels make great intuitive sense and allow for a basic cataloguing of all possible jottle cases.

However, this book pays homage to Hynek's scientific treatment of *anomalous experiences* (i.e., experiences that differ to common or ordinary experience).[1] That means keeping things as clear and concise as possible. So, rather than retain Barrington's six conspicuously different labels I'll stick with my three simpler categories matching Kate, Mark and Martin's jottles, namely *disappearances* (flyaways), *appearances* (incorporating turn-ups and windfalls), and *reappearances* (embodying comebacks and walkabouts). That leaves the troubling category of a trade-in, which, as mentioned, is a hybrid affair—the disappearance of one object followed by the appearance of a different object. Here's a story from Deborah that I frantically wrote down as she told it to me (if I recall correctly, it was at roughly the same time I learned about Martin's egg):

> A year or two ago I went to the library to borrow some books. I got out three or four, one of which was *Foul Shot*. I don't remember the others, but I'll always remember this book because of what happened next. I checked the books out at the counter and put them in my library bag. On the bus I looked at each of them and wondered which I'd start reading first. I know I put them all back when I closed my bag up. When I got home I emptied the bag on the table, and all the books were there except *Foul Shot*. Instead there was another book. I can't remember who wrote it, but it was a historical novel. This wasn't the book I borrowed and looked at on the bus, although it was from the same library. Over the next week I read the rest of the books except this one because it didn't interest me. I took them all back a week later and put them in the return slot. I didn't investigate further. I never went back to the library, even to see if *Foul Shot* was still in the shelves. Also, I never got any correspondence telling me *Foul Shot* hadn't been returned. I've never understood how one book could be replaced by another in my bag on the bus trip home.

I'll label this type of incident a *replacement*—equivalent to Barrington's trade-in. What distinguishes a replacement from a flyaway followed by a separate windfall is that the disappearance of one object—and the appearance of another in the same location—occur in such close temporal proximity that the experient causally links the two events. Whether the *replacing* object is always comparable to the *replaced* object (in Deborah's case, one book swapped with another) is something that can be determined only by collecting more replacement cases.

Armed with these four classes of jottle (disappearances, appearances, reappearances and replacements), stories in the database can be sorted and grouped more effectively. However, this Hynek-like approach still lacks precision. For example, does the type of jottled object vary? And what about the locations where these events occur or the time periods involved? To achieve a deeper understanding of the similarities and differences among jottle class I'll need to add more substance to the basic typology, starting with mysterious disappearances.

Disappearing Objects: Objects and Their Significance

For disappearances, the most obvious feature of any story is the *type* of object that goes missing. That's essential information. However, just as relevant is the *importance* of this object to the experient. This doesn't necessarily refer to the object's raw monetary value but rather its personal value. For instance, Lucy[2] tells how she was in her bedroom when a slightly oversized ring slipped off her finger. She heard it hit the wooden floor and looked down but couldn't find it. It was an inexpensive ring but sentimental enough for Lucy to make a thorough search worthwhile, so she removed every piece of furniture and with the help of a friend (and a powerful lamp) scoured the floor, albeit unsuccessfully. She then vacuumed the room, hoping the ring would be sucked up from a groove in the boards. This approach didn't work either, so she crawled around with a magnifying glass. The ring was never found. Interestingly, Lucy reports she lost two more rings in the same location, this fact suggesting "recurrence" isn't the sole property of disappearing TV remote controls. Nor are cheap rings the only prosaic objects deemed important to the loser. Here's Malcolm's story of his vanishing guitar pick:

> I play guitar and only ever used this one flat pick. I'd had it ever since I first started playing years ago. It was just an ordinary celluloid one, but it was just the right size and shape and I could never find one in the shop bins that matched it. I loved that pick! Anyway, after playing one night I returned it to the little box inside the hard case where it always lived. I'd done that same process for years, and never had a problem. Next day I went to play again but the pick wasn't there. I know it doesn't sound very mysterious, but it was definitely there the night before, and there's absolutely no way it could have got out of that box. I seriously miss that pick. Nothing I've used since comes even close. I put it down to the fact that I had a bad night playing, and blamed it on the guitar and the way it was set up. Maybe the pick heard me, got annoyed and left?

The stories of Lucy's missing ring, Malcolm's lost plectrum and Mark's TV remote not only indicate that a wide range of objects disappear in strange circumstances, but that object *type* cannot predict object *importance*. We might amass plenty of information about common missing objects but find no coherent theme or pattern in it. However, when those same objects are reclassified in terms of their personal worth, a pattern might emerge. For example, sentimental objects might vanish more frequently than everyday objects.

I'll term objects of great personal importance that permanently disappear *high significance,* and to be a member of this category the object must be considered virtually "irreplaceable" by the experient. We could guess that high significance items would most likely refer to things like expensive jewelry and heirlooms and even works of art and classic cars—assuming these large objects can also be jottled. However, Malcolm's anguish over his lost plectrum suggests some flexibility is required when identifying high significance items.

Objects that disappear might also be personally important but possess less emotional significance. Examples would include car keys, a wallet full of credit cards or a cell phone. Although the experients will literally tear their hair out when these items are lost and search frantically for them, keys, cards and telephones can ultimately be repurchased or reordered. Such valued but ultimately replaceable items I'll term *medium significance.* And what about objects that aren't important possessions? These also vanish permanently. Here's Sam's tale of a disappearing brush: "I remember once I was in the laundry cleaning out the tub, as it was dirty and full of black slime. I was using a wooden scrubbing brush that I'd bought specially for the occasion. The state of the tub had been bugging me for quite some time. When I finished the job I put the brush at the bottom of the tub and went to the kitchen to make a cup of coffee. When I came back to clean the brush it wasn't in the tub, or anywhere else in the laundry. No one else was in the house at the time. It was a weekday." This is a *low significance* case. The brush is of little personal value, but it's a possession nonetheless. Such items are inexpensive and easily replaced if the experient could be bothered. Sam's tale is one of many examples I have on file, including those involving a coffee mug, a second-hand paperback novel, and a makeup bag. Mark's TV remote(s) also fit the definition of a low significance object.

Finally, there are disappearing objects of absolutely *no* significance whatsoever—those hardly even worth calling a possession. Ben's case[3] is typical of a valueless item disappearance. He was renovating his house and had suffered from a number of unremarkable disappearances that he mostly ignored. However, he was particularly impressed by one incident that happened when he was soldering pipe in the bathroom. He was using a wet rag to cool the joints and at one staged reached out to fetch it but discovered it was no longer behind him. Like in any good disappearing object story, Ben thoroughly searched the near-empty room and all the gear in it, but the rag was never found.

Other examples of low-value possessions include pen tops, bottle lids and general household rubbish. I'll label these *no significance* objects. While they might be trivial, when they're lost the resulting search can often be as exhaustive as that undertaken for a lost wallet or diamond ring—more out of a sense of frustration than panic. No significance also refers to situations where the experient notices the unusual disappearance of an object that they *don't* own. Take this example: Mandy walked into her doctor's surgery to confirm her appointment and noticed a lone magazine sitting on a table in the middle of the waiting area. Apart from the secretary behind the counter, Mandy was the only person in the room, so she figured she wouldn't be fighting over it with anyone else. When she finished checking in at the counter she turned to take a seat and found the magazine was no longer on the table. Was this some sort of practical joke? Mandy didn't think so and fondly remembers this event as "paranormal."

The Location of Disappearance

With the exception of Mandy's magazine, all stories told so far involve objects vanishing from the experient's home—particularly the kitchen and bedroom. These can be considered *private localities*. However, across hundreds of cases it might transpire that *public localities* are the most common sites of disappearances, for instance a park bench or a restaurant table—or in the case of Mandy, the doctor's waiting room. These are (often) crowded spaces, and it's perfectly reasonable to conclude that objects that go missing from public localities are the result of human interference rather than a paranormal process.

When the disappearance *is* from the home, the exact place of loss should also be noted, for example whether it is from the bedroom floor or living room couch. However, the experient often doesn't remember the object's last known whereabouts in the house, hence two subcategories of *location* are required: *precise* and *imprecise*. The former involves firm knowledge of the whereabouts of the disappearance—Sam's missing brush is a good example of a precise disappearance because she was absolutely certain she left it in the laundry sink. On the other hand, here's an *imprecise* tale from Kevin: "I got a Sportura [watch] for Christmas. I usually take it off before bed and put it in my bedroom. Well, last Thursday I couldn't find it. I hadn't worn it for a few days because I'd been busy with other things, but when I went to look for it in my room it wasn't anywhere.

I really searched the room. I still haven't found it, and no-one would have taken it as no-one goes in my room, ever. It cost a fortune, so I'm really unhappy I can't find it."

This medium significance disappearance is less convincing than Sam's missing brush because Kevin was rather vague about where he left his watch. He assumed he'd placed it in his bedroom but when pressed was not entirely convinced. For this reason, a *precise* disappearance is stronger evidence of an anomaly than an *imprecise* disappearance. If it turns out that most stories are *imprecise* (regardless of whether they occur in public or private localities) then it's more evidence that disappearances might not be mysterious after all.

Time Delays Associated with Disappearances

Another jottle variable worth considering is *delay*. With regard to disappearances, the *last seen delay* refers to the time period between the object last being "seen" or "noticed" and the discovery that it has gone missing. For example, Mark lost his first TV remote from a precise (private) location—next to his lap—and this occurred over a short last seen delay, literally a matter of seconds. Together, these two variables lend credibility to his tale. Another manifestation of a short last seen delay is found in the following story of a vanishing low significance object. Told by Pat, this is the quintessential expression of the disappearing object phenomenon: "I was doing some kit modelling on the dining room table, as it's the biggest in the house and I had lots of stuff laid out around me. By accident I brushed a wheel off the table with my elbow. It wasn't a very heavy piece but it should have made some noise when it hit the floor because that part of the house is tiled not carpeted. I didn't hear it hit the tiles, and I never found the wheel, even when I moved the table and vacuumed around the whole room (I even went through the vacuum bag, to double check)."

In this story, Pat was present when his wheel vanished and immediately noticed something unusual about the circumstances of its loss. Alternatively, it can sometimes take experients minutes or even hours to recognize that an object in their vicinity has disappeared. In these situations, the last seen delay might be long, but the story retains validity if the location is precise and the experient is alone and has remained in the same spot the whole time. On the other hand, when the last seen delay lags and the experient leaves the location, a disappearance jottle is far less impressive. Consider this next example from Naomi. The delay is long, the location imprecise, and she was nowhere near the object when it allegedly vanished without a trace: "The only example I can give you is from a while back when I couldn't find my silver bracelet. I hadn't worn it for ages, and when I last took it off I would have put it back in the box with all my other jewelry and important things. I couldn't find it a few months ago, and haven't seen it since. That's a mysterious disappearance, in my opinion."

Up until now, the disappearing object cases I've included have been quite remarkable—like Mark's vanishing remote controls. His story is so good I couldn't help but use it to open this book. However, the selective use of these narratives might give the impression that all disappearing object stories are this convincing. Instead, it might transpire that the majority of disappearance jottles are as feeble as the tale of Naomi's missing silver bracelet (which she truly believed was inexplicable, so it was included in the story database).

Appearing Objects:
Revisiting Object Type and Significance

Martin's egg is an appearing object—or more specifically a windfall. Indeed, Barrington's classification is (at this stage) more informative than simply calling it an "appearance" because windfall refers to an unowned object. Not only was the egg unowned, Martin also recognized it as something familiar (i.e., an everyday egg!). To account for these two features the revised typology classifies Martin's appearing object as *unowned familiar*. Another example of an unowned familiar appearance comes from the British parapsychologist Maurice Grosse, who described how he'd replaced the lock on his house door following the loss of the key and stored the original 40-year-old lock fitting in a room upstairs.[4] Shortly afterward, his wife discovered a shiny new key on her key ring that didn't fit the replacement lock but instead worked only in the old lock. Although it *looked* like an ordinary key, neither Maurice nor his wife recognized it as ever having been owned.

There's also the possibility that the appearing object is not only unowned but completely unrecognizable! These objects I'll term *unowned unfamiliar*. For instance, imagine an experient fetching his coat from a hook in the hallway, putting it on, and finding an object in the pocket that wasn't there when he wore the garment the day before. He has difficulty determining the purpose of the object and what it is made out of. Is it stone or some kind of plastic? It is dark in color, quite heavy and smooth, with an odd shape as though it's been crafted. In this type of case, some experients might unthinkingly throw it away, but sometimes they perceive it to be so unusual that they keep it as a lucky charm—a gift from another world.[5] Considering the certified strangeness of these unowned familiar and unowned unfamiliar appearing objects, it might be speculated—even at this early stage of the investigation—that these items are in fact other people's disappearing objects!

There's also the possibility that the appearing object is an owned possession, and these equate to Barrington's turn-ups. Owned possessions are, by definition, familiar, so I'll label these objects *owned familiar*. We can also apply a level of significance to these owned objects similar to that applied to disappearance jottles. That way, an owned familiar possession appearing somewhere unexpected might be a precious wedding ring of high significance or a notebook with dozens of important phone numbers (medium significance). Then again, the object might be of low significance, which presents a problem. Such objects are far more difficult to recognize as something owned because they are nondescript and lack identifying features. Here's a story from Chris highlighting this ambiguity:

> I can remember an object that appeared mysteriously. One day my car was parked in the garage at home, all locked up as usual. I got in to drive somewhere and found a box of matches on top of the dashboard. I'm the only one who uses the car, and no-one else has any keys. The matches weren't there the day before, when I last drove my car. I'm convinced the matchbox was the same one that normally lives in the bowl in the living room, where the cigarettes are kept. How they appeared in my car is beyond me, because I keep it very clean.

An object with no significance might also be interpreted as an owned familiar appearance; however, these stories are even less convincing, as it is difficult for the experient to be certain the object is a recognizable possession that has materialized somewhere it shouldn't be. Can the experient really be certain a screwed-up chocolate wrapper sitting on the passenger seat of their car or a small screw found on the bathroom floor are owned objects that have appeared through paranormal means?

Appearance Location

To aid understanding of appearance jottles, we again need to reconsider the variable of location. Rather than the precise and imprecise locations characterizing disappearance jottles, appearances occur at *familiar* and *unfamiliar* locations. Experients spend a lot of time in a familiar location. The home environment is the most obvious, but conceivably this could include a workplace or the house of a close friend or relative or perhaps even a set of clothes, such as a jacket or pants pocket. An unfamiliar location is somewhere the experient rarely goes or has never visited before. Take this appearance of an owned familiar but low significance object, told by Jessica:

> Only once has anything like this ever happened to me, and it's wasn't a disappearing object. It was something of mine that just turned up when it shouldn't have. Two years ago I was having some issues at home and went to stay at a friend-of-a-friend's place down in [____]. I hadn't been there before, so it took some time finding it. I turned up and they were really nice, and they gave me a bed in their spare room, off the lounge. I'd only been there a few hours but was determined to still attend classes at Uni[versity], although I was a bit stressed because money was very tight at that time and exams were coming up. I had a few back-to-back tutorials that afternoon, and when I came back to the room there was my blue woolen beanie on the floor. It was nearly summer and hot, and I'd only packed light when I left home. I certainly didn't pack my beanie. It was definitely my beanie, as my name was in it. My parents hadn't been to the house, and the people who lived there (I didn't know them that well) didn't know anything about it either. I never told my mum or dad about it, as they wouldn't have believed me.

Naturally, I won't consider appearances of objects in unfamiliar locations if they are unowned familiar or unowned unfamiliar, because it's hardly peculiar for a strange object to be discovered in a strange location—which happens to us all the time! However, there is one exception worth acknowledging—the *duplication*.

Duplications as Appearances

Greg was in his room picking through a box of old bits and pieces, taking anything out he thought might be useful and putting these items on the floor beside him. One of those objects was a knife, and when he'd finished sorting through the box he looked down to where he'd placed it and found two knives instead of one. There was the old knife he'd put there just moments before, and next to it was an identical version that looked brand new. Each knife had the same serial number attached, implying that somehow they were the *same* knife, separated in time. Superficially, Greg's story[6] has a lot in common with Martin's materializing egg. Both stories involve appearances of unowned familiar objects in a familiar location. Nonetheless, Greg's is a duplication, which is conceptually very different to a "simpler" appearing egg.

Moreover, the duplicated object doesn't necessarily have to appear side by side with the original object. There are examples where a replicated article appears at a very different place than the original and is recognized by the experient as a familiar possession, but it is noticeably *not* that possession. For instance, this person might own an obscure book that is old and worn and presumably resting safely in the bookshelf at home. One morning the person is far away, visiting friends, and returns to her car to find a much newer copy of that same rare book resting on the car's hood. On first glance this story resembles a walkabout, and yet the book found on the hood cannot be the one that is owned because its condition is far superior. Since the book is so obscure, finding an identical copy in a very conspicuous manner defies all logic, and the experient can barely classify this (apparent) duplication as a *meaningless* coincidence.[7]

Appearance Delays

Recall that for disappearing objects only one time period is measurable—the last seen delay. This represents the time between last seeing the object and finding it missing. When it comes to appearance jottles, things are slightly more complicated, as "delay" now has two facets. For owned familiar objects (high, medium, low and no significance) the last seen delay is still relevant and denotes the length of time between last seeing the article and finding it in a surprising location. Conceivably, this time period could be anything from seconds and minutes to months and even years.

Remember Jessica's appearing beanie? The last seen delay was on the order of months, but unlike a disappearance jottle this long delay doesn't necessarily invalidate her story, because it is the circumstances surrounding an object's appearance that determine whether the event is unusual. These circumstances are represented by a second temporal measurement I've named the *appearance delay* (see Figure 1). This is the period between visually scanning a location and *not* perceiving an object to be present, then scanning that same location once more and finding the object *is* present. In the most remarkable jottle cases this delay may be seconds. For example, the experient might be brushing his teeth over the bathroom sink and momentarily looks elsewhere. Turning back to the sink, he, to his surprise, discovers his wristwatch (the appearing object) now propped up against the faucet. Jessica's tale is not quite as impressive, because her beanie appeared sometime between her leaving the house at midday and her returning later that afternoon. That's a time delay of hours, not seconds, and the longer this appearance delay the less convincing the story because there's a greater probability of locational interference—that is, other people positioning the object where it's later found. In Jessica's case, a skeptic could argue there was ample time for her mother or father to have driven the beanie to the new house and to have placed it on the bed as a message or practical joke (ignoring all the difficulties this entails, such as getting access to the house or even why her parents would bother with such inane behavior).

For unowned familiar and unowned unfamiliar objects, the last seen delay is irrelevant, because (by definition) these objects have never been seen before. However, the appearance delay remains a valuable indicator of a story's validity—the shorter this delay the more convincing the case.

Reappearing Objects: Reappearances— Significance and Location

There are no *unowned familiar* and *unowned unfamiliar* categories for reappearing objects because these items must have been knowingly lost in the first place (implying some degree of initial familiarity). Reappearing objects are therefore *owned* and possess the four varieties of significance found for disappearing objects (*high significance, medium significance, low significance* and *no significance*).

There are also four categories of reappearance location. The first is a *precise return,* involving an object being *returned* to the same location from where it knowingly disappeared (an expression of Barrington's *comeback*). This example from Cameron involves a set of keys:

> I was watching TV in the lounge and fiddling with my keys. I was twirling them around my finger. I leaned over and put them on the coffee table while I was still watching TV. Then I looked down and saw they weren't where I put them. I got up and searched around the table and under the table, because they couldn't be anywhere else. They shouldn't have even left the table so I don't know why I was looking under it. I didn't know what else to do. When I looked back, presto! They were on the coffee table again. Maybe I imagined not seeing them the first time, but I'm sure I would have felt them there with my hands, even if I couldn't see them. This is absolutely a true story.

On the other hand, there is the possibility of a *precise relocation,* where the object is *relocated* to a place different from where it was last knowingly left (an expression of Barrington's walkabout). That corresponds to Kate's story: Her keys were knowingly left in one place, the front door, then relocated to her bed in a completely different house.

There are also stories where the experient is aware they've lost something they own but aren't exactly sure where they left it. The object is later found where it *should* be, at some later time, even though this location had been thoroughly searched. This is an *imprecise return*, as illustrated by Rowan's story. Rowan notices his keys are missing when he goes to fetch them from the sideboard dresser. Standing over the empty drawer, he racks his brain wondering whether he'd put the keys somewhere else the last time they were used. An unsuccessful search ensues, and Rowan returns to the drawer for one last check, only to find the keys sitting within, plain as day.

The fourth reappearance location is an *imprecise relocation*. These describe situations where the experient is uncertain about where an object was lost, but when it reappears it is to a location very different from where it was believed lost—made clear in this case from Robert:

> I noticed my wallet was missing on Wednesday night. I can't remember exactly where or when I had it last—probably the day before. I usually put it in a drawer with my keys and glasses, to keep everything together. It wasn't there when I needed it so I looked around the house. Sometime I put it on the kitchen counter, or the dresser, or next to the bed, or in the front zip of my work bag, but it wasn't in any of these places. I couldn't pinpoint where exactly I left it. Thursday was raining and I was working at home that day, so in my spare time I actually walked the track at the back of my house where I go jogging, on the off chance I accidently took the wallet the morning before and dropped it while running. Of course I couldn't find it. It was cold and wet and miserable, and I wasn't very happy. I cancelled my credit and debit cards over the phone straight after that, and drove to town on Friday to get a new driver's license. I told the lady behind the counter that I'd lost it, but I had a funny feeling it would turn up again, and she agreed with me. Once the license was ordered I felt a little better, and figured I'd replace all the other lost cards more slowly, over time. Friday night is sport night for the kids, and we were leaving about 6pm. I was in the kitchen fetching chewing gum from an overhead cupboard where the wine glasses are kept (I chew gum watching the games, because it gets so tense sometimes). I took out some gum and was fussing around on the kitchen counter when I heard my wife let out a gasp behind me. She'd just opened the same cupboard to get some gum as well, and discovered my wallet on the shelf straight above the gum container. There's no way I would have missed seeing the wallet seconds before, as it's large and fat and made of black leather, and the cupboard is white on the inside and full of clear glasses. It was obvious to me it had appeared between me closing the cupboard, and my wife opening it less than a minute later. She definitely didn't put it there as a trick. She's no joker and takes this kind of thing very seriously.

This story doesn't suffer because the location of loss is imprecise. The freakish circumstances surrounding the wallet's reappearance identifies the event as anomalous.

Reappearance Delays

Reappearance jottles possess three distinct delay phases, irrespective of object significance or location of loss. First there is the last seen delay, once again referring to the time between last seeing an object and finding it missing. Sometimes this delay is almost immediate, as in the case of Cameron and his twirling keys, but it can also be longer; for instance, Robert's wallet was discovered missing overnight. Next is the loss delay. Simply put, this is the period between discovering an object has disappeared and finding it once more. This can be any length of time—in the range of minutes (Cameron's keys) to days (Robert's wallet) to years (Kate's keys). The third delay I'll term the *reappearance delay*. This is the time that separates an object's known absence from a specific location (i.e., it cannot be seen there) and its materialization at this same location. Here's a second imprecise relocation story from Robert to help visualize these three reappearance delays, and how they fit together:

> It was approximately 4 p.m. on a Monday, and the afternoon was unseasonably warm for the time of year. I was at home, and I'd just finished tidying the kitchen bench. Since it was so hot, I decided to water the garden as there hadn't been rain for a few days. There are two gardens, one at the front of the house, and one at the rear, and a single tap services each. Unfortunately, I only possessed one hose fitting, as all the others I had were made of cheap plastic and had long been broken. This surviving fitting was currently screwed to the tap at the rear of the house. I decided to water the front garden first, so I left the kitchen and walked to the back tap to remove the fitting, which I knew was attached to the tap as I'd seen it the previous day. However, it wasn't attached, which I found puzzling. I then walked around to the front tap to see if the attachment had somehow ended up there, but of course it hadn't, because that hose hadn't been used in a week. With no fitting, I couldn't use a hose. I assumed I must have pocketed the connector, so I went to the garage cupboard in the hope that I could find another one. After making a cursory search I was forced to accept that there was only one connector on the property, and decided to go to the laundry basket to check my pants from the day before in case I'd unscrewed the fitting and put it in my pocket. I couldn't remember ever doing that, but it was worth checking out. I found nothing in the pockets, so I walked outside again and tried to attach and use the hose without a proper fitting (and got very wet in the process). Then I gave up completely. By now I figured there was something strange about the disappearance (like my wallet), and I was reasonably convinced that the connector would turn up eventually. I walked back into the kitchen and there, very obvious on the empty bench, sat the attachment. I'd only been out of that room for 15 minutes. I hadn't touched the attachment at all that day, and no-one was in the house at the time.

This story consists of a last seen delay of approximately 24 hours (the time since the attachment had last been seen), a loss delay of 15 minutes (the length of Robert's search) and a reappearance delay of 15 minutes. The latter denotes the time between Robert's leaving the kitchen (the connector definitely *wasn't* on the kitchen counter when he left) and when he returned and it *was* on the counter. In this story, the loss and reappearance delays happen to be identical because the loss phase corresponded with his absence from the kitchen. If the fitting had returned overnight, the loss delay would be in the order of eight or ten hours, but the reappearance delay might still be 15 minutes if Robert had only briefly left the kitchen. There's no necessary relationship among any of these delay variables, although generally speaking the shorter all three delays (especially the reappearance delay) the more convincing the jottle.

Replacements: Significance and Location

Replacements involve the disappearance of one object and the appearance—at the same location—of an identifiably different object. Replacements therefore possess two measures of significance—a value for the object that vanishes and a value for the object that takes its place. For the disappearance phase the significances apply only to owned possessions (high, medium, low and no significance), but for the appearance phase all significance categories are relevant (high, medium, low and no significance and also unowned familiar and unowned unfamiliar). That's because the new object might or might not be recognized property. The story of Deborah's new book recounted earlier is an example of an unowned familiar replacement.

Regarding the location of the replacement, the most appropriate classification is the familiar/unfamiliar dichotomy applicable to appearance jottles. That's because the replacement could occur in a familiar environment, such as the home or office, or somewhere less familiar, such as a path or shopping mall. In this curious case from Colin, the swap occurs in familiar surroundings:

> This is a real disappearing object story, but it really is more of a swapped object story. I was working on the computer at home, in the nook on the landing where the desk is. I went downstairs and made myself a sandwich. Nothing extravagant. I put it on a plate and went back to the nook and put the plate on the table. I then went to my room to get some files from my bag. When I came back the sandwich was gone from the plate, and instead there was an apple. This is a serious story. There was no one else in the house and I was only gone for 5 minutes at the most. I was seriously shocked so I went back downstairs to check I had made a sandwich because maybe I'd imagined the whole thing. But the bread was still on the bench with the spread and the chopping board. The knife in the sink still had spread on it. And there were definitely no apples in the house that day. I've never been so freaked out. I think it was someone telling me I should be eating more fruit.

Complicating the matter, Deborah's book swap occurred somewhere between the bus, an unfamiliar location, and home, a familiar location. In such situations, an *ambiguous* designation is most appropriate.

Replacement Delays

A last seen delay is the only period of consequence to replacement jottles. Conceivably, the swap can occur immediately, when the experient is literally holding the object, looks away, then looks down again to discover a different item in her hand. Alternatively, Colin's last seen delay was five minutes, and Deborah's last seen delay was in the order of half an hour. As with all other aspects of the phenomenon, the longer this delay the greater the chance that the swap has a rational explanation.

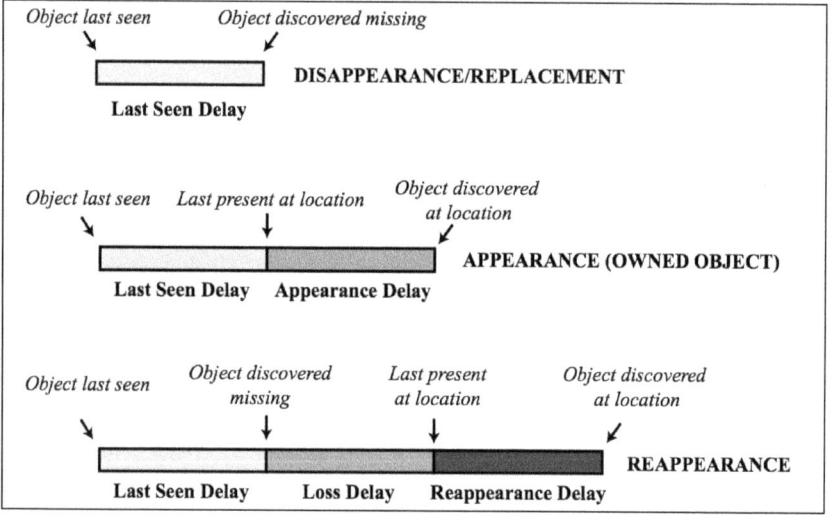

Figure 1: Time delays associated with disappearing, appearing, reappearing and replaced objects.

3

Additional Features Applicable to All Jottles

Alongside (1) object *significance*, (2) *location* and (3) *time delay* are additional variables shared by the four types of jottle. I discuss here the most important.

Object Size

Any jottle story possesses an implicit piece of information—the size of the object that's jottled. In the stories presented so far the objects generally have been small enough to fit into the hand—keys, TV remote controls and a tap fitting. Indeed some articles, such as Malcolm's guitar pick and Pat's model car wheel, were *very* small. It might therefore be justifiable to assume we're dealing with a "small object phenomenon." However, overemphasizing these cases might bias our understanding of the phenomenon. Search the Internet and you'll find plenty of tales of *big* objects jottling. For instance, there are examples of parked cars discovered missing (hence presumed stolen), only to be found a short time later relocated up or down the road—still securely locked with no sign of forced entry. Sometimes they're even relocated back to the owner's garage!

The idea of a car being jottled in *truly* mysterious circumstances[1] is even less believable than a small object vanishing or appearing from nowhere. Even if you're prepared to accept the possibility of keys or a wallet relocating in some bizarre paranormal fashion, you'll likely scoff at the thought of a 4,000-pound car doing the same thing. It just doesn't seem *logical*. And if you do accept these "big object" stories on face value, then you'll need to consider how frequent they are and whether the behavior of a disappearing car is comparable to the behavior of a disappearing key or wristwatch. Information about the prevalence of large-sized object jottles is therefore an important piece of the jottle puzzle.

Sex, Age, Occupation and Other Demographics

Psychological researchers are driven to seek a rational explanation for anomalous experiences, and it's common for them to associate reports of the paranormal with variables such as the experient's sex, age when the incident occurred, occupation and education level. Here's one example of how this is put into practice. Studies have suggested that alien abductees are mainly highly educated middle to upper-middle class white females,[2] engendering (psychological) speculation about why these particular individuals are targeted. In this instance, there is speculation that a mix of stress, expectation and personality encourages fantasies of abduction.

Are jottles any different? From the few stories presented so far, there's an equal balance of male and female experients, and no one type of occupation or education level is overrepresented. For instance, there's a fund manager, a professional musician, a university student and an electrician. Nevertheless, based on such a small sample, this distribution might not be accurate; and out of respect for the scientific method it is important to determine the broader demographics of people who experience jottles. The same applies for age. Our experients so far have been adults, but there's no reason to suspect that children or adolescents are necessarily immune. For example, here is the experience of Shirley, who was 85 years old when her jottle occurred:

> Two evenings ago I removed my hearing aids when I turned on the TV so I could use my headphones. I usually put them into their case, but that evening I simply laid them down as I was rushing in preparing my dinner.
>
> The following morning I went to get the hearing aids to put them on and I could not find them. I distinctly remembered taking them off and laying them down but they were nowhere to be found. I made three careful searches of the entire house, but could not find them. I was without them at two meetings during the day. I prepared my meal as normal that evening and sat at a small table to eat while watching the news. My doors were all closed and locked and the curtains drawn. At seven I went in to my study to do some computer work and just before nine, returned to the lounge room to shut everything down for the night and go to bed. My hearing aids were lying in the middle of the small table where I had had my meal.
>
> I had cleared that table of all books and magazines during the day, and I could not have sat there to eat my meal without seeing the entire table top. It is difficult to describe my feelings. The hair stood up on my neck!
>
> Today on thinking through the event, I realized that over the past couple of years

several of my belongings have disappeared in much the same way. I cannot name them now, most likely because none of them were of great importance like my hearing aids are, and were easily replaced. As well (as I have also told my friend) there was a period of several years when I was awakened at night by someone knocking loudly on my doors, but there was never anyone there when I looked. Is there really such a thing as a poltergeist? And if there is, have I acquired one, and how can I make it go away?

Shirley told me her experiences over e-mail, two days after it happened, so hers was a very recent jottle. However, this might be the exception. How many stories are years or even decades old or perhaps vague recollections from childhood? Wouldn't the passage of time affect the accuracy of these jottle memories? That's another factor to take into consideration.

Witnessing Jottles

When an object mysteriously appears or disappears, the loss delay and appearance delays can both be very short. In other words, the experient is present at the location where (and when) the jottle occurs. However, that doesn't necessarily mean he has *witnessed* the event. For example, Pat was sitting at a table when his model wheel fell to the floor, but he didn't actually *see* it vanish before his eyes. However there are occasions where experients claim to have observed the materialization or dematerialization of the jottled object. This can occur when an experient is alone or even in a group and should be acknowledged. In the following story, Sophia is alone and reports a witnessed imprecise relocation:

> I had a very funny experience from a few years back that I still recall to this day. I have a silver bracelet with little leaves attached by small lengths of chain all around it. There are about 20 or so leaves, and one day I noticed one was missing. The links of the chain were still there, but nothing was on the end. I was upset but didn't think much more about it, as it wasn't that noticeable and I still wore the bracelet. I assumed it had been pulled off the end of the chain somehow. Anyway, about a month or two later I was in my room at home and sort of staring into space thinking of something when I saw this small silver thing appear before my eyes in the middle of the room. It was there for about a second, then dropped to the floor. It was the missing leaf.

Repeaters and Recurrence

Robert has provided two stories for the book so far—his reappearing wallet and the backyard tap fitting. This classifies him as a *repeater*, which is a label given to anyone reporting multiple (alleged) paranormal or anomalous experiences. In the psychological literature, the concept of a paranormal "repeater" typically has negative connotations. This is most apparent in regard to UFO witnesses and abductees. These individuals are widely considered to have various cognitive deficits or personality traits or both that encourage them to fabricate stories (perhaps similar to reports of alien abductions discussed earlier). For example, skeptic Philip Klass regularly used the charge of "repeater" to debunk stories told by witnesses of flying saucers (or to ridicule the photographs they had taken).[3] On the other hand, people who report multiple paranormal experiences have been shown to be no less "mentally healthy" than people who report only one or a few experiences.[4] That would mean the claims of repeaters shouldn't be dismissed outright, if anything because jottles are far more humdrum than the stories served up by UFOlogy or other more spectacular branches of the paranormal. Nevertheless, in light of the ambiguous research findings associated with the status of a repeater, a more measured assessment of jottles might be warranted if large numbers of repeaters are identified as experients.

An associated concept also worth noting is that of *recurrence*. Mark's experiences with vanishing TV remote controls, and Lucy's experience with her rings, suggest a certain *type* of object can undergo persistent disappearances. Whether this is a common symptom of jottles is certainly worth exploring.

Meaningfulness and the "Sense of Presence"

An additional, intriguing aspect of jottles is the extent to which experients interpret their encounters as personally *meaningful*. While some people believe an object's disappearance, appearance, reappearance or relocation is unusual but without apparent reason, others infer a purposefulness tied to the significance of the targeted object. For example, here is Jessica's conclusion to her story of the relocating beanie: "The reason [for the missing beanie]? I think it was because I was stressed, and my Guardian Angel was giving me some comfort with a warm beanie because things got a lot better for me after that." Attributions commonly involve a deceased relative, as demonstrated in Eleanor's story:

> I have a photo frame on the upstairs hallway table with me in it when I was a little girl, standing next to my father and mother. My mother had died a few years ago from cancer, and now my father was in hospital recovering from a stroke. I was the last one to leave the house that morning and drove straight to the hospital to visit

him. When I arrived I found he was beginning to deteriorate so I thought I'd better go home and collect some things as I wasn't really prepared for a longer stay. I arrived home and opened the door and the picture frame was on the floor, propped up facing the door. No one had been in the house, and we have no pets or anything. The photo couldn't have travelled from upstairs to the front door without some sort of help. It turned out that dad died as I was driving home, which came as a huge shock. I think dad moved the frame there somehow, before he moved on, to let me know he was going to be OK.

Reflecting on these examples, we might speculate that some jottles (e.g., an appearance or relocation) are more meaningful than other jottles (e.g., a disappearance). Meaningfulness might also be tied to an eerie feature of certain jottle stories—the *sense of presence*. That is where the experient believes an "invisible presence" is "watching" her during the disappearance, appearance, reappearance or replacement—and this "presence" is somehow responsible for the object's behavior. Here's an example from Jemma:

> I have had a few disappearing objects over the years, at different places I've lived, but I've only had one time when the object reappeared. I was overseas on a short holiday and I lost my phone. I think it fell out of my pocket when I was changing clothes and rushing for a coach. I didn't care too much because it was an old phone and I wasn't using it overseas anyway because of the cost. I know the phone was lost for good because it definitely wasn't in my luggage when I packed, and I travelled really light. When I came home everything was fine, but about a month later I walked into the bathroom and the phone was on the vanity. It was the exact phone, in perfect working order and with my contacts and even holiday photos, up to when I was swimming that day and lost it. Funny thing is when I picked it up I had the strongest feeling that there was someone watching me. It wasn't me feeling scared or upset. It was a different feeling. I just somehow knew that someone was there, wanting to see my reaction to the phone being in the bathroom.

Jottles and the Paranormal

Finally, there's the issue of *isolation*. Are jottles isolated events or do they occur in conjunction with other paranormal experiences? We've all heard of "poltergeists"—spooky stories involving an invisible household force that knocks on walls, moves furniture and throws objects around rooms. Is it possible people who claim jottles also suffer similar, poltergeist-like happenings? That's not to say poltergeists are *real*, in the sense of something paranormal. It simply means that jottles might simply be part of a much wider set of paranormal phenomena. A good understanding of the nature of jottles therefore requires thorough knowledge of *other* events simultaneously affecting the experient.

Gaining knowledge of these extra variables (alongside object type, object significance, location of event and time delay) will help our burgeoning understanding of jottles. The task now is to collect as many jottle stories as possible and seek out each of these variables to determine whether any significant patterns emerge—common threads that might take us that little bit closer to an understanding of what jottles actually *are*.

Part II

4

How Prevalent Is the Phenomenon?

Now that we know what to look for in a jottle story, it's time to conduct the analysis. In total, I have managed to bring together 385 detailed cases of disappearing, appearing, reappearing and relocating objects. The most obvious way to use this database is to determine the frequency of jottles in the population, but this presents a problem. These 385 cases are not a random sample, because the majority is self-selected. That simply means the experients *themselves* have identified an unusual event in their lives and publicized it, either by responding to an advertisement for stories or by mentioning it me or someone they think will listen (who then relays it on to me, with permission, via e-mail or written letter). These stories, while invaluable in telling us about *how* the phenomenon operates, won't tell us how *often* it is experienced by the general public.

Fortunately, I've been able to gain an idea of frequency from a recent, well-controlled scientific study. Eighty people volunteered to take part in an anonymous survey, and since they had no idea in advance about the requirements the dilemma of self-selection was minimized.[1] Their task was simply to answer questions about whether they'd ever experienced an incident resembling a "strangely behaving object" and describe in detail one of those incidents.[2] The initial assumption was that very few *legitimate* jottle cases would be documented, so to hold the interest of participants who had never been "jottled" these individuals were asked to create an imaginary tale about an object that mysteriously disappeared, appeared, reappeared or was replaced. In other words, they would become a (very large) simulation control group.

Quite unexpectedly, there were far more legitimate experients than expected! Forty-two participants (52 percent) self-identified as "having been jottled," which is my best guess of the prevalence of jottles in the wider population. That could mean as many as one in two people have experienced a strange disappearance, appearance, reappearance or replacement sometime in their lives. In comparison, the odds of seeing a UFO are about one in three million, so from the perspective of paranormal phenomena jottles appear to be *very* common. It's also interesting that these experients recounted details that were structurally identical to the remainder of the 385 cases in the collection. However, they rarely provided an unusual explanation to account for it. They either admitted being baffled by the object's strange behavior or tried to brush off the jottle as a consequence of "carelessness" or "distraction," in spite of the evidence to the contrary. Therefore, conceding that a jottle is potentially paranormal is the only difference between people who volunteer a jottle story and people who are asked (for the first time) to recall a similar incident in their lives.

How Many People Are Repeaters?

Just because a person is a "repeater" doesn't mean his story is untrustworthy. There's no mandate requiring a jottle to be a singular life event. Indeed, repetition might be a characteristic of the phenomenon. Examining the full collection of 385 stories, 84 storytellers were identified as repeaters, although the number of repetitions varied considerably among them. Episodes range from two (the minimum required to join the "repeater" club) to double figures. Although it's lovely to have so much additional data, errors can arise if multiple cases from the same person are included. For instance, if we added all three examples of Mark's missing TV remote to the collection as independent stories we're likely to reach a misleading conclusion about the prevalence of disappearance jottles compared to appearance, reappearance and replacement jottles. What is just as important, we would overestimate the importance of TV remote controls as a jottled object. To avoid these potential difficulties, only a single case was allowed in the collection from any one person. Preferably, this was the most unusual incident they remembered, containing the greatest amount of relevant information.

And while I'm on the topic of Mark, the analysis suggests that the repeated loss of the *same* object or same *type* of object is actually an aberration. His is the only story in the database that possesses the characteristic of recurrence.[3] I've written extensively about Mark's experiences because they're fascinating and contain much detail, but they cannot be considered representative of the jottle phenomenon as a whole.

Sex Differences?

There's also no evidence that males suffer jottles any more or less frequently than females—cases are equally shared across the collection (197 males versus 188 females). Nor is there any apparent age preference—some people recall adolescent encounters and some, like Shirley, in their eighties report very recent events. Occupation and level of education are also arbitrary, confirming my earlier suggestion that these attributes have no bearing on who experiences jottles and why.

A Hierarchy of Jottled Objects

There *is* one subtle demographic distinction to take into account, however, and this involves the interaction between the experient's sex and the type of object that's jottled. To appreciate this relationship some basic number crunching is required, reducing the overall number of objects from 385 (the total number of collected cases) to 33 simpler object *categories*. Table 1 shows the frequencies of these categories, with a percentage breakdown for males and females, irrespective of whether the jottle was a disappearance, appearance or reappearance (replacement jottles involve two different types of objects, and these will be considered separately). In the table, I've arbitrarily highlighted any category of object with a frequency above 4 percent as Tier 1, meaning they're the most common jottled object. Objects with a frequency of between 2 percent and 4 percent are shown in Tier 2 and any frequency lower than 2 percent is shown in Tier 3.

Tier 1 Objects

Object type	Number	% Overall	% Males	% Females
Jewelry	37	9.8	11	89
Food and beverages	36	9.5	42	58
Keys	26	6.8	50	50
Clothes	21	5.5	29	71
Computer items	18	4.7	89	11
Grooming items	16	4.2	6	94
Utensils	16	4.2	63	38

Tier 2 Objects

Object type	Number	% Overall	% Males	% Females
Household goods and appliances	14	3.7	64	36
Reading material	14	3.7	64	36

Object type	Number	% Overall	% Males	% Females
Toys	14	3.7	79	21
Minor (no significance) items	13	3.4	62	38
Money	13	3.4	62	38
Telephones	13	3.4	31	69
Eyeglasses	12	3.2	58	42
TV remote controls	12	3.2	58	42
Wristwatches	11	2.9	73	27
Tools and building materials	10	2.6	100	0
Cards (credit/debit cards, etc.)	10	2.6	10	90
Medical supplies	9	2.4	56	44
Smoking (cigarettes)	9	2.4	78	22

Tier 3 Objects

Object type	Number	% Overall	% Males	% Females
Smoking (drugs)	7	1.8	86	14
Purses/wallets	7	1.8	71	29
Stationery	7	1.8	29	71
Media	6	1.6	67	33
Artwork	4	1	25	75
Linen/bedding	4	1	25	75
Musical instruments	4	1	50	50
Ornaments	4	1	25	75
Furniture	2	0.5	100	0

Table 1: A hierarchy of the categories of jottled object, sorted by frequency.

The Most Commonly Jottled Objects

From the table it is clear that jewelry items are the premier jottled objects, making up nearly 10 percent of all cases. This category consists of earrings, rings, wristbands and necklaces, although the first two articles are by far the most represented. As small items they're also the easiest to permanently lose or temporarily misplace, which needs to be taken into account when assessing the veracity of claims. The other interesting finding is the percentage breakdown for jewelry between the sexes. Females have their jewelry disappear, appear or reappear far more often than men, the candid explanation being that women own more jewelry than men—or at least pay more attention to its behaving strangely.

Although jewelry items are predominantly of high significance, there's no evidence that frequently jottled objects are always so valuable. That's made clear by the second most popular category, *food and beverages*. The objects in this category are of no personal importance since people don't consider "owning" food in the same way they own a ring or a bracelet. These foods are mostly raw and include bread, cheese, fruit and vegetables, although the occasional processed food article is reported being jottled (e.g., a salt shaker or a chocolate bar). These foods are all single items of a smallish size—a sole apple or tomato or a lone carrot or a single fried chip. We're not dealing with whole meals on a plate or large bags or boxes of assorted products. Beverages are rarely jottled (only six of the 36 cases) but where reported they also vary quite widely, from water to a can of soft drink or a box of fruit juice. Sometimes the liquid disappears *from* (or appears *in*) a glass or bottle, so the actual vessel itself is not necessarily affected. And unlike jewelry, there's no obvious sex difference for jottled foods and beverages, nor is there a discernible item that males lose (or gain) more than females, perhaps because no single type of food is targeted more than twice. It seems as though all small food items are at risk.

The third most popular category is *keys*, which can refer to a single key but more likely is an assortment of house and vehicle keys attached to a key ring. In common with foods and beverages they're jottled equally between males and females, and although keys aren't as sentimental as jewelry they *are* more functional, and their loss can cause considerable annoyance and frustration. Anecdotally (from stories such as Kate's), keys are classically associated with disappearing and reappearing objects—an assumption supported by this cursory analysis.

Number four on the jottle hierarchy are *clothes*, which typically come in all shapes and sizes; stories involve strangely behaving headwear, coats, shirts, trousers, underwear, socks, buttons and shoelaces. Although everyone wears clothes, females tend to claim more experiences of clothing jottles, but no specific style of clothing item is favored.

This sex stereotyping persists over the next few categories. Men have been significantly underrepresented so far in terms of jewelry and clothing, but they make it up fast when it comes to *computer items*. These are small peripheral objects rather than large pieces of equipment like towers, monitors and printers. Items include "mice," USB sticks, cords, cables and memory cards. As well as being a predominantly male problem, these jottles occur overwhelmingly in a home environment rather than, say, the workplace. This might represent nothing more than the outcome of a typically male pastime—playing around with computers in the bedroom or study (e.g., online gaming).

Contained in the sixth category of *grooming* are small hand-held objects such as combs, brushes, hair clips and tweezers, with the seventh category, *utensils*, including forks, spoons, strainers, trays, knives and mugs. Interestingly, grooming items are strongly influenced by sex, with over 90 percent of cases affecting females, in contrast to *utensils,* which slightly favor males (63 percent).

Reflecting on what these seven most frequent categories have in common, an intriguing possibility arises. If we consider only events that comprise a disappearance phase (whether a "gone for good" disappearance or a reappearance), perhaps the object's initial dematerialization has less to do with the importance of the item that disappears or whether the experient was female or male and more to do with the issue of human **interaction**. Interaction is the degree to which the object was actually touched or handled before it was jottled, and as you can see from the types of objects that feature in the top tier they are very interactive. Accounting for sex differences, males just happen to interact more with computer devices such as mice, USBs and cables than they do with jewelry. Females, on the other hand, might handle brushes, hair clips and tweezers more frequently than men.

That still doesn't explain the sex disparity found for clothing jottles. We might expect men and women to interact equally with their apparel, as everyone wears *something.* That's certainly true, but (at the risk of digging myself further down a controversial hole) this might simply reflect a situation where females are more *aware* of their clothing than males and more attentive to the possibility of jottles. Recognizing that an article of clothing has disappeared is not necessarily easy, since it requires a degree of attention and analysis. For example, a male might have taken a pair of socks from the drawer and laid them on the bed. They disappear when his back is turned, but he's too disinterested or distracted to take notice because there's a drawer full of replacement socks in the dresser.[4] This is hardly scientific reasoning, but the concept of interaction at least provides a potential clue for *how* jottles might be initiated.

Less Frequently Jottled Objects

If you read the jottle stories freely available on the Internet—and some of the tales included in this book—you might get the impression that cell phones, glasses, watches and TV remotes are regularly jottled. However, these items emerge only in the second tier of the hierarchy. This tier is headed by *household goods and appliances,* which encompasses low significance, hand-held objects that people use a lot—things like toilet paper, candles, dishwashing liquid, toothpaste and the parts of a vacuum cleaner. Perhaps unexpectedly, males are more likely than females to report these objects being jottled, although not too much can be read into this breakdown since the range of objects in the category is so diverse that it's not possible to come up with specific predictions about which articles are specifically "male jottles," and which are "female jottles."

The number of cases comprising each category declines in Tier 2, hence sex differences become less informative. Nevertheless, in eyeballing the table one might concede that *telephone* jottles[5] tend to affect females; jottles of *TV remote controls, eyeglasses* and *medical supplies* (e.g., pills and Band-Aids) occur equally between sexes; and jottled *wristwatches, reading material* (books and magazines) and *toys* are predominantly experienced by males. *Minor* (no significance) items similarly favor males, although like household goods and appliances this is a generic category holding an inconsistent array of worthless items, for example discarded timber pieces, the orphaned lid of an empty jar and paper trash.

Tools and building materials are also a class of male jottle comprising small things you'd expect could easily be lost and found. Examples include drill bits, screws and nails, although sometimes larger hand-held items such as hatchets, saws and electric drills are targeted. Likewise, males overwhelmingly report jottles of *smoking* items—cigarettes and cannabis joints (in the third tier)—which perhaps reflects their slightly higher prevalence of usage in the population.[6] On the other hand, jottles of various types of *cards* appear to be the domain of females (these are debit and credit cards and driving licenses rather than actual playing cards). Therefore, notable sex differences exist among the jottle categories in Tier 1 and Tier 2. However, all items within these categories have one thing in common—they are all *interactive*.

I've left until last a Tier 2 category which I believe is the most intriguing of all jottled objects: *money*. Admittedly "money" and "disappearance" are two words that go together in a very un-mysterious way. However, this isn't the case for the 13 stories in the collection. Most involve single coins, not wads of cash, and as I'll shortly explain these coins *don't* disappear from wallets and purses, never to be seen again.

Rare Jottles

Tier 3 consists of object categories holding between two and seven cases—too few to achieve a meaningful frequency distinction between males and females. Nevertheless, the category labels in this tier are very interesting. On first glance, they represent objects that grow physically larger the lower we scroll down the list. Starting at the top of the tier, the category *stationery* includes small things like sticky-notes and pencils, and *media* refers to DVD boxes and videos cassettes. But as frequency declines, the categories of *artwork, linen/bedding, musical instruments, ornaments* and *furniture* are represented. While these lower category labels might epitomize "big things," the objects comprising these categories are not themselves big. For example, artwork doesn't refer to a large dusty-framed canvas hanging on a wall over a fireplace, but a sheet of paper with a drawing or painting on it. Likewise, linen/bedding could be a single pillowcase (not a whole quilt), musical instruments are things as small as a guitar pick, and furniture is a reference to loose doorknobs and drawer handles—not an actual dresser or cupboard sitting unused and untouched in the corner of a living room.

Reflecting on the Data So Far

From this superficial analysis, the type of object you would *expect* to be jottled *is* jottled. To reiterate, these are articles found around the house or on the person. Differences between female and male reports are also predictable. Females tend to report jottles of "female" things, and males tend to report jottles of "male" things. Furthermore, objects are the type that are routinely touched, handled or used at the time they're jottled. That's why I suggested that interaction is a variable worth exploring further.

It is also apparent that larger objects (bigger than that which can be held easily in the hand) are only very rarely jottled. This relationship is surely a boon for skeptics. Taking furniture as an example, large articles are much harder to accidentally misplace than diminutive earrings or keys, so that's why tables and chairs (rather than knobs and handles) are hardly ever reported as having been jottled. That's a perfectly reasonable criticism, although it conveniently ignores the context in which small objects disappear, appear, reappear or are replaced. To appreciate this context, we'll need to explore the data more deeply.

Object Significance

Significance	Number	%
High	31	8
Medium	188	49
Low	127	33
None	8	2
Unowned Familiar	27	7
Unowned Unfamiliar	4	1

Table 2: A breakdown of object significances across the collection.

Rearranging the raw data from Table 1 leads to the creation of Table 2—a breakdown of the different significances of jottled objects. Examining these percentages, it's easy to see that objects of low to medium significance most frequently disappear, appear, reappear or get replaced, which counters the argument that jottles involve nothing more than "expensive stuff that's stolen." Indeed, half of all jottled objects are of medium significance—things like inexpensive pieces of jewelry, car keys, driving licenses and credit cards that are all considered replaceable. Moreover, when it comes to the high significance category, there are just as many ordinary objects considered precious or sentimental as truly valuable items. They are as likely to be an old moth-eaten teddy bear as an heirloom diamond wedding ring. Low significance objects, like food items and household possessions, are also strongly represented across the jottle collection, which again supports my earlier claim that it isn't necessarily the most valuable articles in a person's life that are impacted by the jottle phenomenon—it's the stuff they *use* the most.

What Are the Most Common Object Behaviors?

Jottle Type	Number	%
Disappearance	142	37
Appearance	44	11
Reappearance	192	50
Replacement	7	2

Table 3: A breakdown of jottle frequencies in the collection.

A further juggling of the data gives rise to Table 3—the percentage breakdown of the various types of jottles across the data collection. You'll notice that reappearances make up half of all cases! I've previously indicated that a comprehensive reappearance story is one of the best pieces of evidence that jottles are truly anomalous. The sheer number of these cases in the collection therefore undermines any simplistic assumption that jottles are nothing more than tales of things that disappear—and if they involve rings or money it's because of thievery, while everything else that goes missing is nothing more than forgetfulness. That's not to say objects don't disappear regularly, although Table 3 shows this proportion is only a little over one-third of all cases. Another surprise is the very small percentage of appearance jottles (11 percent), and the even smaller number of replacements (2 percent).

But there's a catch! Cast your mind back to the small study that determined the relative prevalence of jottles in the population. Of the 80 stories provided by participants, 38 were *imagined*. While these stories don't contribute to the collection, they do provide important information. Table 4 shows the percentage breakdown of imagined jottles for this small group, and you'll notice it's quite similar to the distribution of "real" jottle stories (Table 3).

Imaginary Jottle Type	Number	%
Disappearance	16	42
Appearance	6	16
Reappearance	14	37
Replacement	2	5

Table 4: A breakdown of object behaviors for "imaginary" participants.

It also turns out that the objects from these imaginary tales closely match those listed in Table 1. Apart from a single, flippant example of an "appearing elephant," participants made up jottle stories featuring USB sticks, jewelry (rings, bracelets, earrings and necklaces), camera and computer accessories, books, a hairbrush, a knife, keys, shoes, telephones, and a wallet. Put simply, without any prior knowledge, these novices were able to fabricate a jottle narrative that is, in many ways, identical to a "real" tale (at least in terms of jottle *type* and jottle *object*).

This lends credence to the skeptical argument that experients consciously (or unconsciously) fanaticize their "true" reports. However, I'm not prepared to write off jottles on the basis of this very small sample of "imaginaries." After all, "real" jottles are actually quite simple events—in fact, *so* simple that the circumstances surrounding them might easily be concocted by naïve participants in a simple experiment. That doesn't mean these "real" stories are *false*. Rather, they are intuitively easy to imitate.

How Objects Disappear

To learn more about what distinguishes the different types of "real" jottle stories it's necessary to study each in turn, starting with a close inspection of disappearances. Disappearance aren't restricted to one particular sex (75 females, 67 males), although repeaters are relatively common. Indeed, it turns out that 30 percent of experients report multiple jottles in their lives, and of these a large majority claim they'd only ever experienced *other* disappearances—not appearances, reappearances, or replacements. That suggests people who suffer disappearance jottles possess a very particular disappearing "trait."

Furthermore, disappearing objects are more likely to go missing from a precise location than an imprecise location. This lends further credence to the anomalous nature of jottles, as it confirms that most stories of disappearing objects are *not* vague recollections by gullible individuals of situations where something they owned vanished from "somewhere." In fact, if a disappearance does occur from an imprecise location, individuals are more likely to believe it has been misplaced, stolen or thrown away by accident. The event is rarely considered mysterious.

Regarding *where* disappearances occur, as you might suspect the answer is also straightforward: home. The majority of disappearances occur in a room of a house, the front or back yard, the driveway or the garage. Only on rare occasions do objects go missing in strange circumstances from a restaurant table, doctor's office or some other very public place. Moreover, when it comes to *what* disappears, there's another surprise. It's not jewelry that most frequently vanishes permanently (as indicated by the *combined* data in Table 1), but foods and beverages—twice as often as any other type of object! I've included the percentage frequencies of the top five disappearing objects in Table 5, and you'll notice the category of food and beverage is way out on top.

Object	% of Total Disappearances
Food and Beverage	16
Jewelry	9
Clothes	6
Household goods and appliances	6
Utensils	6

Table 5: *The most frequent disappearing object categories.*

Disappearing Food, with Some Utensils Thrown In

I've already mentioned that food and beverage is a low significance category which favors food items rather than beverages, since examples of jottled drinks are relatively uncommon. When it comes to disappearances, it's not surprising to find food items vanish from the kitchen, although other rooms around the house are sporadically represented—in particular the dining room and living room. It's also intriguing to learn *how* these food items disappear. Most stories are associated with a short last seen delay, whereby the experient is present in the room—usually the kitchen—

during the period of time when the food vanishes. This doesn't mean they actually witnessed the disappearance. I can find no good case where an experient has seen a piece of food dematerializing in front of them. Rather, it's commonplace for them to have taken their eyes off a slice of bread or single biscuit as it sits on the countertop, only to return their gaze to find it gone. Also emblematic of food disappearances are items that fall temporarily out of eyesight, having been knocked off a bench or table onto the floor. When the experient goes in search of the item, either immediately or a minute or two later, they cannot find it (and *never* find it). Here's a great story from Ed that specifically involves a disappearing food product:

> I once made a salad sandwich and put everything on it including a big slice of tomato. I stuffed it too full, and half of it slipped straight down onto the floor when I picked it up. I saw the bits and pieces fall in one big plop out of the corner of my eye. None of it flew anywhere. I am sure it all landed in the same place at my feet. I managed to pick it all up except for the tomato piece. It wasn't still in the sandwich and it wasn't on the floor, or anywhere in the kitchen. I just found this strange. I don't know why it happened. It's stupid.

Kitchens are communal spaces, so it's satisfying to find that over three-quarters of these "rapid" disappearance stories are shared by one or two other people in the experient's company—although these peripheral actors also *do not* witness the food "winking out of existence" before their eyes. They are merely present in the kitchen or dining room when the disappearance occurs and take part in the subsequent, unsuccessful search. That's good evidence to suggest these kitchen disappearances aren't purely imaginary.

While we're on the subject of objects disappearing from kitchens, it's worth mentioning that utensils (knives, forks and spoons) also vanish from this location and in the manner of foods they're low significance items. The overwhelming majority of cases similarly possess trifling last seen delays. The disappearance occurs either immediately (a dropped fork vanishing before it has hit the ground) or within a few seconds (a spoon that goes missing from the tabletop when the experient's attention is drawn elsewhere). Apart from the difference between organic raw food items and inorganic utensils, there's very little to distinguish the two types of disappearance—particularly in terms of how the item is being used at the time. Foods and utensils are usually handled moments before they disappear. Therefore, a brash suggestion might be that disappearing items are not only interactive items, but also that they disappear because they have been only *recently* interacted with. Of course there are exceptions. Plenty of tales can be found (on the Internet and elsewhere) of individuals opening a fridge or cupboard door only to cause an apple or tomato to come loose and drop to the floor. The piece of fruit rolls between their feet and is never seen again. While these examples don't involve the fruit's being touched, it is possible that the *motion* of this object is the more fundamental property of disappearances, and interaction through touch simply facilitates this necessary movement.

Disappearing Household Goods and Appliances

Household goods and appliances are hand-held objects of low significance commonly used for menial jobs around the home. Unlike food items, the rooms from which these goods vanish vary greatly. It all depends on what these items are. Toilet paper disappears from the bathroom, detergent from the laundry shelf and the head of a vacuum cleaner from the hall closet. These are all useful items, and like food their loss is frequently associated with a small last seen delay of seconds or minutes following recent interaction.

Why such a short last seen delay? That's straightforward. The only reason why anyone would bother acknowledging the mysterious disappearance of a lowly toilet roll or unimportant detergent bottle is that the circumstances surrounding the disappearance are considered "weird." When an ordinary object rapidly vanishes from the vicinity of experients they are jolted out of their complacency. Imagine rushing desperately to the bathroom, checking there's toilet paper in the holder by giving it a spin, sitting down, then turning to pull a sheet off the roll only to find it's now missing. That's a humorous event worth remembering and retelling at some later time. Likewise, you might fill a capful of laundry liquid and pour it into the machine, but when you go to screw the lid back onto the container it isn't where you *know* you just left it. That's another tale that might stay with you for a long time.

Stories of low significance items vanishing over much longer last seen delays aren't remembered with such clarity. Picture yourself opening the laundry cupboard to fetch a cleaning cloth you last used two weeks ago, and you find it's not there. Given the passage of time, you're unlikely to interpret this loss as "supernatural." It never crosses your mind *why* the cloth isn't there anymore. You assume it must have ended up as an unidentifiable rag in the garage or garbage can, and you simply grab another cloth as a replacement. Who knows how many similar objects found missing over time have the characteristics of jottles but are never recognized as such?

Disappearing Jewelry and Clothing

There are plenty of examples of experients recently handling jewelry and clothing before these items disappear—with bedroom locations figuring prominently. Rings and brooches are placed on dressers and vanish in the period when the experient is briefly out of the room. Shirts, underwear and trousers swiftly disappear from the floors on which they've been hastily discarded or the bedcovers where they've been hurriedly laid. Here's an example from Michelle:

> I once threw a pair of leggings on the bed and went back to the wardrobe to find something else that would go with them. I had my back to the bed for no more a minute, but when I went to put the leggings on they were gone. No-one had been in the room with me, because I'd closed the door and would have heard someone if they'd come in the room. I looked everywhere but I never found them again.

However, this isn't to say that short last seen delays are an orthodox feature of disappearing objects. Stories of vanishing jewelry and clothing frequently describe much longer last seen delays, often overnight. For example, it's common for rings or earrings to be removed and placed on a dresser or nightstand before the experient retires to bed. She wakes the next morning only to find the articles inexplicably missing. Similarly, a shirt might be hung in a cupboard one afternoon but is no longer there the next morning.

Last seen delays can also be in the order of weeks or months where high significance heirloom rings and necklaces and favorite items of apparel are concerned. These are often stored untouched for a very long time; for instance a new shirt or dress might be packed away over winter or saved for a special night out and is noticed missing only when it is eventually sought from a drawer, chest or closet. The event is interpreted as a jottle because the storage was performed in private and the experient is certain friends or siblings couldn't be responsible for taking such a valuable item without permission.

Superficially, a lengthier last seen delay distinguishes stories of disappearing jewelry and clothing from stories of vanishing foods, utensils and household goods. Can these different styles of disappearance be reconciled, specifically in terms of interaction or motion or both? The answer is "yes" if the following two arguments are accepted. The first is that jewelry and clothing items are more personally significant than foods, utensils and household goods, hence their loss is more salient even when a protracted last seen delay is involved.

Second, it's simply not possible to determine exactly when a jewelry piece or clothing article vanished during the last seen delay—regardless of whether the time period is in the order of hours, months or perhaps even years. Assuming the object has dematerialized (which is a *big* conceptual leap), we really can't be sure this didn't happen only moments after the ring or garment was last touched while being stored away! In these circumstances, a *long* last seen delay may still be compatible with recent interaction.

The Curious Nature of Appearing Objects

According to Table 3, mysteriously appearing objects are much rarer than either object disappearances or reappearances—making up only 11 percent of the database. Nevertheless, this percentage is still big enough to work with and some interesting findings emerge. The first is that appearance jottles are shared equally by males and females (26 males, 18 females), and the second is that they occur in familiar locations, particularly around the home. In fact, well over three-quarters of object appearances take place in various household rooms, as well as backyards and driveways. A home focus is to be expected, because personal objects must be *very* well-recognized to be unexpectedly discovered at an unfamiliar location.

If the object does appear somewhere other than the home or yard, it's most likely to be at the experient's workplace. Strangely enough, the other location is on or beside a road or sidewalk. For example, the experient might be strolling along a verge or driving down a deserted road when they spy a wallet or purse lying just ahead of them. Only when they stop walking or pull over to examine the discarded item more closely do they realize it actually belongs to *them* and isn't where it *should* be (in other words, their coat pocket, glove compartment or handbag). Although dramatic, these outdoor cases are truly the exception rather than the rule. The five most frequent object categories are shown in Table 6 and make up roughly half of all appearance jottles (there's a huge drop in case frequency from 5th most frequent to 6th most frequent).

Object	% of total appearances
Food and Beverage	11
Jewelry	11
Clothes	9
Household goods and appliances	9
Money	9

Table 6: The most prevalent appearing object categories.

This list looks familiar! You'll notice the top three most common appearing object categories are exactly the same as the top three disappearing object categories. There are food and beverage items at number one (again), jewelry items at number two (again) and clothes at number three (again). Here's another important finding: only three of these appearance stories come from "repeaters." That means very few individuals claim to have experienced multiple appearance jottles, let alone episodes of object disappearances or reappearances. Appearing objects are therefore a "surprise" event—something singular in a person's life, whereas I've already suggested that people who suffer from disappearances are often plagued by them over a lifetime.

Foods and Beverages as Windfalls

I have a prediction. Should you ever experience an appearance jottle, chances are it will be a small item of food turning up somewhere in your kitchen. Expect it to be a raw food, although there's also a small chance it will be processed and in a package.[7] In the fashion of disappearing foods, you won't necessarily witness the materialization and you will probably be on your own when it happens. Unfortunately, I can't forecast whether you'll recognize the food item as something that's yours (owned familiar) or something you don't own (unowned familiar), because both types of objects feature prominently in the collection.

If you do recognize the food item as something you own, then the last seen delay and appearance delay are usually in the order of hours, overnight, or at the very most a few days. Here's a typical example. Katrina last remembers placing a small half-filled plastic bag of cooking chocolate in the pantry on Tuesday afternoon. On Thursday evening she tidies the kitchen, turns off the light and retires to bed, waking on Friday morning to find the same chocolate bag, with the same amount of chocolate in it, now sitting on the countertop. The last seen delay was approximately two days, and the appearance delay was overnight.

In terms of an explanation, Katrina has no idea how or why the chocolate bag appeared where it did, but she prefers the simple rationalization that because her husband and young children were also in the house on Thursday night they *might* have been responsible—although judging from the way she tells her story she doesn't really believe this to be true. I'd go as far as to suggest many appearance jottles haven't made the collection because an unlikely explanation is better than no explanation at all. And even though the appearance of a food item in the kitchen may be surprising, most of the time the event is soon forgotten in the hubbub of everyday living.

Nevertheless, the appearance is particularly memorable when the food is unowned familiar and not recognized as something that's ever been purchased. In other words, the food is a true *windfall* in the manner of Martin's egg (discussed earlier). While the last seen delay is not relevant to these examples, the appearance delay varies significantly among cases. Sometimes the period is short, as in Martin's story. At other times it can be much longer—24 hours in this story from Greta: "I once found a bag of plain biscuits in the bread bin. I don't know where they came from, as I didn't put them there. I'd never seen them before, and they weren't in the bin last time I looked, the day before. I don't live alone, but I was on my own at the time as it was Easter-time and everyone else was away." This highlights how food *appearances* differ from food *disappearances*. Food that vanishes from your kitchen naturally belongs to you, but an item of food that materializes in your kitchen is very often NOT yours!

This thought-provoking feature of appearing food items allows me to return to a profound question I first brought up on at the beginning: If owned familiar food items are the most frequent type of disappearing object, and unowned familiar food items are very common appearing objects, does that imply someone's edible flyaway is another person's edible windfall? For instance, a banana disappears in unusual circumstances from the kitchen of Person A. Hundreds of miles away, Person B unexpectedly finds the same banana in *her* kitchen, for no apparent reason. From this perspective, appearances and disappearances are implicitly linked. That's hardly a novel proposition. Back in the 1920s the outstanding investigator of anomalies, Charles Fort (whom we will meet again later in this book) contemplated stories of objects that disappear and others that appear. He pondered "whether something that mysteriously appears somewhere had not mysteriously disappeared somewhere else (568)."[8]

If you're prepared to countenance this wild speculation, then you might surmise that my made-up story of a disappearing/appearing banana is initiated by a "rule of recent interaction" and is driven by the experient who first lost the fruit. As an active agent, the experient touches or gives motion to the food item, causing it to vanish (in some as yet unknown way) and randomly end up somewhere else. This in turn might account for why—at the receiving end—the appearance delay is so variable. The appearance of the unowned familiar food item is simply a passive event not instigated by the receptive experient at all. Perhaps that's why people who report the materialization of unrecognized food items around their homes are unlikely to be repeaters—they are simply random bystanders in someone else's disappearing jottle dilemma!

Of course, this creates more questions than answers. For instance, why must the food item appear in a completely different kitchen and not *any* room of the new house or even in a house at all? And what do we make of stories of owned food items mysteriously appearing, like Katrina's chocolate? Do food turn-ups and food windfalls have different causes? Let's dig further.

Materializing Jewelry

Materializing jewelry is a female predicament (as we might expect from the overall analysis) and these pieces tend to be unowned familiar. They include strange rings, earrings, necklaces and bracelets, and the bedroom is the most common appearance location. At all times, the experient is alone when the item materializes, so these jottles are very private affairs. The jewelry piece looks and feels quite ordinary in every respect, and there's no evidence of strange markings or hieroglyphics to indicate a bizarre, otherworldly origin (unowned unfamiliar objects do not feature in the database). These items also appear over a consistently short appearance delay. That is, the experient had left the room only momentarily or had remained in the room and turned her back, only to find a ring or necklace on a nearby dresser or nightstand. There are even a few examples where experients actually see the article appear in mid-air before it drops to the floor. This surprise, coupled with the fact that the object is not recognized as being owned, has a long-term, personal impact. Experients are far more likely to consider this appearance as "meaningful," compared to the person who reports a stick of celery showing up overnight next to the dish drainer. The latter is thought of as outlandish and a good (if inexplicable) yarn. The windfall of a ring or necklace, however, is construed as a gift from a deceased loved one or an angelic being.

Appearing Clothing, Household Goods and Money

Only three other appearing object categories contain enough cases for consideration: *clothes, household goods and appliances,* and *money*. Like food and jewelry, all three possess a surprisingly large number of unowned familiar cases.[9] With regard to clothes and household items, a peculiar shoe could be found resting in the shoe rack, or an odd wax candle sitting on the living room coffee table. There's no apparent reason for the objects to be where they're discovered. No one in the house admits responsibility or claims ownership, and there's no evidence the appearance is a practical joke. With variable appearance delays in the order of minutes to hours, these cases better resemble food materializations than they do jewelry materializations. The experient also finds the event arbitrary and meaningless.

Money, however, is a different matter. I've already suggested that these are some of my favorite jottle stories, and that's because they consistently involve the appearance of a single, unowned coin in spectacular circumstances. The coin is in good condition and originates from the country where the jottle takes place. It could be five, ten, twenty or even forty years old—but it's never anything truly antique. Uniquely, these coins are *active* objects, which means they are heard or seen to drop to the floor rather than being found resting passively on a chair or desk. They're also the only object that appears consistently outside a home environment, although still within the confines of a building. Reports of appearing coins have involved a public hallway, a public toilet and an office building.

The strange behavior of appearing coins can be quite eerie. I can't match for quality this story from an Internet blog that I'll now paraphrase (although like all such tales I've avoided using it in the database). One evening the male narrator was alone in his house taking a bath when he heard the noise of an object hitting the floor somewhere up the hallway—out of sight—and rolling toward the open bathroom door. A silver coin then appeared in the doorway and made a neat turn toward the bathtub, ending up just within reach as it fell over. Needless to say, the narrator was quite disturbed by the event.

Building a Theory of Jottles

The inclination for appearing objects to be unowned familiar further advances our nascent theory of jottles. So far, I've argued that recent interaction or motion or both is a feature of many disappearance stories. The experient has often touched or held the object moments before it vanishes forever. For appearing objects, the concept of interaction is less relevant if that object is recognizably owned, because the last seen delay is frequently quite long. Indeed, these objects generally haven't been handled for hours, days or even months until they turn up somewhere unexpected. For example, food items that have lain dormant in the pantry for days or weeks appear on the kitchen counter overnight or during the day when the house's residents are at work or school. The experient appreciates the event is strange but attributes very little purpose to it.

And of course if what materializes is *not* owned there has been no prior interaction; however, the appearance delay is usually short and the experient interprets the event as purposeful. These jottles therefore hold an *intentionality* not found with disappearing or appearing owned objects. As single small windfalls, they might not be terribly valuable in their own right but they represent value and could be considered a "gift." This is particularly the case with jewelry, but there are several examples of appearing unowned foods which might also possess a gift-like quality depending on the experient's current circumstances.[10] For instance, Martin was in need of an egg to complete his recipe and one was provided. In this way we're not simply dealing with *how* a jottle occurs, but *why*.

Assuming this paranormal conjecture is legitimate, and intention has some bearing on the appearance of an unowned object, then how can it be determined which appearance jottles are intentional and which aren't? There are no rules to guide us, other than the following simple dichotomy: *explicit* and *implicit*. *Explicit intention* refers to situations where the experient easily perceives a logical context for the appearance, like Eleanor's story recounted earlier. There is an indisputable connection between this jottle and the death of her father. Another, less morbid example of explicit intention is contained in this appearance tale from Dave, involving a cricket bat and an upcoming finals match:

> On a Saturday afternoon in February I turned up to the oval to watch my team play a cricket semi-final. I was carrying a rib injury from the week before and consequently wasn't playing, but I would be playing next week if we won this game and made the grand final. I was pretty nervous about that game, and whether I would be able to bat well enough to make a contribution. So, I made a conscious decision to mentally prepare myself during the week, and practice every day with a bat. I didn't actually own a proper bat—I always borrowed one from the team kit—but I knew there was a "junior" bat somewhere in the garage at home I might be able to use. I'd have to search hard for it, though, as it would be buried somewhere in all the junk that was piled up against the back wall. I hadn't seen it, or thought about it, in months. Anyway, I left the game about 3 p.m. to go home, as I'd agreed to go out to a friend's place for dinner that night. We left as a family around 5 p.m. and I locked up the house once I was sure everyone was in the car. We returned home at 9 p.m. and I was the first inside, turning on the light in the lounge room. Immediately I noticed, propped up against the bookshelf, the junior cricket bat. It was the one from somewhere in the garage. It absolutely should not have been there. It wasn't a practical joke from one of the kids because I was the last one to leave the house, and the first one inside. No one else had been in the house—we don't exactly live in a populated area, and besides ... only I knew about my worries with batting. I hadn't told anyone else. There's no conventional explanation for why that bat appeared

where it did, and when it did. There was definitely a reason for it happening, it was to make me focus on the next weekend.

On the other hand, *implicit intention* corresponds to situations where the jottle seems purposeful, but the reason simply cannot be discerned. Judgment is based more on "gut feeling" than on common sense. There's no objective way to determine whether a jottle possesses implicit intention, other than assuming the appearance of an unowned object is interpretable as a gift, but the appearance of an owned object has a deeper, symbolic function.

Revisiting Interaction and Intention for Reappearance Jottles

Recall from Table 3 that "reappearances" are the most common jottle. Unfortunately they are also the most complex because they involve both a disappearance and an appearance phase. Luckily, 85 percent of stories in the collection involve both the disappearance *and* subsequent reappearance taking place in the same home environment, which makes interpretation of the data much easier. Of the remaining cases, 10 percent claim *only* the disappearance *or* the reappearance occurs in the home (that is, the object disappears or reappears somewhere else), and a meagre 5 percent have no home involvement whatsoever.

And of the 192 people who claim to have experienced a reappearance jottle, 29 are self-confessed repeaters. Seven report additional reappearances *only*, while the remaining 22 also recount disappearances *and* appearances. These figures are very different from what we found for (1) disappearance jottles, where repeaters are plagued only by *other* disappearances, and (2) appearance jottles, where repeaters are uncommon. Therefore, the analysis shows that reappearances are a more flexible style of jottle compared with either disappearances or appearances.

Furthermore, the types of object that reappear don't resemble those that disappear or appear, as shown in Table 7. This table is arranged in an alternative fashion to Tables 5 and 6 as it lists the frequencies of the top five reappearing object categories in the first column but in two additional columns also shows the frequencies of those *same* objects for disappearance and appearance jottles. You'll notice that in terms of raw percentage, the top five reappearance categories are very different from the equivalent disappearance and appearance categories.

Object	Reappearance (%)	Disappearance (%)	Appearance (%)
Keys	11	4	2
Jewelry	11	9	11
Computer items	8	2	0
TV remote control	6	1	0
Food and beverage	5	16	11

Table 7: The most prevalent reappearing object categories, compared with their frequency as disappearing and appearing objects.

Specifically, *keys* are by far the most frequent reappearing object, but are rarely reported to have permanently disappeared or appeared from nowhere. And just as strikingly, the strong presence of *computer parts* and *TV remote controls* in the overall collection (see Table 1) is entirely due to these objects reappearing! These variations suggest that a disappearance jottle is not simply the first stage of an unrealized reappearance jottle.[11] Based on the evidence of what objects most commonly disappear and what objects most commonly reappear, it seems clear that whatever is behind a disappearing object is different from whatever "causes" an object to disappear but *come back again*.

Reappearances: The Answer Is with the Keys

The collection provides five stories of permanently disappearing keys and key rings and only one story involving an appearing (unowned familiar) key. On the other hand, there are 23 strong cases of reappearing keys or sets of keys. Although a great deal of outward variation exists amongst these tales, when judged as a whole a subtle pattern emerges. To recognize it we need to consider where the keys went missing, where exactly they reappeared, and the length of the return phase.

When the keys initially disappear, some stories purport the loss to be in minutes, some over hours, and others involve days, weeks and even months. As you might expect, if the last seen delay is on the order of seconds or minutes, the experient is usually present in the room when the keys go missing. Alternatively, if they only recognize the loss overnight or after a few days, they are typically uncertain of the time or place where the keys were last seen or placed. Of the two circumstances, the latter is far more common for reappearing keys. I'd suggest this has something to do with the fact that keys are not in constant use. We tend to seek them out when we need them, once or twice a day in the place where they're usually stored (perhaps a hook on the wall or drawer in the hallway).

The *loss delay* also varies considerably, from minutes to hours or even many months (Kate's story comes to mind here). However, there's a noticeable consistency in the relationship between the last seen delay and the loss delay. When the last seen delay is short, so too is the loss delay. The keys quickly disappear then reappear after only a few minutes—or an hour at the most. This also implies a small reappearance delay—the experient is generally in the act of searching when the keys are (thank goodness) found.

Here's an informative story that exhibits a short last seen, loss and reappearance delay. Christian places his keys on top of his bag on the kitchen counter when he comes in from school, ducks down the hall to change, and returns to fetch them only to discover they aren't there anymore. He is alone in the house, or so he assumes. Since the keys aren't in the kitchen, Christian searches the porch, hallway, bathroom and bedroom before returning to the kitchen to find his keys—back on his bag on the counter.

Keys can also be noticed missing overnight or after a day or two. That's to be expected when you hang them on the rack once you've opened the front door, not needing them again until it's time to take the car out of the garage the next morning. Matching this longer last seen delay is a loss delay that's also consistently of the same magnitude.[12] Stories that include longer last seen delays and loss delays also show more variable reappearance delays.

Fast Loss/Fast Returns and Long-Delayed Relocations

Considering these different patterns of time, a more sophisticated model for reappearance jottles can be proposed. In the manner of Christian's encounter with the phenomenon, if we've only recently seen our keys but can't find them where we just left them, then we shouldn't panic; we can expect to see them again shortly. On the other hand, we might discover our keys missing after a considerable period of time. We search the house, without luck, and put the loss down to forgetfulness. However, if we suspect the disappearance is something atypical (perhaps one of those unfortunate jottles haunting us time and again over the years), we might seek solace in the knowledge that they *will* eventually reappear. After all, the evidence suggests that keys are apt to reappear rather than disappear for good. Unfortunately we might also have to accept that, because it's been a long while since we noticed the keys missing, we might have to wait just as long for their return!

Informed by this data, I can make a further suggestion about *where* the keys will reappear. As it turns out, there's a dearth of precise return cases involving keys. If you recall, this is where an object goes missing from a known spot (such as the key hook or kitchen drawer) and is later found back in this spot despite a previous, thorough search. In the few detailed cases available (e.g., Christian's), it is usually only a matter of minutes before the keys are discovered missing and only a few minutes pass before they reappear in the location.[13] So expanding on my original prediction, if we find our keys missing not long after we've put them down on the kitchen counter not only should we expect them to show up again shortly, but they also should reappear in the *same* location we left them. Typically, that's sums up Christian's experience. Therefore, short last seen and loss delays lead to *precise object returns* (a "fast loss/fast return").

It's not possible to supplement the few precise return (key) cases with the addition of imprecise returns, because there aren't any of these cases in the database. As mentioned in chapter one, imprecise returns have a respectability problem. After all, if you're unsure about where you've lost your keys (if they're lost at all), search for them thoroughly—including the place where they're usually kept—then find them back in this same spot a little later, couldn't this simply reflect carelessness on your behalf? Or has someone in the family felt guilty about taking them and put them back without owning up to it? That's certainly possible in light of the tales you find on the Internet rather than in the current database of stories. In one Internet example, keys for a motorcycle went missing from around the house (a last seen delay of four days) and a search ensued—particularly around the place where they were usually kept. The experient appears to have searched sporadically in different rooms of the house over the next few days, a search culminating in another hunt through the house, where they were subsequently found, back on the key rack where they belonged.

The problem with this story—like many low-information Internet tales—is that no good reason is given *not* to suspect that someone else hadn't taken the keys and returned them a few days later. It seems the most obvious explanation because the experient never mentions they were alone in the house during the loss delay. I'm certainly not claiming that the experient is mistaken in regarding the incident as anomalous, only that there's not enough information to confidently rule out a mundane explanation for the reappearance.

On the other hand, precise relocations are the most striking example

4: How Prevalent Is the Phenomenon?

of a reappearance jottle, with many stories in the collection centered on keys. These cases also contain plenty of detail. Keys vanish from one known location—chiefly around the house—and reappear in a completely different (house) location. In the manner of key returns, the way they reappear suggests a core logic. Seldom is a relocation associated with both a short last seen and loss delay. Rather, you might not have seen your missing keys for hours, although you know exactly where they should be. In these circumstances, not only can you be confident they *will* eventually reappear, you can also predict the reappearance to be at some completely unexpected location around the house or yard. There's also a greater chance you'll view the event as *meaningful*. The return of your keys to the hook where they are normally kept might be brushed off as "strange," but you'll be more disturbed if they relocate to the inside of a shoe instead. In this context, you'll start asking questions about who or what was responsible for the relocation, and why.

As has been pointed out previously, if there's been no recent interaction with a set of keys and the last seen and loss delay are long, an object will likely *relocate* (a "long-delay relocation"). A representation of the time differences associated with fast loss/fast returns, and long-delay relocations are shown in Figure 2.

It is worth augmenting this model with the leftover *imprecise relocation* cases from the database. These are situations in which the experient has only a vague notion of where he last left his keys and discovers them

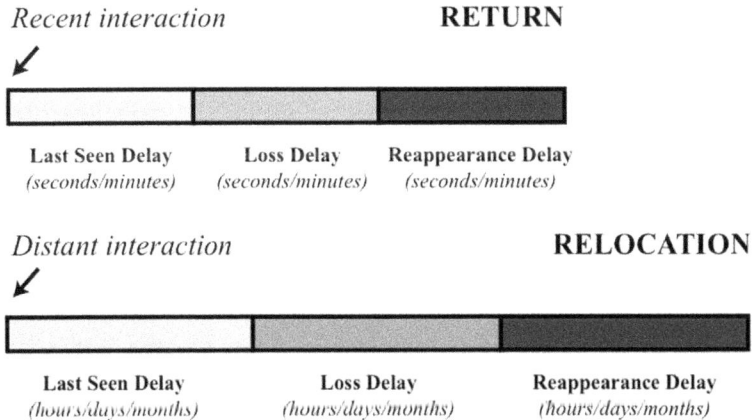

Figure 2: The different delay times associated with object returns (top) and object relocations (bottom). Both returns and relocations are expressions of a reappearance jottle.

relocated to somewhere completely unexpected—the backyard shed, the attic, or even a seldom-used drawer in a filing cabinet at work. These stories are structurally very similar to precise relocations, as they possess comparable last seen delays and loss delays. Here's a story about my own encounter with a relocating key, extracted from a previous book:

> In late 2004 I lost a key to a padlock for an outside gate near my house. I distinctly remember taking it out of the lock and, since all the pockets of my trousers had holes in them, I carried it inside my house. I can't remember what I did with it after that–I presume I must have put it on a table or a bench. A few days later I needed the key, but couldn't find it anywhere. I even tore the house apart looking for it. In the end, I had to hacksaw through a chain to open the gate. I commented out loud how annoying it was that things were going missing around the house (the key being just one of a number of frustrating disappearances) and I wished it would stop. The very next day I was working in a paddock on the property that no-one had entered for over a month. For some reason, I decided to shift a pile of rotten firewood that had been there for many years, and under the very bottom log, where the grass was brown and dead, sat a shiny silver padlock key. I knew instinctively it was my missing key, so I wasn't surprised when it opened the padlock perfectly. If I recall, various (unremembered) incidents had been occurring in the lead up to this particular one, which may explain why I asked it to "stop" on this occasion [81].[14]

Returns and Relocations

In view of the relationship between time delay and the *return* or *relocation* of keys, it's also worth determining whether there's any connection between *loss delay* and distance travelled. Returns are associated with short loss delays and the keys don't travel very far.[15] However, there are also examples of short-distance relocations taking place over slightly longer loss delays; for example keys that are found missing from the bedroom dresser one morning turn up that evening on the bathroom floor. And of course there is Kate's story of her missing keys, relocating from one house to another, very far away, following a year-long loss delay. However, considering as a whole the many tales of jottled keys, I cannot find a systematic correlation between the distance separating the initial loss and subsequent reappearance and the loss delay. Losing your keys from the chair in one room of the house and finding them on a table in the next room *can* involve a period of minutes—or many months, although one would expect the farther away the object is discovered the longer it will take to find it.

What, then, can we conclude about reappearing keys? Although there is no strong evidence of a relationship between temporal delay and distance travelled, the home environment does figure heavily. There is also evidence for two styles of key reappearance—a rapid return to the *same* house location, or a much longer relocation to a *different* (and unexpected) house location, an event imbued with intentionality. This is particularly noticeable when experients consider that the explicit placement of their keys was done with purpose, as if to create shock—for instance on a pillow (Kate), or under a log, as in my story above. This distinction may be a function of recent interaction. Physically handling keys is synonymous with a short last seen delay, and as we've seen from Christian's story this largely results in a short *loss* and *reappearance* phase before the keys are returned. However when there's *no* recent interaction the last seen and loss delays are lengthy, and the reappearance delay is variable. This culminates in a relocation jottle.

Jewelry Also Reappears!

Of the top four reappearing object categories, only *jewelry* finds its way into both the disappearance and appearance hierarchies, although recall that appearing jewelry items tend to be unowned familiar rather than an existing possession—a necessary feature of any reappearing object. Despite this, jewelry items are the same regardless of jottle type (i.e., earrings, rings and bracelets). And, like disappearing jewelry, reappearing jewelry pieces are not something constantly worn, but rather they are handled intermittently or only on special occasions. When not in use they are safely stored out of sight in the bedroom. So if you discover your favorite necklace missing from a dresser drawer it's almost certain that a long time has passed since you last noticed or interacted with it. That accounts for a last seen delay of days to weeks. These similarities also suggest that *some* cases of disappearing jewelry might be unfulfilled reappearances.

Accompanying the long last seen delay for jewelry is a long loss delay and a variable reappearance delay. In common with keys, these delays go hand in hand with relocations, and that's exactly what emerges in stories of reappearing jewelry items. They are discovered somewhere unusual in the house rather than where they first went missing. Indeed, three-quarters of jewelry cases are precise and imprecise relocations, and many months or even years pass before a ring or bracelet that's been lost from one room reappears in another, so large travel distances aren't relevant. For example, Linda tells the story of a single earring that went missing from her nightstand overnight, only to reappear ten months later resting on the carpet at the front door as she returned home one evening (to an empty house, of course). This so disturbed Linda that she considered moving from a house she now believed was haunted by a particularly creepy ghost.

Let's Not Forget Reappearing Computer Parts and TV Remote Controls

Following my initial analysis, I made the claim that *computer items* (memory cards, floppy disks, USB sticks and "mice") are "male" household objects since they are jottled from the bedrooms and home offices of male experients. According to the collection, they also *only* reappear. Computer peripherals rarely disappear for good, and there are no cases where an owned or unowned item mysteriously *appears* in the house. Furthermore, like keys, computer items are of low to medium significance and useful. They're not stored away in a safe place for long periods in the manner of jewelry. Where the reappearance of computer peripherals differs from keys is that they're seldom moved to, or used at, external locations (keys lock doors and start cars and are carried around in handbags). Occasionally loose items such as a USB stick might reappear after vanishing from a coat pocket while it is being carried from place to place, but this is the exception rather than the rule. Typically, computer items are permanently and publically stationed in a fixed spot on a study table next to the hard drive.

Computer items also go missing while in the process of being used. For instance, Steve is busy working at his computer and is momentarily distracted by an event behind him. When he turns back to continue typing, he discovers the mouse is no longer sitting on the mouse pad. The last seen delay is therefore very short, followed by a rapid loss delay and a precise return. Steve drops to the floor and searches under the desk on his hands and knees to see if the mouse has fallen, and when he lifts his head he finds himself staring at his mouse, returned neatly to the pad. Once more, this "fast loss/fast return" scenario is not indicative of anything meaningful. On telling his story Steve didn't perceive any obvious purpose, although he was adamant the mouse had actually disappeared and he hadn't been hallucinating.

To the contrary, discovering a computer item missing after a long last seen delay then finding it has mysteriously returned to where it was last seen is exceedingly uncommon. In those few cases where the last seen delay is long (signifying no interaction) there is instead a longer loss delay and a meaningful relocation. These items also tend to be more valuable than a mere cable or mouse. This example of an intentional relocation comes from Mitchell;

> I remember when the CD with all the holiday videos on it went missing from the CD drive in the computer. It was there one day, the next day it wasn't. I asked everyone in the family "who took it," but no one owned up. I don't think anyone else knew what I was talking about. They weren't that interested, and I know they weren't playing any tricks. I gave up looking, figuring it would turn up eventually. The very next morning I found it sitting right in the middle of the driver's seat of my car. The car was locked all night, and I have the only keys, so no-one else could have put it there. It wasn't there when I parked the car the night before. I would have felt it when I sat down. The reason? It's got something to do with what was on the video. I'm yet to work out the meaning, but it was something supernatural, for sure.

And it gets better. TV remote controls also go missing—and are mostly *returned*—to a household environment (largely the living room). The remote vanishes in seconds or minutes (a short last seen delay) and is returned just as quickly following a brief, frenetic search (a short loss and reappearance delay). By and large the remote has recently been used, and perhaps placed on an armrest before disappearing. A search ensues before the experient notices it sitting on the armrest again. These precise returns account for 80 percent of TV remote cases in the collection, and recent interaction with the remote control appears to predict the characteristics of the reappearance. Furthermore they are mostly a "one-off" jottle. Mark's problem with recurrently disappearing remote controls is therefore very unusual. His is a wonderfully detailed narrative, but it doesn't represent the manner in which most TV remote controls are jottled.

The remaining cases of jottled TV remote controls involve a last seen delay on the order of hours to a day and a loss delay of at most a week. "Repurchase" is an interesting aspect of these longer delay cases. Generic TV remotes are relatively inexpensive, so the experient will set out to buy another one. You might remember that's just what Mark did after he lost his first remote. So too did Andy. His remote went missing from the living room table on Sunday night. After a few days of fitful searching, he decided to replace it. Returning home on Tuesday from shopping, he discovered that he was now the owner of two remote controls—one still in a box in the shopping bag and the old one now sitting on the kitchen counter. This is an example of a precise relocation with intention. Andy concluded that "something" was playing a spiteful game with him and had deliberately waited until he'd acquired a new remote before giving the old one back.

Foods Also Reappear

Food items are fifth on the list of most frequent reappearing objects. Most cases are precise returns consisting of a short last seen delay subsequent to handling the food and an equally short loss and reappearance delay concluding with a return to the kitchen a few minutes later. In keeping with a pattern of interaction and intention, the longer the last seen delay the longer the loss delay, and the greater the chance the food will relocate somewhere else. However, unlike other relocating objects (e.g., jewelry), we're not dealing with a displacement from the kitchen to another room in the house, the front porch or the garden shed. Food items instead rematerialize *back* to the kitchen, although to a spot far enough away not to be interpreted as a "return." This could be the window sill rather than in the cupboard where the item was last seen. This is a rare variety of relocation, matched only by one other reappearing object category: *wristwatches*.

Although stories of reappearing watches are uncommon in comparison to food items and don't make the hierarchy in Table 7, it's worth mentioning that these possessions disappear from bedrooms and display—in equal measures—either a fast loss/fast return or long-delayed relocation habit. And like food items, when a watch is relocated it is consistently *back* to the same bedroom, albeit in a slightly different spot (e.g., from a nightstand to a drawer or under the bedcovers). By the end of this book I'll try to get as close as I can to explaining jottles, having teased apart the database to the best of my ability. However, one thing I won't be able to provide is a clear reason why *only* food items and watches relocate within the same room. I'll admit that this completely baffles me.

There's a second feature associated with reappearing food items not encountered with other objects, but this time I'll at least *attempt* an interpretation. Not only is a longer loss delay associated with relocation, but foods that relocate also are typically preserved—they're not fresh like many disappearing and appearing food products. It could be a salt shaker, a container of cat food[16] or a single wrapped chocolate bar knowingly lost from the pantry or kitchen table that pops up again (seemingly without human intervention) on top of the wine rack or accidently found balanced behind the fridge when the experient is vacuuming. The "faster" the food reappears, invariably the fresher it is. Returned foods include bread rolls or a banana, an apple or a tub of yogurt. These vanish immediately from the kitchen counter and turn up a short time later *back* on the counter. It might sound bizarre, but based on this analysis it seems only preserved foods capable of enduring a longer loss phase are targeted for relocation!

In no case is there direct evidence that the reappearing food item has turned rotten during the loss delay or that a food that should have spoiled has remained remarkably well preserved. From the experients' point of view, intentionality is not a strong feature of reappearing foods, i.e., they do not interpret the incident as purposeful, compared with their attitudes towards a more significant relocating possession such as a ring or set of keys. Nevertheless, the differential behavior of fresh and processed foods suggest there's an element of shrewdness behind the choice of reappearing food items, implying (dare I say it) some element of intelligent activity behind the process.

Things That Don't Make the Reappearance Hierarchy: Clothes, Credit Cards, Wallets and Purses

Half the jottle stories in the collection concern reappearing objects, so many of the categories outside the reappearance "top five" still contain plenty of useful information. For instance, in the manner of computer items, TV remote controls, and food and beverages, there are stories of recently handled clothes that vanish and return to the original location of loss. For example, Mia placed a pair of shoes on her bed, and when she returned from a brief foray to the walk-in closet she discovered one of the shoes was missing. She walked around the house, somewhat aimlessly, hoping it would show up somewhere. Giving up, she walked back into her room and found the missing shoe returned to the bed.

However, there are just as many clothes cases where *no* recent interaction has occurred, and the result is a relocation jottle. Take this second reappearing shoe story from Mia. She sought out a pair of shoes from a bag in the walk-in closet but found only one shoe present. After a long search lasting a number of days she discovered the second shoe in an upstairs cupboard where it had never been before. Mia was adamant that no one could have, or would have, put it there.

Lost cards also tend to relocate over a long time period. Credit cards and licenses are usually kept in purses and wallets and are only brought out intermittently, so cases involving missing cards possess a significant last seen delay. They're also precise relocations, as illustrated in this story from Nicholas:

> I was paying bills online and went to get my credit card from my wallet. I found the wallet but the credit card wasn't there, so I panicked a bit. I couldn't understand

> where else it would be, as I'm very careful to always put it back in the same place. I've never left a card anywhere by accident in my life. I couldn't actually remember the last time I had it, but that doesn't mean I'd left it somewhere else. I'm convinced it was back in my wallet, but I just didn't know 100%, so I checked the balance over the phone to see if it had been used, and it hadn't which was a relief. I then rang the bank and spoke to someone to get it cancelled. A new one came in the mail a few days later, and the very next day to that I found it in a mug in the bathroom. That's why I remember it so well. It shouldn't have been in the bathroom at all. I was only in there an hour before. Who would have slipped in and done that? Not my wife, that's for sure.

In other stories, the card relocates (without apparent human intervention) to a coat pocket, a shoe box in a bedroom closet, and a living room table. Experients also project *intention* onto card returns, maybe due to the incongruity of a valuable item—found only in a wallet—standing out so starkly in the new location. Because he ordered a new credit card, Nicholas's case matches stories of remote controls that reappear following repurchase. Nicholas was suspicious that his card reappeared just as a new card arrived in the mail. Since no one else other than his wife knew about the cancellation, he assumed a "bad spirit" was responsible.

If cards can go missing from a wallet or purse, how often does the actual wallet or purse itself disappear then reappear? Wallets and purses are handled more frequently than the cards contained within, and as a consequence there's less certainty about where they were last left. Robert's story is one such example (recorded earlier). This means the last seen delay is overnight or a few days. The item then relocates days, months, or even years later. There aren't nearly as many cases of wallet and purses making a quick return, but when they do the stories don't necessarily conform to the rules followed by other returned objects. Here's a story from Jeff:

> I clearly remember leaving my wallet on the dining room table when I walked in the door. I was the only one home. I went to put it away a little later and it wasn't on the table anymore. I found it instead on the chair seat, tucked just under the table directly underneath where I first put it. It couldn't have slipped there. I have absolutely no idea how it got there, or why.

By all accounts this a relocation jottle but has the "feel" of a typical return. It also lacks the intentionality found with more definitive relocations, such as the story of Robert's wallet.

Surely, Telephones Reappear?

Just about everyone has one, so you'd think that cell phones would be a common reappearing object. Not so, as the number of cases is simply no match for jottled keys or jewels or even TV remote controls. Cell phones are much-handled objects, but they also get stowed away in handbags and drawers. As a result, a broad range of last seen delays are found across stories of reappearing cell phones—a more unpredictable pattern than found for TV remotes and credit cards (which persistently suffer short and long last seen delays, respectively). Most interestingly, phone reappearances are not confined to the home. Cell phones are just as likely to go missing from your friend's house, your locked car parked outside the home, your workplace or even a hotel room where you are staying. Nevertheless, interaction remains a relevant variable. A shorter last seen delay means the phone will be found after a small loss delay in the location it was last seen—in other words, they return to your friend's armchair, your car seat, your office desk or on top of your suitcase in the hotel room. Alternatively, a much longer last seen delay entails a long loss delay resulting in a relocation to just about anywhere—inside *or* outside the home. Here is Marcus's contribution:

> I leave my phone on the middle console of the car when I'm driving. I knew it was there because it rang when I was driving home, but I didn't answer it. I got home and forgot to bring it with me because there were people at the front door and I got distracted. I remember locking the car, though. First thing next day I got my coat on to walk the dog before work. My phone was in the coat pocket, but I hadn't worn that coat for over a week. My phone had moved from the car to the coat overnight, but it wasn't me that did it.

Again, I don't have a worthy explanation for why phone relocations are more flexible than other items, apart from the reasonable observation that there aren't many examples of reappearing telephones in the collection, so the unusual nature of the relocation might be an anomaly. Or perhaps cell phones are just different in some way?

Reappearing Objects with Idiosyncrasies

That concludes my basic analysis of reappearance jottles. However, there are two (rare) categories of item–*glasses* and *toys*—that possess distinctive behaviors worth discussing, as they apparently violate the rule of fast loss/fast return versus long-delay relocation. "Glasses" refers to prescription glasses rather than sunglasses, and the experient is unlikely to have handled them recently. He seeks them out in the place they were last left. That could be beside the bed or on the hall table, but most frequently they are recalled as being stored inside a handbag or backpack. They're discovered missing the next morning or during the day when the experient needs them to drive or read the newspaper. Frequently, the bag in which they're usually kept is tipped upside down and brutally shaken, but no glasses fall out. Nor are they found anywhere in or around the house. The loss is accepted as permanent, and the experient frequently purchases a new pair later that week or early the next. Lo and behold, the glasses then reappear, after weeks or months—back in the handbag or backpack. This behavior seems to contradict an *interactive* fast loss/fast return. After all, based on what we've learned about other reappearing objects, a longer last seen delay means a greater loss delay, resulting in a relocation jottle rather than a return. However, when glasses are found returned to the bag from which they were lost, the discovery occurs in a different physical environment, so in a sense a relocation has occurred after all! Here's an example from Samantha:

> I lost my glasses case from my handbag, with my glasses in it. I ended up getting another pair, as well as a spare pair on two-for-one special because I do have a habit of mislaying glasses quite often. Sometimes I find them again, sometimes I don't. This time was different because they reappeared back in my handbag! I was out shopping a few weeks later and went to get my purse and found my old glasses case instead. I'd been using that handbag constantly and I'd emptied it out in the meantime, so there's no way I could have missed them. My new case was in there as well, right down the bottom. Maybe someone could have slipped them in there as a practical joke, but I don't see why.

This style of relocation isn't found with other items frequently found in bags, such as wallets, purses and phone. It seems to solely affect behavior of prescription glasses.[17]

Regarding toys, I have eight strong cases in the collection, and as you might expect all involve children—or at least the experient *was* a child when the toy disappeared. In common with most jottled objects, the toys are single items—a ball, trinket or small soft animal. They're not complicated things like multipiece games. That is, a single Lego brick will disappear then reappear, rather than the entire Lego set. These toys initially vanish from bedrooms, living rooms and yards where they're being played with, and most commonly it is an immediate disappearance (i.e., a very short last seen delay). The loss isn't visually witnessed by the child—instead the toy drops out of her hand and can't be found in the place where it should have landed. The child makes as good a search as possible (for a child), confused and perhaps a little upset if the item was considered sentimental. For half of the eight cases, the child finds the missing toy shortly afterward in the place it should have been, regardless of the earlier fruitless search.

This pattern of loss and return is unconvincing. Taking into account the child's age when the jottle occurred and the time that's passed until the story is told, it's quite reasonable to argue that the experient simply missed seeing the toy the first time she looked. However, the remaining four toy reappearances have an added element that not only boosts their respectability but contradicts the novel pattern of a "fast loss/fast return." In these additional childhood stories, the toy returns after many years when the child has grown into a young adult and is still living in, or visiting, the same house! The toy is found very near to where it was originally lost many years before, in the same condition and in spite of all the activity that has occurred in that location during the intervening years—countless hours of vacuuming and tidying, not to mention the constant human traffic!

How Common Are Replacements?

In my initial classification of jottles, I brushed over replacements because they are a complicated chain of events involving two distinct objects rather than one. As it turns out, snubbing them was justified, as they rarely occur. Making up only 2 percent of all cases in the database, replacements contribute very little to a broader understanding of the jottle phenomenon. With so few stories to consider, they're best discussed on a case-by-case basis as a mere curiosity. Methodical analysis simply isn't possible.

One thing that can be said from the seven available replacement cases is that they are similar in characteristics to disappearances, appearances or reappearances. The items that are replaced are of low to medium significance indistinguishable from any other style of jottle. Alongside a book and a food item, these include a credit card, a key, a toy, a pen and a TV remote control. The objects are replaced by unowned familiar items, recognizable as something that *could* be owned and possessing a strong connection to the original, vanished item. No unfamiliar or "alien" objects ever seem to be reported. Thus a book is swapped with another book, a food item is swapped with another food item, and a pen is swapped with another pen. All these replacements happen at home (Deborah's bus trip being the exception) and as expected the swap phase is relatively rapid—otherwise they wouldn't be recognized as a replacement. All occur in the space of minutes to hours, with the experient in close vicinity when the swap takes place. That suggests interaction is a factor in the replacement.

Nevertheless, in all cases the actual "transition" is hidden from view within a purse, bag or suitcase. So like most jottles the experient doesn't actually *see* the pen or book dissolve into thin air and a different object materializing in its place. The swap happens anonymously, and the experient has the sense that the new object has always been there.

Not only does interaction appear to play a role in replacements, there's also a hint of intention. The replaced object is very much like the original, so it can't be considered some arbitrary "paranormal" occurrence. If so, surely *anything* could appear in place of the original article? Take Deborah's book swap. Why was *Foul Shot* replaced with another book and not a rock or a TV remote? Colin (discussed earlier) certainly felt *something* replaced his sandwich with an apple for personal health reasons. I'm not sure how Deborah interpreted her experience, having never asked, but I'm sure she also wouldn't consider as "meaningless" the cryptic choice of a new book to replace the one she'd personally selected only half an hour previously.

5
Collating Case Studies—Finding the Common Threads

That concludes a very basic analysis of the jottle collection, and with so many ideas open for discussion it's worthwhile to halt momentarily and (at the risk of sounding repetitive) examine *as a whole* the findings for disappearing, appearing, reappearing and replaced objects.

Jottles: The Facts

Here are the general features of jottles:

(1) Experients vary in age, and their stories are just as likely to be recent as distant in time. However, there's no particular emphasis on childhood or historical cases.
(2) There is no overall favoring of one sex or particular occupation, although objects more strongly associated with one sex (e.g., jewelry for females, computer parts for males) are more likely to be reported by *that* sex as having been jottled.
(3) There's nothing unique about the personal possessions claimed to have been jottled. They are indistinguishable from similar possessions that *haven't* been the focus of a jottle.
(4) Jottled objects tend to be hand-sized. They are single items in the most basic sense, although multiple objects attached to one another (e.g., keys on a key ring) or contained in a package (e.g., peanuts) are sometimes targeted.
(5) Jottles overwhelmingly occur in the home environment (private localities), specifically the house, but also in the garden, the car parked in the driveway and occasionally outbuildings (a stand-alone garage or workshop).

(6) Examples of witnessed materializations or dematerializations of objects are exceedingly rare. For example, even in the many disappearance cases expressing small last seen delays, it's very unlikely the object will be *seen* to vanish, although the experient is very close to the jottle location.

(7) There's no evidence that a "sense of presence" is a feature of jottles—the environment is, and remains, completely normal. Jottles are also isolated events not accompanied by additional paranormal activity.

(8) Very rarely is the *same* object recurrently jottled (i.e., Mark's experience is unusual).

There are also specific features for the different varieties of jottle that deserve separate attention. Here's what we can take from a *disappearance*:

(1) All object significances are represented, however *low significance* items in the form of food are glaringly conspicuous. Consequently, there's no reason to suspect that more expensive things necessarily disappear more frequently than inexpensive things.

(2) Disappearances are often suffered as a recurrent event by individuals identified as "repeaters." In other words, these people appear to be "haunted" by disappearances of various objects they possess. Offhandedly, it's like suffering from a disappearance disorder!

(3) Experients more often recount a *precise* location for the disappearance than an *imprecise* location. This is because they rarely interpret *imprecise* disappearances as mysterious.

(4) Disappearances at *precise* locations are strongly associated with short last seen delays and recent physical interaction with the object. This suggests that *interaction leads to a rapid disappearance*. It is not yet known whether the handling of the object, the motion generated by handling, or an interaction of the two is the driving force behind the disappearance event.

(5) There's no particular emphasis on *meaningfulness* in stories of mysterious disappearances. For instance, there's no evidence that experients were cursing an object (and wishing it would disappear) in the moments leading to its disappearance. Objects disappear without obvious reason. This leads to the postulation that *disappearances are not necessarily implicitly or explicitly intentional*.

Appearance jottles possess a different array of features, as follows:

(1) *Unowned familiar* objects are strongly represented in the collection. These correspond to Barrington's *windfalls*. Owned *familiar* items are also common (Barrington's *turn-ups*). All these objects are of *low* to *medium significance*. Duplications are infrequent, and there are no *unowned unfamiliar* items in the story database.

(2) Appearances are singular events in people's lives. That is, most experients have only one memorable encounter with an appearing object. However, because many of these objects are foreign, the appearance is considered so peculiar that it is frequently committed to long-term memory and easily recounted at a later date. This differs from stories of disappearing objects, which must be frequent enough to be registered as a series of anomalous events. This in turn might account for the disparity of repeaters in the disappearance and appearance categories respectively.

(3) The appearance of an *owned familiar* object is associated with a long last seen and appearance delay. In other words, these objects haven't been recently seen, and when they appear unexpectedly around the home the experient (and any observer) has been absent from that location for a considerable time. In comparison, *unowned familiar* objects display a more rapid appearance delay and the experient is often present at the location when the object materializes, although it is rare that they see the jottle occur. For example, they are more likely to hear a coin fall to the floor than see it materialize and then fall.

(4) Experients often interpret appearances as meaningful, particularly when the object is unowned. This leads to the postulation that *unowned objects appear with implicit intention*.

Reappearance jottles demonstrate the following unique features:

(1) Reappearing objects range in *significance*, although objects of lesser personal value (low to medium) prevail.

(2) Experients often report recurrent reappearances throughout their lives. However, they also claim additional disappearances and appearances. These people might be labelled *universal repeaters*.

(3) There's little evidence that *precise* or *imprecise* knowledge of the original location of a missing object influences how it reappears.

(4) Where the last seen delay is short, the loss and reappearance delays are also short and the object overwhelmingly *returns* to the original location. This relationship is also associated with recent object interaction. The return does not strike the experient as particularly meaningful.

(5) Longer last seen delays are associated with longer loss delays, variable reappearance delays and a *relocation* over a short distance—generally somewhere else in the house. The experient frequently interprets this relocation as *implicitly intentional* because they feel that someone (or something) is seeking their attention, although they do not know why.

Finally, *replacement* jottles are very rare, although the few good cases that exist feature both interaction and intention. Perhaps it's a gross oversimplification, but it appears that two variables—interaction and intentionality—emerge from this summary and act in a mutually exclusive fashion. Specifically, this means:

(1) Disappearances are *interactive* and *non-intentional*.
(2) Appearances of unowned familiar objects are *non-interactive* and *intentional* (although some examples might simply be the reappearance phase of another individual's random disappearance, hence intentionality is misinterpreted). The appearance of an owned familiar object can also be interpreted as meaningful (e.g., Dave's cricket bat story recounted previously), although these might be expressions of an unrecognized relocation.
(3) Returns are *interactive* and *non-intentional* (i.e., a fast loss/fast return).
(4) Relocations are *non-interactive* and *intentional* (i.e., a long-delayed relocation). For certain objects, relocations occur following repurchase (e.g., remote controls) or cancellation (e.g., credit cards), enhancing the theme of intentionality.
(5) Replacements are different from other jottles—they are both *interactive* and *intentional*.

Jottles in the "Real World"

If this representation of jottles is bewildering, I'll express it again using "real world" examples:

5: Collating Case Studies—Finding the Common Threads 75

(1) If something you've just handled mysteriously disappears from where you last saw it, chances are it might reappear just as quickly to the same spot (a return). If the object doesn't come back in a short space of time, it's likely you'll never see it again (a disappearance). Where is it? Well, it might have randomly ended up with someone else as an appearance (their windfall), or perhaps it is still floating around somewhere in "higher space" (whatever that means). Prior interaction seems necessary to generate the disappearance, however the outcome is judged as non-intentional.

(2) If you just happen to find a small, unowned but familiar object lying around the house (an appearance), you'll likely to have been in close spatial and temporal proximity to the item when it appeared. This object might be an article of jewelry or an item of food, and you consider it a supernatural gift—its appearance is implicitly intentional. Since you've never seen it before, let alone touched it—the event is non-interactive. If you're savvy with the topic of jottles (having closely followed this book), you might concede that the object is someone else's disappearance jottle!

(3) If one of your possessions has been uncharacteristically missing for a short while, there's a good possibility it will reappear in a different but seemingly calculated place elsewhere in the house (a relocation). This is a non-interactive event that you'll interpret as intentional (either explicit or implicit, depending on object and personal context).

(4) If you find one of your (owned familiar) possessions in a different spot from where it should be and you've no logical explanation as to how or why it got there (an appearance), then depending on the object and the circumstance you might consider this an inexplicable but unmemorable event or you might project onto it personal significance. The appearance is noninteractive but can be non-intentional or intentional based on how the object is presented (tucked away in a corner or situated in a very prominent position).

That concludes the analysis, whittled down into four basic points. Although the findings are rudimentary, the discovery of a loose pattern in the jottle data confirms the value of Hynek's approach to researching paranormal phenomena. Now it's time to critically assess these findings.

6

Thinking Skeptically About Jottles

Maybe I'm getting too far ahead of myself. After all, jottles aren't exactly mainstream science. People may report with the utmost sincerity their weird jottle experiences, but surely their stories aren't *real* in the sense of being paranormal, in which case the research I've just conducted has been a complete waste of time. Although I've come to the view that jottles are truly anomalous events, it's important to appreciate the critical perspective because some stories in the collection—perhaps all—might be perfectly explainable.[1]

So, let's place ourselves in the position of a skeptic—someone who will not countenance the strange nature of *any* of the jottle stories told so far. We'll even make ourselves knowledgeable of the topic—appreciating that the phenomenon manifests in different ways rather than merely encompassing "disappearing objects." That's more that can be said for most detractors. Here's how I'd broach such a criticism, as a rather rude essay directed to myself:

> It doesn't matter how many stories you've accumulated, each one has a perfectly straightforward explanation. Why did you even bother analyzing the so-called "database"? Your claims about "interaction" and "intention" are ridiculous, and here's why:
>
> First, there's a big problem with the stories that comprise your collection. Only one in nine derive from a proper "scientific" study. Can you even trust these tales, let alone the ones you've been told by believers? These people might claim the stories are true, but who's to say they're not just made up? You even present findings which show the basic features of an experient's story can be imagined!
>
> And even if I accept that not all stories are fabricated, that doesn't mean rational explanations for these can't be easily found. For example, let's pretend there's a situation where an object disappears from a room in the home—that's where most of this stuff happens according to your analysis. The object is likely to be small, so it has either been dropped and bounced somewhere across the room or it's been stepped on or kicked into the corner by accident. Of course, it's not going to be

6: Thinking Skeptically About Jottles

where you think it is! It might never be seen again, because it's now gathering dust under the refrigerator or the vanity. Eventually it will be vacuumed up as a featureless lint ball. That solves "mysterious" disappearances. Of course, if the lost possession is found at a later date, it's because the object has recently been knocked out from where it was hiding. That explains a "mysterious" return.

For other jottles, even ones involving bigger objects like keys or remote controls, have you considered absent-mindedness? That's where you think you remember where you put your keys, but when you set out to find them they're not there. That's not paranormal; it simply means you've been mentally distracted and convinced yourself you knew where the keys were when they were in fact somewhere else. Moreover, finding them again at a different location from where you think they should be does not constitute a relocation jottle—your keys are simply where they've always been! That's not your fault. We all get distracted at times and often we aren't able to construct accurate memories of the events that happen to us.

And don't get me started on memories! Can you really trust what these "experients" of yours have told you when the event happened 30 years ago? I mean, some of these stories come from childhood, for goodness' sake! How valid are they? Over time, people forget things that have happened to them and replace the segments they've forgotten with embellishments that weren't there originally. That's a proven psychological fact.

Here's another explanation for the remainder of your cases—perceptual blindness. That's where you stare at an object but don't actually register that it's there. We've all experienced it at some time or another. For instance, remember that time you couldn't "see" your car even though it was parked in front of you and you were looking right at it? Perceptual blindness is particularly applicable to everyday domestic items that go missing. They're so familiar your brain starts to ignore them because it has more important things to think about, and as a consequence they aren't processed deeply enough for recognition. Then, a little while later, your brain kicks back into gear and you see them again. It's a "now you don't see it, now you do" situation! Perceptual blindness is another psychological fact. Read some textbooks and educate yourself. It easily accounts for appearance stories and the rest of the return cases not solved by accidental object movement or poor memory. That's why large things hardly ever disappear or reappear—the smaller the item the more prone it is to perceptual blindness.

I've saved the best for last: an explanation of those "inexplicable" cases, such as the story of the woman who found her missing keys on a pillow a year later and hundreds of miles away. Well, if someone truly thinks that has happened to them, I'd say take a close look at that person. Is it possible that if they're not attention-seeking weirdos deliberately making up their stories that they have deeper unregistered psychological issues contributing to their strange experiences? Presuming the missing key story actually happened the way the experient said it did, perhaps this person has carried around her keys for a year and for some reason put them on her pillow when she was sleepwalking or in some kind of bizarre unconscious state that she can't recollect. There are a lot of people out there with psychological problems you wouldn't even begin to guess at. And if you won't believe that, what about all the other people who might be involved in leaving the keys where they were found—friends, relatives and strangers who move things around the house without telling anyone, take things without permission and secretly return them later. Your "experient" won't have access to that information, so you'll never know if it's a relevant cause.

> I'll end by saying this: there are dozens of straightforward solutions that rationally explain every one of these allegedly paranormal "jottles," and they're a whole lot more convincing than telling me a fairy has stolen someone's keys then returned them!!

Wow. On the basis of that argument, I've almost convinced myself! This is certainly a powerful diatribe, and I don't think it can be dismissed lightly. Obviously the next step is to systematically evaluate each of the criticisms laid out in the passage above to determine how well they undermine our fledgling theory of jottles.

Can We Trust the Collection?

The first pejorative statement is directed toward the trustworthiness of stories, a criticism made stronger by the fact there's no physical evidence a jottle has ever happened. The analysis shows that objects that appear and reappear look and feel perfectly normal. They're not possessed with some kind of radiant supernatural energy that can be measured in a scientific laboratory. Put simply, there's nothing inherent in these objects that tells us where they've been, presuming they've been somewhere extraordinary in the first place. Jottles are also a *spontaneous phenomenon*, like seeing a ghost or experiencing a precognitive dream. They happen unexpectedly (even to repeaters), and there's simply nothing to suggest their manifestation can be anticipated in advance. Interaction and intention might emerge as points of interest from the collection, but *predictability* is certainly not a feature.

This doesn't "prove" jottles are necessarily illegitimate. It simply means they can't be scrutinized in a controlled experimental setting. Unfortunately this unpredictability and the lack of any physical variable to measure (such as energy fields or temperature) make the topic of jottles off-putting to even the most serious parapsychologists. All we're left with are a collection of historical stories, mostly from lone witnesses.[2]

Then again, transcribing stories of people's life experiences is a standard method of gathering data in social research, so I am satisfied that the tales in the collection were genuine in intent. They possess internally consistent details associated with the measured criteria (such as *delays* and *location*), and I can find no systematic differences between these tales and stories derived from other sources, such as the Internet. Furthermore, the apparent pointlessness and complete absence of any thematic development of jottle stories help their authenticity. Experients gain nothing from telling them; and when it comes to object disappearances there isn't even a satisfactory resolution. They lose their possession forever and for no good reason.

However, while the collection (by and large) is made up of honest recollections, this doesn't mean any of them are *true*. The hard-boiled critic would argue that this admission shows the jottle phenomenon is no different from eyewitness stories about UFO sightings or encounters with Bigfoot—a load of pseudoscientific nonsense. And yet without these firsthand accounts there wouldn't be a database, and by association this book couldn't be written. So, accepting that the bulk of stories aren't deliberate fabrications and comprise the best possible information available, let's concentrate instead on how reasonable they are as evidence for something truly anomalous.

Jottled Objects Are Merely Lost or Stolen

Are disappearance jottles a simple case of theft? After all, the longer the last seen delay, the greater the probability an object has been removed (or stolen) by someone else. We're already familiar with the dubious nature of disappearing money. Here's one from a person ("Lauren") who genuinely believed she'd experienced a jottle:

> My story is about an object disappearing. Early this year I had about $100 dollars in my purse and when I went to get some of it out later there was only about $60 left. I had my purse at home but I don't see why anyone would take money without telling me. My sister usually tells me if she needs cash. If it was a person who stole it, they would have taken the whole lot. I would have taken it all, not just $40. I believe there's a spirit in the house, as I feel very strange in some rooms and there are cold places there.

Lauren's assumption is based entirely on the premise that her sister (or perhaps someone else in the household) couldn't have stolen the money. The problem is that people unwittingly project positive traits onto affiliates, such as friends or relatives, even if they are potentially guilty of wrongdoing. This is an expression of a psychological effect known as *positive bias*,[3] which is conceptually related to the more famous tendency of *cognitive dissonance*. Made famous by psychologist Leo Festinger in the 1950s,[4] cognitive dissonance holds that individuals who possess conflicting ("dissonant") attitudes, beliefs or opinions resolve the tension by altering one of these cognitions to conform to the others. Applied to Lauren story, she *implicitly* understands her money was stolen and her sister is the prime suspect. However, this conclusion is personally uncomfortable. The easiest (and least stressful) way to reconcile her inconsistent thoughts is to conclude that the money wasn't stolen by a human after all but that it disappeared into a "time vortex" or was pilfered by mischievous spirits.

Positive bias and cognitive dissonance therefore interfere with an experient's introspection of an otherwise prosaic event. However, Lauren's case is an exception. The majority of "money" cases in the collection involve single materializing coins rather than notes vanishing from wallets and purses.

Of course, plenty of objects of medium to high significance can be stolen. However, there needs to be evidence that humans were responsible. Generally speaking, if an object disappears over a long last seen delay and people other than the experient are present in the location during this period, then that's either admitted in the story (whether the experient realizes it or not—as in the previous narration) or there *is* no story, as the experient does not consider the loss mysterious. That's why so few long last seen delay disappearance jottles feature in the database.

Rather than being lost to thievery, an object may have simply been moved without the experient's knowledge.[5] Or, as argued by our skeptic, it's been accidently lost. A measured response would make reference to the frequency of cases where the loss occurs in a closed environment (e.g., a small room) over a short last seen delay and where there is a concerted effort on behalf of the experient to search the room thoroughly. As we've seen from some of the earlier stories, this search involves removing furniture, sweeping and vacuuming (followed by a careful exploration of the bag), the use of lamps and flashlights, and even a magnifying glass. If a thorough search isn't made, then the event isn't considered a jottle. It's the unsuccessful outcome of the search that makes the circumstances anomalous, not so much the fact that the object has vanished in the first place (unless it's one of those rare, witnessed dematerializations). Furthermore, these objects aren't necessarily tiny earrings or pins or small buttons. They're apples, shoes and bottles of detergent—things that cannot be so easily concealed.

What about "return" jottles? Dropped objects can bounce across the bedroom or bathroom floor and become temporarily lost, only to be found under the bed or sink a few days later. However, these occurrences are seldom identified as mysterious. When returns *are* reported as jottles, the object has *not* fallen to the floor. Instead, it first disappears from a stationary position—usually elevated—and returns to that same position after a short period. The object is not found covered in dust in the corner of the room or show signs of having been concealed somewhere accidently.

Relocation jottles are even less likely to be the result of accidental loss. The analysis shows that most relocated objects travel between rooms, rather than being discovered on the floor where they were dropped. Surely the objects in these stories haven't been unwittingly dragged around the house in a trouser cuff? And like returned objects, relocated objects are *never* discovered in places where they might have been unwittingly discarded. Rather, they turn up in prominent positions like the top of a pillow or locations which require considerable effort to access (e.g., a closed shoe box in the bedroom closet). Therefore, while it is reasonable to suggest that human involvement explains a small minority of disappearances and reappearances, taken as a whole it's difficult to conclude that jottles are the product of thievery or accidental loss.

Jottles Are Forgotten Objects

A more effective rationalization of jottles focuses on the vagaries of memory, a problem acknowledged by psychiatrist Donald West during the study day held in 2003. He pointed out that it's difficult to separate jottle cases where someone has simply forgotten an object's location from those that might involve a reputed paranormal "relocation."[6] And when it comes to memory deficits, the untrustworthiness of childhood reminiscences is especially evident, especially anything recalled before the age of three (*childhood amnesia*).[7] By five or six years of age *some* resilient memories can be formed and retained for long periods; however, children still cannot successfully articulate the date, time, duration or sequence of a straightforward past event.[8] Nor can they express the emotional context of the event or what they were thinking about at the time. This has serious implications for childhood memories of jottles.

To avoid this problem, stories from adults regarding their early childhood experiences were not included in the database, although I have allowed adult recollections of incidents occurring after 10 years of age—specifically the jottling of toys. That's because proficiency with the temporal aspects of a recalled event *is* possible from early adolescence onwards,[9] reassuring us that the encoding of relevant information has occurred (e.g., temporal delay and location). That said, only eight of these adolescent stories are contained in the database, so the question of memory should really center on the dependability of historical *adult* memories, rather than events alleged to have occurred in late childhood or as a teenager.

The renowned cognitive researcher Daniel Schacter and colleagues list various ways in which an adult's mental processes can deliver a flawed recollection of their (adult) past.[10] The most prominent obstacle to accurate memory is *forgetfulness,* and two aspects have relevance to jottle stories. The first is the concept of *transience,* which describes how memories decay with the passing of time. This can happen to recollections of how to do things (*episodic memories*) and also of life events (*autobiographical memories*). The current investigation relies on the latter—accurate autobiographical memories detailing the type of object that was jottled, the associated delays in the disappearance, appearance, reappearance or replacement phases, and the location where the jottle occurred. Some of the stories in the collection are a decade or more old, so naturally the information they contain is prone to deterioration.

Transience can also potentially affect contemporary jottle stories. For example, events considered to be quite recent are often much older than the experient realizes. This is an example of a *telescoping error*[11] and will result in a potentially flawed memory unless there's a definite context to draw on (e.g., "I'm certain my watch disappeared on the morning of my thirtieth birthday"). Nevertheless it's perhaps unfair to discriminate against historical (or more recent) jottle memories because transience potentially affects *all* types of memory. Indeed, even old jottle memories may be insulated from transience, compared with everyday recollections, because the events they represent are so *unusual.* Their peculiar nature, and the emotionality that is often engendered by the experience, allows subsequent memory to better focus on a central event (e.g., the object's behavior) rather than peripheral details.[12,13]

Flawed Memories of Jottles

A stronger skeptical argument is that a jottle memory might not have been appropriately formed *in the first place.* As our skeptic sensibly suggested, objects disappear for good, and often reappear, because of *absent-mindedness.* This is an everyday error of cognition associated with tasks that are so well practiced, repetitive or tedious[14] that they can be completed using very little attention. There's simply no need to utilize the thinking resources normally required for multifaceted or complicated behaviors or learning something new. Absent-mindedness can also manifest when the task is relatively complicated but the individual becomes distracted by an external stimulus or an internal state (e.g., emotionality).

Without the "spotlight" of attention, memories of a current activity won't be accurately encoded. This is particularly relevant to the initial disappearance of well-handled objects around the home. We are often unsure of when and where we put down our car keys (a repetitive routine) or the last location of the TV remote control. Of course, it's unlikely we'll lose these objects for good, because even if we're uncertain about where we left them one would assume they're still in an exposed and safe location (rather than having been thrown in the trash can!). In this way, absent-mindedness is best applied to reappearances rather than to disappearances. That's not so much a precise return or relocation as an imprecise relocation. You might have absent-mindedly tossed your keys down on the bed rather than hanging them as normal on a hook by the front door. When you visit the rack a little later in the day you can't find them, but after a search you are most disturbed when they turn up on the pillow. Did you really put them there? You just can't remember. Surely not—? You blame it on a jottle, but it's nothing more than absent-mindedness in action.

The analysis tells a different story. Recall that relocation jottles are strongly associated with a long loss delay. The object can be rediscovered in an obvious and previously searched location *or* is found somewhere hidden—frequently a shoe box tucked away at the back of a seldom-used closet. Therefore it's the *manner* in which the object relocates that makes the event memorable (specifically the length of time that's passed and the new place where it's found), not the fact that it relocates.

Naturally there are individual cases that might be attributed to absent-mindedness, but this is not a blanket explanation for jottles. In fact, it's just as likely that individuals are absent-minded about their own *real* jottle experiences, and these are quickly forgotten in the rush of everyday life. Parapsychologist Michael Thalbourne, when writing about his own experiences with a "disappearing poltergeist," admits it took a long time for him to realize that things around his house and workplace were disappearing in a mysterious fashion. Like many people, Thalbourne was happy to accept he had merely "lost things" through forgetfulness. Eventually the experiences became so unequivocal that he was forced to admit they were anomalous.[15]

Preexisting Beliefs and the Distortion of Jottle Memories

Dismissing absent-mindedness as a universal solution to jottles won't deter the hardened skeptic. They'll argue that the memory of an event that's been adequately encoded and stored might still be influenced by current beliefs and attitudes. Consequently, recollection will no longer be an accurate representation of what originally occurred.[16] For example, an experient meticulously searches his home but cannot find an object he is seeking. Since he possesses preexisting beliefs about the reality of paranormal phenomena (e.g., jottles), these beliefs subtly transform this unremarkable quest into a bewildering story of a disappearing object.

However, in the same way that transience can affect all memories, it can be argued that memories of *any* life event can be altered by prevailing beliefs, leading to a tit-for-tat debate. We all hold beliefs about various matters, so why can't these also affect the precision of everyday memories? If you don't believe my jottle story that the TV remote control mysteriously disappeared from the couch, then I won't believe what you say you had for breakfast. You assume you had cereal, as that constitutes a typical breakfast, but perhaps this belief has distorted your memory of what you *actually* ate this morning—toast!

I'll admit that's a petty and implausible retort, so here's a more valid defense of jottle memories. In turns out that most of the experients contributing stories to the collection did not hold prior beliefs about the reality of paranormal phenomena, let alone knowledge of "jottles." Therefore, we might need to be wary only of stories told by repeaters, as they are the ones most likely to interpret their experience as being anomalous. However the tales of repeaters aren't necessarily more detailed, smarter, or told more confidently than those of "non-repeaters." I can also present an alternative psychological theory that supports the genuineness of jottle memories. There is some evidence that existing beliefs may in fact *facilitate* recall of an event if they are consistent with that event, compared to people who do not hold these beliefs or who possess conflicting beliefs.[17] Therefore, if you are a repeater and discover your watch has gone missing (again) and the characteristics of the event are consistent with your (supportive) attitudes about jottles, then memory formation may actually be enhanced! So, like absent-mindedness, the possession of existing beliefs about jottles doesn't undermine the legitimacy of a jottle tale.

Influences on a Distant Jottle Memory

What about the influence of more recent information on the recall of a jottle experience? These are known as *errors of commission*, and two aspects are relevant to jottles: *suggestibility* and *confirmation bias*.[18] Suggestibility refers to the incorporation of unrelated information into an existing memory trace.[19] Individuals often have a vague recollection of a jottle event sometime in their lives but are unable to verbally articulate what actually happened. Simply asking them whether they've encountered an object "behaving anomalously"—and leaving it at that—is unlikely to extract a detailed story. Clarification will be required in the form of an example, and this in turn might prompt a story. However, elements of the example might unwittingly become incorporated into the individual's expanded tale. For instance, imagine you've been asked to remember an incident in your life where an object "behaved strangely," and for guidance you are told Mark's story of his disappearing TV remote control. You have a flashback of watching TV on the couch, something you do regularly, so the memory for this context is strong. You also recall that a remote control was permanently lost around the time this memory was based, so you conclude that these events constitute a mysterious disappearance. It might transpire that you *didn't* lose the remote control in these circumstances, but this salient point has been overpowered by the questioner's influential example. That's why the questioner should provide only minimal guidance, in order to reduce suggestibility.

The good news is the majority of stories in the collection were told spontaneously, rather than being the product of probing enquiry. That means the impact of suggestibility is minimized. Although it might still exert an impact it does so in a way opposite to expectation! It's just as likely that experients will come to believe an authentic, autobiographical jottle recollection *hasn't* happened to them for three reasons: implausibility, a lack of corroborating evidence, and, most important, suggestibility—in this case the influence of other people telling them the event *can't* have transpired.[20] That's because jottles *are* implausible and are usually experienced alone, so there's no confirming proof they've ever happened. And if the experient confides in a friend, but her tale is, to her embarrassment, belittled, the experient might start doubting that her memory is true and accurate. For this reason, suggestibility is a cognitive variable that may *prevent* good jottle stories from ever being told, rather than helping to create false tales.

Whereas suggestibility acts passively, confirmation bias is an active, agent-centered process. It involves modification of the memory of a past event such that the recollection now conforms to *current* attitudes or beliefs.[21] This is the end stage of a reconstructed memory whereby information accumulated following the jottle encounter is integrated into the experients' worldview (whether they realize it or not). Confirmation bias helps ensure past memories match current attitudes and beliefs in order to preserve an individual's "self-stability." Aspects of the recollection that are consistent with current beliefs might be *sharpened* and exaggerated, while deviating aspects are *levelled*—meaning they are downplayed, or reduced in significance.[22] Moreover, these actions are reinforced over time through repeated retelling of the story, so what's eventually narrated is very different to what actually happened.

Blaming memories of a jottle on confirmation bias might be a little unfair, as it implies a past event has been incorrectly reinterpreted because of more recently acquired beliefs (e.g., knowledge of jottles gained from the Internet). However, there's no evidence that experients hold *current* jottle beliefs, even following their encounters. When questioned about *why* something they owned disappeared or reappeared or why something they didn't own appeared in their homes, experients mention "wormholes" and "fairies" offhandedly—with humor. They certainly aren't hardened believers in the paranormal, and this attitude is not conducive to confirmation bias. It might even be suggested that, as a consequence of processes such as cognitive dissonance *and* confirmation bias, the experient would prefer to interpret the encounter as "normal" rather than supernatural. To conform to social expectation, they will dismiss the event as something mundane even when it is actually very strange. That's what seems to be the case for the experients in the formal study. Deep down they *know* their experience is anomalous, but they have great difficulty accepting this to be true.

Jottles and Perceptual Blindness

Now I will recap. I've suggested that absent-mindedness might rationalize some disappearance cases, but as an explanation it is most effective when applied to *imprecise* and *delayed* relocations. Simply put, the experient is uncertain about where and when they last saw an object that is eventually found in the place it was (wrongly) left. Absent-mindedness is less effective in explaining other jottle types (e.g., rapid returns), but there is another psychological possibility that might be a better solution. Take this passage from Peter Rogerson found on the online Magonia blog, where he compares jottles to a paranormal phenomenon known as *streetlight interference (SLI)*. This is a peculiar characteristic possessed by certain people that allows them to turn streetlights (and other light sources) off and on when they walk past:

> Logic suggests that if something is impossible and it can neither be recorded nor publically demonstrated then it isn't happening in the external space of physics and geography at all, but in some kind of inner perceptual space. In the phenomenon of SLI, this might mean that in these cases electricity still flows to the lamp, it still emits photons which hit the SLIers retina, [but] from time to time it stops producing the internal experience of seeing a light, a kind of negative hallucination. This

would perhaps place it in a similar character to the phenomena described by Mary Rose Barrington, whereby objects seem to disappear only to reappear later in the same place, or in plain view. We have all had the experience of loosing [sic] things, searching high and low then finding them when not looking. Rather than assume they had been removed by boggarts and returned it is simpler to assume that they were there all along, but just fell out of perceptual space....

Regarding many anomalous personal experiences as happening in an internal perceptual space has the interesting result that many of the massive anomalous features—the physical impossibility, the inability to duplicate at will, the strange personal connection—now become just what one would predict.[23]

"Falling out of perceptual space" is a good way to describe perceptual blindness. In the manner of absent-mindedness, perceptual blindness is an error of directed attention but it applies to jottles in a different way. Better known in the psychological literature as *inattentional blindness*, it involves a person's being so engrossed in a task that they are oblivious to objects and events that are present or taking place in the surrounding environment.[24] For example, imagine a participant in a psychology experiment who has been asked to judge the relative lengths of the arms of an "X" intermittently presented on a computer screen. While performing this task, there's a 25 percent chance he will fail to notice an image briefly flashed onto one of the X's quadrants. Underwhelming? Absolutely! However, the effect is also demonstrable in the "real world." For instance, if people are concentrating fixedly on something happening right in front of them, like a basketball game or their cell phone, they are less able to process unexpected events taking place in their peripheral vision. That event could be someone running past who's dressed in a gorilla suit[25] or unicycling and wearing a brightly colored clown costume.[26] Perhaps this is how experients fail to notice missing objects around their home.

Unlike distortions of memory, inattentional blindness accounts for "here-and-now" situations where a person searches for an item that can't be found, then all of a sudden finds it in the place they've just been looking. Think of rummaging around a kitchen drawer for a pair of missing scissors. You know they're there, but they become visible—right in front of your eyes—only after you've been searching for a minute or two. When it comes to *single* items in a *less-cluttered* environment, consider the following example involving Belinda and her eyeglasses. A few moments earlier she was aware that her glasses were sitting on an empty kitchen countertop in plain sight. However, Belinda becomes distracted by other events that require her immediate attention, so she is no longer able to visually process the glasses. They become temporarily "invisible," but they are perfectly visible to anyone else who might happen to be in the room at the same time. When the necessary resources become available once more, Belinda will be able to see her glasses again (a *return* jottle). Alternatively, Belinda might not be aware that her glasses are "lost" in the first place, but she is still "blind" to them as they sit motionless on the countertop. When attentional faculties are restored, she is surprised by the object's apparent materialization—the exemplary appearance!

The argument is strengthened by the fact that it's been demonstrated that inattentional blindness goes hand in hand with people who believe in, and experience, paranormal phenomena.[27] Apparently these individuals display poor working (short term) memory. They are also prone to becoming absorbed in whatever task they're performing and—compared to regular people—lack the facilities to attend to their surroundings. These people are therefore at risk of misperceiving the behavior of objects around them and might fail to recognize and remember causally connected events (e.g., physically picking up an object *causes* it to relocate). Most important, they will also decipher the loss, appearance or reappearance of this object as a paranormal phenomenon.

Inattentional Blindness as an Explanation for Disappearing Objects

Like Belinda, imagine you also discover that your eyeglasses (or any other small possession) are no longer where you recently left them on the kitchen counter. There's no distracting clutter to hinder the search, so you must have missed seeing them because you're looking *around* them and not *at* them. Since the glasses soon return to view, this "blindness" can only be temporary—before long attention will be restored and directed to the correct position on the counter. Your glasses are visible once more.

That might apply to a situation where the missing glasses are stationed in the visual periphery, but how does that account for *direct* searches in the *correct* location? How could we be blind to our glasses when we're staring at them? One solution is to accept that the "cognitive drain" is internal rather than external. You might believe the missing glasses are the primary focus of your attention during the search process, but in fact you are mentally preoccupied and your attention is instead focused inward on a myriad of pressing life issues. You might even start to panic about the loss, which further exhausts the available search resources.

There is experimental evidence supporting this proposition. Studies have shown that certain stimuli are unable to capture a person's attention even when they are positioned in the observer's direct line of sight rather than on the periphery.[28] These unattended stimuli might still be processed implicitly, meaning you are *unconsciously* aware of where they are even if you can't *consciously* see them. The problem is these experimental findings have limited "real world" application. To be "inattentionally blind" means you must be so engrossed in your search that you can't see what you're searching *for*. That doesn't really make sense, and it's not how *real* people search for *real* missing objects. One of the most common complaints about disappearance jottles is that attentional resources *were* available and utilized, and every effort was put into the hunt. Take Belinda's example. She harnesses these available resources to call up an internalized representation, or *schema*[29] of what her glasses look like and uses this schema to scan for the missing possession, purposefully directing all her focused attention across the entire countertop—especially the location where her glasses were seen only minutes before. She *won't* be prevented from seeing her glasses due to inattentional blindness. If they're on the countertop, she *will* see them. Furthermore, rarely do experients show debilitating panic or emotionality when searching for jottled objects. The evidence instead suggests that most experients conduct a thorough, rational and directed pursuit of the lost item.

A skeptic might be happy to attribute disappearance jottles to "inattentional blindness," but I think they're actually referring to an entirely different psychological process. I'll term this "*attentional* blindness," in the sense that you are allocating attention to an object search but you *still* can't see the object, even when it is right in front of your eyes. Without delving into altered states of consciousness (which I'll discuss shortly), the closest I can suggest would be the equivalent of a *scotoma*, or blind spot, in the visual field on the retina or higher in the visual cortex.[30] In these circumstances, attention is directed toward seeking an object which the blind spot prevents the searcher from apprehending. Borrowing from Charles Bonet syndrome,[31] perhaps there's a black void in the center of your vision that masks an object from perception, but your unconscious brain cleverly "photoshops" this void with an empty background borrowed from the surrounding environment, thereby disguising the object but also leaving you blissfully unaware that your vision is faulty. I'm not aware of any model of visual processing that fits this improbable claim—at least one that's not based on demonstrable retinal or cortical (brain) damage. And of course, once "attentional blindness" is used to rationalize jottles, there's nothing stopping its being applied more generally—which leads to these awkward questions: Why is "attentional blindness" overwhelmingly restricted to the home environment and specific types of objects? Shouldn't the experient suffer from it all the time and everywhere?

Inattentional Blindness and Appearing Objects

Inattentional blindness, and to a certain extent absent-mindedness, is far better suited to explaining object *appearances*. The characteristics of an object that captures attention include how conspicuous it is compared to background *(sensory conspicuity)*,[32] how relevant it is to you *(cognitive conspicuity)*, and what people think an environment *should* look like *(expectation)*. I've also previously mentioned that a person's attention can be consumed by what she's thinking about at the time *(mental workload)* and whether she's currently engrossed in a complicated behavior *(task interference)*. Also important is how capable a person is *(capacity)*, a reference to intelligence level, age, and whether there have been drugs or alcohol involved.[33]

With this in mind, imagine a situation where a cream-colored coffee mug blends in neatly with the cream-colored tiles on the kitchen wall near the sink. As you walk past you don't notice the mug because it's an object that's completely irrelevant to your current needs. You also have a strong preconception of how your kitchen should be arranged (mugs NOT left messily on the countertop), and you are deep in thought. With respect, you are also not the brightest person and perhaps even a little drunk. Consequently, you never notice the item of crockery until some later time when—quite unexpectedly—your attention becomes focused and you "see" it for the first time. Hey, presto! An appearing object! Of course, this doesn't explain how the mug got there in the first place—something particularly relevant when considering that many appearance jottles involve owned familiar items turning up where they shouldn't, for no apparent reason (and of course unowned familiar items that should be in the house in the first place). I'd argue that a *very* particular array of conditions is required for an appearance jottle to match the requirements of inattentional blindness. I just can't find those conditions in any appearance tale in the database.

Altered States of Consciousness

In my opinion, the skeptic's final criticism of jottles—an ad hominem attack on the experient as an impartial narrator—is the most effective. I'll openly admit I don't really know how many experients are well-disguised attention-seekers or possess mild schizotypal tendencies causing them to interpret random events as meaningful. I've no reason to suspect dysfunction in any of the cases analyzed so far, although I can't rule it out completely. As far as I'm aware, no one claiming a jottle experience has ever undergone psychological assessment for the purpose of determining whether the jottle story might be a function of mental health. And even if experients aren't exhibiting overt mental dysfunction, they might still have suffered a *transient* (temporary) break from their normal state of consciousness that would explain their jottle encounter.

"Consciousness" plays a large role throughout the remainder of this book, so I'll start here with a simple definition. Generally speaking, a person who is "conscious" is roused or awake[34] and aware of themselves as a sentient person possessing thoughts and emotions. They also understand the distinction between themselves and the surrounding environment. This self-awareness is relatively consistent throughout life, and the experience is interpreted as *subjective reality*, different from the objective reality of the "real world" beyond the senses. When this process is disrupted, an *altered state of consciousness* is generated. Put simply, the person is no longer attuned to her normal self or surrounding environment or both. This concept applied to jottles, an experient might have suffered from a subtle brain seizure—perhaps in the temporal lobes (that part of the brain that sits just beneath the skull surface in the region of the temple). This in turn triggers a *fugue* state where the sufferer lacks self-awareness but their outward behavior appears normal to an observer (a situation corresponding to our skeptic's "unconscious state"). During this period, the experient might be unwittingly rotating objects around his home to be lost here and rediscovered there. When the seizure resolves, the experient has no recollection of his behavior and interprets the movement of objects as paranormal. This of course assumes that the experient has overlooked the fact that a significant period of his life is blank—a feature of fugues. As that doesn't feature in any story in the database, I think it's unlikely that this variety of altered state is responsible for jottles.

On the other hand, there are altered states where some degree of self-awareness is maintained, and these are far better at accounting for typical jottles. One way to visualize how this maintenance of self-awareness might occur is to imagine there are two types of consciousness, *primary* and *reflective*. Primary consciousness is the domain of subjective experiences. These include motivational states, sensory experiences, emotions and body image.[35] Primary consciousness gathers its constituent materials from both the outside world and the internal world of the psyche.

Reflective consciousness, on the other hand, takes the elements of primary consciousness and contemplates them. For example, it might name and categorize objects or judge and evaluate events, then choose behaviors that best suit those judgments. Roughly speaking, it's the deeper, more personal aspect of consciousness. Now, for various reasons primary consciousness might be affected by an alteration of the elements of subjective experience. However, reflective consciousness still processes these changed or misrepresented elements as though everything is normal. In the words of the eminent paranormal researcher Hilary Evans, "The subconscious mind can present illusionary visual experiences to the waking mind that are so lifelike as to impose total conviction (239)."[36]

Alternatively, a person might be fully aware she is in an altered state, as happens when experients report "spirit journeys" or "astral travel" to other realms. Experients understand that the global input they're receiving is vastly different from everyday reality, but that doesn't make the experience any less real or impressive. In mainstream psychology, both experiences would be classed as *hallucinations*.

Hallucinated Jottles

When it comes to jottles, the former style of hallucination is more applicable. The experient is unaware that what he *believes* to be reality (with absurdly behaving objects) is actually *not* reality. This is a pretty serious claim, because hallucinations have strong associations with mental disorder and substance abuse, although Hilary Evans is careful to point out that it's not the mental illness (whatever the etiology) that causes the hallucination but the altered state of consciousness that is induced by the illness.[37]

Therefore it's conceivable that for any number of jottle cases, objects have been methodically hallucinated *into* and *out of* existence. Nevertheless, strictly speaking, a true hallucination requires a total misrepresentation of reality, and not even the hardest skeptic could argue that experients are trapped in such a state. To make the claim stick the skeptic would need to argue that jottles are the consequence of a milder form of hallucination involving small, specific changes to normal consciousness, where individual objects are imposed on, or removed from, everyday reality. This is known as a *content-specific delusion*, which is a type of *pseudo-hallucination*. These content-specific delusions fit perfectly into the experient's everyday life and go unnoticed because they are seamless with previous, and subsequent, non-hallucinated states of awareness.

Imagine you arrive home and find a miniature elephant standing forlornly in your living room. You race from the room to call the police and upon your return discover it's no longer there. In hindsight you might come to accept you've been the victim of an astonishing content-specific hallucination, since the elephant *can't* have been subjectively real. However, jottled objects are nowhere near as unbelievable as a living room elephant, so you will hardly consider your disappearing eyeglasses or reappearing coffee mug to be the product of a content-specific delusion.

As skeptical explanations go, content-specific delusions are arguably the strongest solution for jottles, although there are awkward issues to acknowledge. The first is that a jottle hallucination is necessarily multimodal rather than simply visual. Experients doesn't just *see* something that *isn't* there or *not see* something that *is* there. They can also *feel* it is there, or *not feel it*, depending on circumstance. For disappearing and appearing objects, there's also the *noise* an object does or does not make when it falls to the ground. That's a very sophisticated type of hallucination.

Second, and perhaps more important, the analysis doesn't support jottles as content-specific delusions. Across stories, jottled objects are much more consistent than would be expected from a random delusion, assuming the delusions *are* random. That's clear with the consistency of jottled objects and jottle locations. Just as damaging is the fact that content-specific delusions are rare and not widely considered outside of gross psychopathology.[38] I've never heard of anyone admitting he's seen an elephant in his living room in the absence of any other symptoms of mental disorder, so why should a jottle be a similar but more frequent type of hallucination? There's no support for the view that experients are mentally ill to the point that they're prone to these types of pseudo-hallucinations or experiencing the effects of a psychedelic drug.

If mentally healthy people experience delusions in the form of jottles, by extension these same delusions must be an unknown component of the rest of our waking lives. Who, then, can tell what *is* hallucinated and what is *not*? Indeed, a disappearance is by definition *forever*, so does that mean the lost object still resides at the location it was last seen but has been deleted from perception for the rest of the experient's life? Such reasoning leads to this curious exchange:

> *Experient*: Last week, an apple disappeared from the countertop when I had my back turned. I haven't seen it again.
> *Acquaintance*: Do you mean the apple that's sitting there now? It's been there for days. It hasn't moved. Can't you see it?
> *Experient*: No. I must have hallucinated it out of existence. Thanks for letting me know. Now I might be able to see it again.

Admittedly this is a comical conversation, but it does illustrate the wider implications of jottles as content-specific delusions. A final feature of content-specific delusions that tends to be brushed over but troubles Hillary Evans more than the concept of hallucination itself is that these powerful images require what he terms a "producer." If imaginary objects can be adapted effortlessly *into* an environmental context (and real objects *out of* the same environment) without affecting any other aspect of conscious self-awareness, then this "producer" is—as Evans suggests—very resourceful. By attempting to explain one unknown (jottles) we're left with a bigger unknown. Who or what is the "producer"?

People obviously can and do hallucinate. However, the highly specific circumstances associated with most jottle cases don't suit the content-specific delusion hypothesis. Flippantly brushing off an interesting and sincere jottle story as "mere hallucination" shows little insight into the hallucinatory process.

Hypnosis and Jottles

Surely there must be some psychological state that isn't as rare and pathological in the fashion of content-specific delusions, but is still applicable to jottles? Perhaps *hypnosis* is the answer, as in the following: "Belinda has been hypnotized not to notice her glasses on the kitchen countertop." It is common knowledge that hypnosis can be induced in volunteers participating in a stage show, causing them to enact crazy public behaviors. Could a variety of hypnosis be the source of jottles? Quite possibly, since hypnosis isn't a "trance" state where people walk around like zombies. Rather, when people are hypnotized they are placed in a form of deep relaxation where their attention shifts from the external world to an inward consideration of mental experiences. That's a bit like saying the spotlight of awareness has shifted its beam from observing the stuff of primary consciousness to be fully fixated with reflective consciousness. However, these people are still perfectly "awake" and enact the instructions from the hypnotist only because they no longer have the necessary "psychological energy" to resist them.

If we apply hypnosis to jottles, experients might be affected by *post-hypnotic suggestion*. For example, they've recently been hypnotized and as they return to normal consciousness the hypnotist suggests that from this time forward they are to "not see" a certain object sitting in plain view around their homes. Superficially the experients look and feel perfectly normal, but the implanted suggestion means their perception of the environment will no longer be entirely accurate. The obvious question that arises is how so many people could have been hypnotized by skilled practitioners *not* to see objects around their home. Surely that's more implausible than the reality of jottles.

To avoid this problem, it may be argued that the experient is responsible for hypnotizing *herself* to either see or not to see random objects around the home. The trouble is, to achieve such *autohypnosis* you have to follow all the standard procedures used by a trained hypnotist. You would need to lie or sit in a comfortable manner and fixate on a point, then work yourself into a progressive state of relaxation while at the same time remaining in complete control of the hypnotic process (through self-instruction) so that you don't simply fall asleep. With practice, that's perfectly achievable, although to assume that jottles are a consequence of experients putting themselves through this rigmarole simply to have things vanish or appear to them around their homes is not supported by any evidence.

Assessing the Skeptical Position on Jottles

Overall, there's very little justification in concluding that *every* disappearing object has been stolen or is small enough to be accidently misplaced. Only a minority of cases possess a long last seen and loss delay indicative of something that's been routinely lost. There are also very few vintage cases in the collection (e.g., stories from childhood), and the analysis suggests that absent-mindedness, suggestion and confirmation bias aren't applicable to most jottle cases either. Nor is inattentional blindness a strong explanation unless you're prepared to accept convoluted assumptions that are yet to be empirically demonstrated.

It's easier to blame jottles on a transient altered state of consciousness—hypnosis, hallucinations and fugue states. These are all perfectly acceptable possibilities, but I don't believe they pass the common-sense test. That's best shown in the following counterargument involving a disappearance jottle. It's a created story (like the skeptic's denunciation);

however, I've drawn on the elements of an actual account to give it some level of authenticity (specifically, the type of object that went missing and the circumstances surrounding the loss):

> This story isn't made up.
>
> I lost an object in a secure location—a small, sparsely furnished room. I was present when it went missing, although I didn't see it vanish. The object was a large hairbrush, not a small needle or earring. It was physically impossible to have misplaced this brush, as every piece of furniture in the room was removed when I performed the search. There was nowhere for my brush to be hidden. No one else was present when it went missing, so it can't have been stolen.
>
> I was fully attending to finding the missing brush. I wasn't "absentminded" at all. My attention was completely focused, so I can't see how my inability to find the brush has anything to do with this nebulous concept of "inattentional blindness." If that's the case, why don't I lose things all the time? Why just this one brush? My search process involved more than simply looking—I was also down on my hands and knees feeling around. Are you telling me that inattentional blindness affected my somatosensory system so that I couldn't feel the brush on the floor, the same way that I couldn't see it? That's a ridiculous assertion and in no way reflects my experience.
>
> And don't try to tell me I possess an "attention seeking" personality trait or was sleepwalking, over-emotional, or stuck in some other unnatural psychological state at the time. I'm not medicated, mentally ill, or physically sick. I felt perfectly fine when my brush disappeared, and I can honestly say I wasn't hallucinating. The situation was as normal as any other time in my life, but the event itself was not normal. That's why I remember it clearly. Nor was it something that happened way back in 1983. It occurred only a few months ago. And it's not as though I unconsciously said to myself, "Wow, I've always believed in jottles, so I'll just subtly change a few of the more important details associated with my disappearing brush (like finding it again under the dresser) to make the story sound mysterious." I had no interest, or knowledge, of these kinds of supernatural disappearances until one happened to me, and I haven't changed my memory of it in the meantime (don't try to tell me I have).
>
> If I can't trust this memory of a real event, I can't trust any memory I have.

If you have no intention of accepting this articulate rejoinder, then you will be happy to accept that one or more of this experient's claims is wrong—whether she knows it or not. However, if you are not so absolutist in attitude and accept the experient is sincere and convinced of the anomalous nature of the disappearance and also agree that skeptical rationalizations aren't watertight, then where does this leave us? Surely we can't go blaming fairies or time warps for the disappearance, can we?

Part III

7
A New Approach

Some jottle stories may be dismissed as examples of physical misplacement and psychological error—indeed *all* stories if you're prepared to accept that experients are inherently untrustworthy and possess subtle psychological traits that generate delusions. If your mind has been made up, there's no use trying to convince you otherwise. However, stealing from the flying saucer literature, I'm now inclined to believe that a large "irreducible minimum" (or perhaps I should say "irreducible maximum") of jottle stories *are* inexplicable—at least in terms of a mainstream "scientific" solution. That being the case, it's worth examining jottles from an entirely different perspective. That means evaluating the more popular fringe scientific and paranormal "explanations" that have been suggested over the years. I've already alluded to some of these explanations—outlandish concepts such as fairies, spirits, poltergeists, parallel universes, alternate dimensions and time warps. These I've appropriated from the experients' own rationalizations, the thoughts of enthusiasts blogging on the Internet, and even the discussion points of participants attending the 2003 study session on jottles. From these diverse perspectives I can discern three primary classes of explanation:

(1) Jottles are caused by fundamental, natural and mechanistic processes beyond current scientific validation (although widely speculated on). The four most popular explanations are *invisibility, teleportation, multiverses* and *"other dimensions."*
(2) Jottles are caused by paraphysical entities that are independent of the experient. The three most popular entities mentioned by experients are *spirits, poltergeists* and *fairies*. Again, the processes operated by these entities are beyond current scientific comprehensions (as are these alleged entities themselves). However such processes may be implicitly related to the mechanisms underlying "natural" explanations (see 1).

(3) Jottles are parapsychological events unwittingly caused by the experients themselves for various obscure subconscious reasons. Once more, these processes are beyond current scientific comprehension but may be the same as or similar to those associated with natural causes and external agents (see 1 and 2). Agent-centered *psychokinetic* ability is the single most popular attribution.

Let's work through these three options in turn to see how well they fit with a conceptualization of jottles as something *real*. That is, can one or more of these radical theories account for the current findings, specifically *interaction* and *intention*?

The Mechanistic Universe

Consider the following remarks:
"My shoe somehow became temporarily invisible."
"My credit card was teleported to the other side of the house."
"My wedding band went through a wormhole to somewhere else in the galaxy."
"The car keys ended up in a parallel universe."
"A vortex sucked my pen into another dimension."

These are all attempts to explain an inexplicable jottle. Unlike the physical and psychological attributions in the previous chapter, the experients are claiming objects are behaving in a manner that is—in our current paradigm—paranormal. Nevertheless, these perspectives all touch on fringe scientific concepts, so it's not completely unreasonable to consider whether they are compatible with our findings.

Invisibility

Perhaps the most straightforward (sympathetic) explanation for jottles is that disappearing and reappearing objects have, at some stage, literally become *invisible*. This is not the same as claims of inattentional blindness, since invisibility is not a function of subjective perceptual error but an exotic property of the object itself. There's some evidence that real objects can actually be made invisible, or at least invisible to certain types of radiation. Researchers at Duke University and Imperial College have recently constructed metal rings implanted with special impurities and microcircuits. Microwaves projected onto the rings are deflected by these impurities in such a way that the object within the rings is made "invisible" to this narrow band of *electromagnetic radiation*. The prediction is that a system could eventually be constructed whereby objects of a single color, reflecting another narrow band of the electromagnetic spectrum, can also be rendered invisible. Over time this may be expanded to a broader range of visible wavelengths and ultimately allow multicolored objects to disappear from sight completely.[1] Therefore, the concept of "real-life invisibility" is scientifically feasible, if only in a laboratory context and requiring specialized equipment to realize it.

That doesn't help our explanation for jottled objects, as a large conceptual leap is needed to accept there are similar *natural* processes causing normal, everyday items to disappear (and perhaps reappear) around the home. The kitchen isn't a Duke University physics laboratory, and there's no current or practical discussion about processes underlying "natural" invisibility—if in fact it happens at all. There's certainly no explanation for where the energy might come from to sustain the deflection of light rays or why it might happen in rare and particular circumstances—singling out keys and TV remotes as favored objects and kitchens and bedrooms as favored locations. One wouldn't expect the physics of invisibility to discriminate in such a fashion. Even more seriously, the word "invisible" means just that: in-*visible*. By definition, an invisible object should still be perceptible to all the senses *apart* from vision. I mentioned earlier that jottles could be visual hallucinations if you assume that this altered state of consciousness simultaneously affects all the senses, not simply vision. The same reasoning cannot salvage physical invisibility. That's because an object made invisible to the eye through advanced technology or rare but natural physical process is still *there*. It can be felt during the search process or heard if knocked off a table.

In spite of this problem, there might still be a place for invisibility when applied to rapid returns. The object is temporarily in disguise but the experient is too shocked to have time to feel around for it with her hands or she looks for it in the wrong place before it reappears. However, this explanation is even more torturous than inattentional blindness. There's no indication that this is how experients search for a jottled object. Therefore, while invisibility might sound reasonable at first glance, I'd suggest it is not a solution to jottles and shouldn't receive a passing mark.

Teleportation

If there's a favorite word to account for jottles, it's *teleportation*. In the fashion of "hallucination" the term doesn't really *explain* anything. Instead it's simply a description of how an object can move through space in an instant across any distance. While just about everyone is familiar with teleportation as a concept, very few people *really* believe it can happen outside science fiction. Nevertheless, teleportation is a good match for jottles. It suits permanent object disappearances and situations where the same object ends up somewhere else as an unexpected appearance. It also matches both types of reappearance jottles—returns and relocations. A complicated chain of teleportation events might even account for those rare replacements found in the collection. One object is teleported to a distant location, and at the same time a similar object is teleported *back* in its place.

To appreciate teleportation as a potential explanation for jottles rather than a vague description of what the process entails, there's no better place to start than with the man who invented the term and appreciate what he had to say about the context and purpose of this purported phenomenon. Such an understanding is highly relevant to an investigation of jottles because the word "teleportation" wasn't invented by a screenwriter to assist the plot of a science fiction movie but to account for *actual* disappearing, appearing and reappearing objects!

From the turn of the 20th century right up until his death in 1932, Charles Fort led a quiet and unassuming life as a writer, spending much of his adult life perusing a huge range of newspapers and journals and visiting libraries in the U.S. and England to browse catalogues for articles that didn't fit conventional scientific (and societal) thinking. He wrote up these oddities in reams of notes that he eventually published in book form, making him very much a pioneer of documenting events that didn't interest even the psychical researchers or scientists of the day. In 1919 he published his first successful tract of nonfiction, *The Book of the Damned*, which contains a mishmash of documented historical, and at times contemporary, events that had been "excluded" (in other words, ignored) by orthodox science. These are the "damned" facts of the title. *The Book of the Damned* is a rather turgid read, and the interesting array of stories is overshadowed by Fort's grating hostility toward university professors and any other "expert" on record who dismissed evidence undermining the mainstream scientific paradigm. In Fort's mind these pig-headed champions of "established preposterousness"[2] unreasonably ignored good evidence irreconcilable with sensible science. Consequently, he uses almost as many words discussing their—in his view—ridiculous rationalizations as he does presenting the "damned" evidence. And there was plenty of evidence to present, although the most numerous stories involve strange objects that rain from the sky—for instance thousands of living fish showering a village street many miles from the coast. Fort felt such a mystery couldn't be explained as the consequence of an accidental whirlwind or as morsels dropped from the beaks of a hungry pelican family. Here's another example from the late 19th century: "[I]n the province of Macerata, Italy, an immense number of small, blood-colored clouds covered the sky. About an hour later a storm broke, and a myriad of seeds fell to the ground. It is said that they were identified as products of a tree found only in Central Africa and the Antilles (Fort 257)."[3] The seeds were also beginning to germinate, which to Fort confirmed they hadn't been hovering in the air for very long. Instead, these seeds could only have recently germinated in their warm homeland, travelling the vast distance to Italy in a very short space of time.

Object showers can involve just about anything, as demonstrated by the large collection of cases Fort assembled. The objects might be living things—like fish or frogs, worms or crabs or seeds. They could also be nonliving things—like dead fish, dead frogs, dead worms or dead crabs. Also of interest were falls of inanimate objects, like pebbles or a heavy stream of water falling from singular points in the sky (imagine a running tap) drenching a single peach tree[4] or small stretch of barren ground. Mainstream science has never accepted these stories as anomalous. They're either rationalized as explainable meteorological events or dismissed as fabrications. Unimpressed, Fort described people who display this close-minded attitude as "exclusionists."[5]

In *The Book of the Damned* Fort remains cagey about the cause of wondrous object showers, although he does obliquely refer to extraterrestrial sources. However, by his third book Fort was more confident in his solution. *Lo!* (1931) is a much easier read, and Fort happily discusses the origin of the objects that shower from above (and those that just seem to appear from nowhere). Apparently these showers are a method to distribute, or *re*distribute, matter from one place in the universe to another where it was more in demand. That matched his existential philosophy that "reality" is fluid and interconnected, constantly fluctuating to the point that all phenomena ultimately merge with one another. Should some fertile place here on earth (or on another world in the solar system) be overstocked with minnows, through universal interconnectedness these surplus fish might instantly relocate via a nonaqueous shower to a pond in Hampshire where they're in short supply. Or perhaps through a singular error of navigation they're dropped on the roofs and streets of a town in New Hampshire.

Fort uses the metaphor of the human immune system to show how no one thing is directly responsible for the redistribution. Osteoblasts mend a broken bone, and this *seems* purposeful. However, these living cells are not conscious of their own behavior. The organism *as a whole* selects and distributes material around the body, but these decisions aren't necessarily volitional either.[6] In a similar way, while the redistributive forces of nature appear to behave with purpose, they merely operate in a mechanistic fashion. Fort was aware of the work of Spinoza, so rather than making God responsible (in an "old-fashioned theological" sense) as the cogent director of operations, he preferred contemplating a pantheistic universe, or "Existence as Organism," which "drools comets and gibbers earthquakes."[7] The redistributive showers he wrote about could therefore be compared to the actions of a terrestrial living system maintaining homeostasis. However, rather than travelling through blood vessels to reach their destination, objects in this universe use a far stranger technique. Fort says, "I shall specialize upon indications that there exists a transportory force that I shall call teleportation (553).[8] He then explains: "In every organism, there are, in its governance as a whole, mysterious transportations of substances and forces, sometimes in definite circulatory paths, and sometimes specially, for special needs. In the organic view, teleportation is a distributive force that is acting to maintain the balances of a whole, with the seeming wastefulness ... providing, or sometimes providing, new islands with vegetation, and new ponds with fishes ... always dwindling when other mechanisms become established, but surviving spasmodically (667)."[9]

To support his argument, Fort presents plenty of obscure and forgotten stories he collected over many years. In one newspaper article he discovered than an English drought in 1921 killed off a large variety of insects—creatures like aphids, mosquitoes, dragonflies, ants and midges. In a separate newspaper article he learned that shortly after the drought ended the affected location was covered in clouds of exotic insects. They'd arrived seemingly from nowhere, "like fireflies."[10] Connecting these two outwardly unrelated events was the compensating actions of teleportation—the same process behind showers of seeds and other organic matter.

More difficult to account for are reports of showers of butter, beef, blood, paper, wool, silk, resin and even stones with unusual inscriptions. These were common stories in Fort's day, and they remain so today—particularly within dwellings. For example, parapsychologist Alexander Imich[11] alludes to cases where water and other unidentified liquids appear from the walls and ceilings of affected homes, startling the residents.[12] And of course there are the famous stories of "stone throwing" within houses. Spiritualist author Frank Podmore refers to a Dutch oil company explorer named Grottendieck who travelled through Sumatra in 1903.[13] Grottendieck was sleeping in a hut when, at 1:00 a.m., he witnessed small black stones falling gently to the floor from the ceiling in an arcing motion. He investigated the hut inside and out but couldn't explain how the stones were penetrating the roof—a *kadjang* made of dense dry leaves. Even stranger, the rocks changed direction mid-flight to prevent him catching any of them, and when he did he found they were warm to the touch. Typical of Fort's exclusionists, commentators at the time suggested the stones were actually seeds dropped by fruit bats lodged in the ceiling!

Fort didn't believe the rains of nonorganic material *within* houses were any different from showers of organic matter *outside* houses. He simply offered the view that these internal showers were the product of a senile universe misapplying the once great—but now redundant—process of teleportation.

Teleporting People

This teleportatory "malfunction" may also explain the disappearance or relocation of actual *people*. One famous tale that's been told and retold for years in paranormal books and on the Internet concerns a Spanish soldier named Gil Pérez. In October 1593 Pérez was found in a confused state in Mexico City and arrested because he was wearing the uniform of a regiment stationed in the Philippines. It was assumed he was a deserter, but he claimed he'd been in the Philippines only the day before, on guard duty in Manila. As he felt tired, he had briefly closed his eyes only to open them again and find himself in the Mexico City Plaza. In support of his claim, he had knowledge of the very recent murder of Philippines governor Gómez Pérez Dasmariñas by the Chinese crew of a naval galley. That was confirmed two months later when a vessel arrived from Manila with passengers who knew of the disappearance of Gil Pérez—and the violent death of Dasmariñas. Luckily for Pérez he avoided further charges (authorities were apparently unsure quite what to do) and was sent back to the Philippines. This is considered a "true" teleportation story,[14] although it's difficult to be certain if it is actually true or if a soldier named Gil Pérez even existed. Indeed, most stories about mysteriously appearing and disappearing people derive from lost or missing historical documents or old newspaper articles of dubious authenticity or containing ambiguous information (e.g., the James Tedford incident).

Fort himself acknowledged that it was difficult to find genuine examples of people remembering being teleported from one place to another (Gil Pérez being a rare exception). This leaves open the possibility that the affected individual was in a psychological fugue state, and travelled between locations in a perfectly normal way—a ship, train, bus or by foot.

If we accept that evidence for human teleportation is weak, the process nonetheless makes sense of various paranormal phenomena involving people, something Fort cleverly acknowledged. Picture someone falling asleep in his own bed and entering an altered state of consciousness. Quite unexpectedly he manages to activate the universe's dormant force of redistribution and accidently relocates somewhere else, then back again. However, since he's asleep he's only dimly aware he's made such an "astral voyage." When he wakes, a trace memory is all that remains, but it's one that's strong enough to jolt him with a sense of recognition—of "being there before"—if he later revisits that same distant location in the flesh. That's a neat paranormal (as opposed to psychological) account for déjà vu. Better still, if someone else is present at this distant location and sees the sleeper in his night clothes[15] briefly appear then vanish again, that person might mistake the teleporter for a ghost![16]

Jottles and Teleportation

Describing object showers and the teleportation of people as the random workings of an enfeebled universe's redistributive machinery is one thing, but where does that leave jottles? Are they a different manifestation of this same phenomenon? Outwardly, showers of objects from the heavens are *appearances*, although the falls of fish or stones don't resemble the characteristics of eggs or bananas that materialize around the kitchen and dining room. Granted, around half of the appearing object stories involve unowned familiar articles, but by the same token half of the cases do not—they're recognized as owned familiar objects hence they don't fit the mold of a typical redistribution.[17] Experients also report that appearing objects *feel* natural, as though they've always been where they're found.

That's very different to the stones that fell from the ceiling of the Sumatran house at the turn of last century, which were hot to the touch.[18] Moreover, in a great number of these anomalous showers the objects were *seen* to fall, something rarely reported for jottles involving owned or unowned objects. Showering objects also fall more slowly than expected (that is, they don't plummet to the ground), and their motion is curious. In the case of living things like frogs and fish, they are often unhurt after hitting the ground. Charles Fort explained these features as the actions of "counter-gravitational" forces,[19] and that makes sense in terms of the "purpose" of teleportation. Care in deposition would help to preserve both the objects themselves and the environment in which they land.

Only jottled coins share the features of a typical Fortean "shower." As mentioned, single coins are *sometimes* witnessed appearing in mid-air, and their descent has also been described as *slower than normal*, although this is atypical of appearance jottles in general. If anything, jottled objects appear to be a closer cousin of lone teleporting people. James Tedford disappeared forever and Gil Pérez (allegedly) relocated, instantly and for no apparent reason. Consequently, it might be more practical to disassociate "teleportation" from its redistributive origins and propose that the ability of an object to disappear or reappear is an expression of a little understood natural mechanism potentially affecting anything or anybody in the right circumstances—and not expressly for the purpose of universal homeostasis.

"Real" Teleportation

In "proper" science, teleportation doesn't refer to the actual transport of an *object* between locations. Rather, teleportation is all about transferring *information*, and to appreciate this concept I need to dabble in some amateurish quantum physics. The *quantum wave function* mathematically represents everything about an object at the most fundamental level, specifically the properties of its component subatomic particles—like electrons and photons.[20] When it comes to "real" teleportation, the idea is that the *information* contained in the wave function is transferred from one place to another rather than the object itself. Conceivably that could be done using existing methods of information transfer, such as a very sophisticated cable. Material present at the new location can then be sequestered and used to rebuild the object using the transmitted information as a blueprint. Meanwhile, the original object at the initial location is destroyed in the process.

This proposition provides an interesting theory for one of our jottle types. What if the original object isn't destroyed and the new, teleported, object is reconstituted only centimeters away? Would that account for object duplication? Unfortunately, there's a large obstacle to overcome before this style of teleportation can be accepted. Knowledge of the quantum wave function is theoretically impossible—particularly in terms of real physical objects like a TV remote control or a set of keys. These objects are made of countless subatomic particles, each possessing a vast range of variables, including motion, location and magnetic field. Such information needs to be pinned down and measured,[21] but the very act of measurement violates *Heisenberg's uncertainty principle*[22] whereby knowledge of, for example, the *motion* of a particle excludes knowledge of its *location* and vice versa. It's simply not possible to know *precisely* the value of every necessary variable in the object. The wave function of a particle isn't a fixed range of measurements but instead represents the various probability states the particle may hold simultaneously—a characteristic known as *superposition*.[23] When applied to complex objects like a set of keys, this array of potential states is indescribably complex and realistically cannot be determined, let alone projected to a distant location.

Therefore, when it comes to "real" teleportation, we can't be dealing with conventional information travel—not even the wave function of something as small as a single electron. Instead, physicists turn to the concept of *entanglement*, which is also best understood at a subatomic particle level. If two electrons are brought together and share identical properties, such as the same frequency of vibration, they become connected by an essential wave that allows them to remain in contact, even if they are then separated by a vast distance. Measurement of the first electron will alter its state (the uncertainty principle in action), and this disturbance will immediately manifest in the second electron. This effect has actually been demonstrated in physics laboratories,[24] although what's been "transmitted" is information about a *change of state*. The electron hasn't been physically relocated from one place to another, nor has its wave function travelled through space. Communication takes place at a far more fundamental level, and the effect is termed *quantum teleportation*.

The reason why quantum teleportation is viable is that the quantum wave function of the material to be teleported *doesn't need be to known*. Only the alteration in the behavior of the first particle has been conveyed to the second particle. That is different from the concept of material teleportation suggested previously, where the quantum state is known and transferred elsewhere to act as the master plan for a reconstituted object.

In quantum teleportation, the target electron is *already* elsewhere and entangled with the first electron. Applying quantum teleportation to the "real world," we might imagine two completely identical TV remote controls, side by side and entangled. Take one TV control to the bathroom and leave one in the living room. Measuring the first control will change its elementary state, and you'll subsequently find the same change has instantaneously affected the remote in the bathroom. Unfortunately, this treatment of teleportation bears no resemblance to a jottle.

Despite this setback, there's something attractive about jottles being the product of wave state teleportation. Apart from duplications, the idea also fits nicely with object disappearances and returns. Recall that prior interaction is a feature of many of these jottles, whereby the object had been touched only moments before it vanished for good, returned to the same spot a little later or perhaps even duplicated side by side. It's easy, although hardly respectable, to argue that physical contact with the object could—in some unknown way—record its fundamental information array, energize it and then project it elsewhere. Alternatively, the disruption might be transient and without physical projection; the object temporarily dissolves then reconstitutes at the same location a short time later. I'm certainly not going to fight for this idea, but it does allow teleportation to remain an intriguing explanation for jottles, even if the idea is literally hanging by its theoretical fingernails.

Jottles Through the Wormhole

If quantum information transfer across distance is unconvincing, then maybe it's worth removing the necessity that jottled objects travel through actual physical space. To explore this notion, I'll need to start with a brief description of *space-time*. Everyday reality consists of three *spatial* dimensions—length, width and height, with time as a *nonspatial* dimension. Local events occur at coordinates in this four-dimensional space-time continuum. However, Einstein's work showed that space-time is a curved system with the addition of mass, which in turn generates gravity. This is represented in popular physics as a stretched rubber sheet.[25] A heavy object placed in the middle of this sheet will distort and curve the fabric, so that a light object moving along the sheet will be forced to follow a curved orbit around the heavy object. That represents gravitational attraction.

Taking this analogy to its logical conclusion, the object could be so heavy—thus space-time so curved—that the sheet folds in on itself. A *wormhole* is a mathematical shortcut representing the meeting place of two of these folded regions, even though they are far apart when the sheet is stretched.[26] If both sides of this wormhole are "open" then an object might be able to shoot across this short distance (if there's any distance at all) to another place that ordinarily seems very distant.[27] In three dimensional space, the holes are spherical, but it's not necessary to try to imagine what *that* looks like. It's just important to appreciate that a wormhole could be a vehicle for rapid teleportation of an object across great distances, irrespective of the object's quantum state. The problem with wormholes is that they are mathematically unstable. If they are even actualized in real space-time, they must collapse just as quickly—so fast that even light can't enter them. What's worse, even if an object like Kate's set of keys did manage to enter the throat of the wormhole floating near her front door lock it would take an infinite amount of time (based on external observation) for them to fall through to the other side—wherever that may be. From this perspective it's a one-way trip, as there's no inevitability for the object to ever complete the journey—or come back, for that matter. Maybe that fits the profile of a disappearance but not any other style of jottle.

Various clever physicists have played around with mathematical equations to determine the conditions needed to keep a wormhole open and traversable—ensuring there's an exit as well as an entrance. This requires the ingredient of *exotic matter*—a type of strange energy that works in an opposite way from gravity to keep matter apart and, by that assumption, keep the throat of the wormhole open. This presents a problem for the wormhole's viability, as anything passing through the wormhole wouldn't want to brush up against the sides, as the exotic matter might exert exotic effects on the object. There are all sorts of numerically complicated solutions to prevent this happening, such as the wormhole entrance being in the form of a cube rather than a sphere. In this treatment, exotic matter is arranged in the straight edges of the cube, allowing an object to pass through the face unhindered.[28] As cosmologist Max Tegmark suggests, while wormholes are theoretically unstable, it is yet to be verified that they *can't* be stabilized with exotic energy in this fashion. It might be assumed but not proven.[29] Therefore, functioning wormholes are unlikely but not completely impossible.

That's about all I can come up with for jottles as the translocation of objects through wormholes. It requires the assumption that wormholes exist in the first place and an acceptance that the universe is riddled with them—and that they are popping into and out of existence all around us without being noticed or measured. And, obviously, they're most prevalent at home, lurking in the kitchen stealing the contents of your fridge and sending it to some other house as an unexpected windfall.

In summary, claiming your keys were swallowed by a wormhole and teleported elsewhere is theoretically possible but beyond anything currently conceivable.

A Parallel World of Jottles

Before moving on to other potential jottle solutions, let's stop for a moment and consider the topography of teleportation through quantum wave transfer and wormholes. At the simplest conceptualization, these processes involve the physical transport of an object from one place to another within a static universe. The important word here is *static*, meaning a solitary universe created following the "Big Bang." This universe operates as a single environment in which things travel around in three dimensional space and through time, a concept known as the *standard paradigm* for reality.[30] Even curved space-time possesses this static trait.

However, jottles are quirky by nature and the framework of the standard paradigm may be too restrictive. Progressing from the notion of an object's being transported around three-dimensional static space in *this* universe (either through teleportation or a wormhole), we could instead consider the possibility that it has travelled to a completely different, *parallel*, universe. The French paranormal investigator Jacques Bergier uses a nice metaphor to describe these parallel universes and how they might interact with each other:

> [W]e are able to influence other universes, and other universes can influence us. The mechanism is similar to that in chess when one bishop traverses the white squares only and the opposing bishop only the black. They cannot come into direct contact with each other: The same situation exists in regards to two different universes. But bishops in a chess game can and do have power over each other through the mediation of other pieces (9).[31]

Bergier argues quite correctly that the term "parallel universe" is not appropriate, as to be parallel implies no contact is possible, *ever*. Instead we are dealing with "alternative universes," which *can* subtly interact with one another, and this makes possible the idea that jottles involve the movement of objects amongst these universes.

Lerina García and the Tokyo Taured

To examine this prospect, I'll start with two stories popularly believed to be evidence for alternate universes. They involve people rather than objects, but the context is applicable to jottles. The first is an Internet favorite about a man called the "Tokyo Taured." As it's told on various excitable forums, back in 1954 (or the early 1990s or last week, depending on your source) a man of European extraction arrived in Tokyo on an international flight. He had in his possession European money and an international driver's license and he was fluent in several languages. What alerted Japanese customs officials was the discovery that the man's passport identified him as a resident of a country named Taured. The passport seemed perfectly legitimate—with customs stamps from real countries (including a previous one from Japan). However, Taured *isn't* a real country, so he was detained for 14 hours at the airport. This naturally made the Tauredian angry and convinced that he was the butt of a practical joke. He was insistent that Taured had existed for 1,000 years—apparently in the location where Andorra currently resides between France and Spain. Unconvinced, the Japanese authorities transported their mystery guest to a hotel for safekeeping while they debated what to do with him. The hotel room door was guarded by two immigration officers, but when morning arrived the man was discovered missing, even though the only other exit from the room was a window 15 floors above the street. An extensive search was made, but the Taured was never found.

The Tokyo Taured is accepted by many in the paranormal community as evidence that people have been transported from one universe to a very similar one and back again. However, the story has all the hallmarks of folklore. Searching for the Taured's origin, he makes a cameo appearance in various old mystery books alongside similar stories of people arriving from the uncharted countries of Sakria and Lisbian.[32] No references to primary sources are ever provided, so it's hard to know what to make of these tales (other than that they're fabricated).

There are also more recent stories suggestive of alternate universes, and some are even told by the protagonists themselves. One of the best hails from 2008, when a 41-year-old Spanish woman by the name of Lerina García posted a tale of woe on the Internet. As she tells it, she woke one morning in her normal bed, in a place she'd been living in for seven years, and everything seemed normal apart from a few minor inconsistencies. For example, her bed linen was different from the night before, although she paid little heed to this at the time. As the day wore on these small aberrations began to accumulate. Arriving at work—a place where she'd been employed for 20 years—Lerina discovered she wasn't assigned to her normal department but another one with an entirely different supervisor she didn't know. Needing headspace to think, she feigned sickness and returned home only to learn her partner was not the man she was currently seeing but someone she'd been with for seven years but had separated from six months previously. This man acted as though everything was normal and no breakup had ever occurred. And to make things worse, Lerina discovered her new, current, partner didn't even *exist*. Despite her assertion that she wasn't drug or alcohol affected and was perfectly sane, physicians blamed stress-induced hallucinations. That didn't sit well with Lerina, who instead viewed her plight as the result of a "decision or action" she'd performed in one "plane" of existence that caused an irreversible "jump" to another plane where history had taken a different course: "[I]t's as though I had lost my memory five months ago and woke up having dreamed those five months, with the exception that everyone remembers me during that time, and I've done things that I'm not aware of having done."[33]

This story is easily attributed to psychosis brought about by organic brain dysfunction, and that's even assuming Lerina exists *at all*. The story could be entirely fictitious and posted on a Spanish blog for a lark. I haven't attempted to assess its legitimacy because it really doesn't matter whether it's true or not. The story of Lerina García simply fuels speculation that alternative universes are real and people can shift between them. If they come *here* from somewhere else, they are *appearing* people. On the other hand, people like James Tedford might *disappear* into another universe, forever. What is more, if these people return they show evidence that differences exist between these universes, including the experience of time: "An interesting story (if true!) about a man who may have passed into a parallel world is that of a Chilean army corporal, Armando Valdes. On 25th April 1977 he apparently vanished in front of six of his men; fifteen minutes later he reappeared. His men noticed that the calendar on Valdes' watch had advanced five days and that he had grown a five-day beard. Unfortunately, Valdes could remember nothing of the abduction, nor of what happened during the fifteen minutes/five days he had been missing."[34]

Where does this leave jottles? The following story was told to me after a public talk I gave on the topic. I didn't get enough information for it to be an addition to the collection, but it's worth retelling here because it has all the elements of an appearance jottle while suiting the notion of travel between "alternative universes":

> This happened at my in-law's house at [___]. We visit weekly and one time there was a large mound of dirt in the backyard near the rear fence. I asked [___]'s dad how long it had been there because it wasn't there last Sunday. He said it had been there ever since he'd dug the pond and hadn't got around to having it removed. It was completely covered in grass, so it must have been there for years. But like I said it hadn't been there the week before, or ever since I'd been to the house and we'd been married three years. I asked [___] and he said it had been there that long too. I thought I was going mad but now I think it's related to jottles.

From this perspective, jottles don't involve objects being teleported around this universe. Instead, it is the *experient* who moves *between* universes! Last week our experient occupied a world where there was no pile of dirt in her father-in-law's backyard. This week she's ended up in another, similar, world (unbeknownst to her) where there *is* a pile of dirt. Applied to household jottles, it's easy to imagine a similar situation where small objects like nail clippers and apples exist in one reality but are absent from another, almost identical reality.[35]

The Multiverse

To evaluate this outrageous idea I'll need to indulge once more in some amateurish cosmology. To start, "alternative universes" implies *multiple* universes, and currently the most popular way of imagining such universes being side by side is as part of an overarching *multiverse*. The word was created by the great early psychologist William James in 1895 in an address to the Harvard YMCA, when he spoke of the natural world as a moral *multi*verse rather than a moral *uni*verse[36] and made the claim that no "divine Spirit" exists in nature alone. James's argument is rather challenging, although he does mention that if divine Spirit cannot be revealed in nature, then "what we call visible nature, or *this* world, must be but a veil and surface-show whose full meaning resides in a supplementary unseen or *other* world (44)."[37] So in an oblique theological way William James was touching on the idea of other, greater, realities. Nowadays, the word "multiverse" is used more pragmatically, referring to the notion in popular physics that there are an infinite number of universes concurrent with the one we're residing in right now. However, as might be expected from such a thorny idea, there are a lot of different perspectives on how the multiverse might have arisen and how it currently operates.

To begin, let's go all the way back to the scientifically respectable beginning of the "standard universe," *very* shortly after the Big Bang about

14 billion years ago. Recent claims are that *gravitational waves* have been detected in space, and this is used as evidence for a rapid inflation of the universe over a very short period following the Big Bang (a factor of 10^{78} in 10^{-30} seconds).[38] At this moment of inflation[39] there was a massive amount of latent energy driving a state of immense gravitational repulsion which acted to blow the universe up like a balloon.[40] This widely accepted idea helps explain many observable features of the universe, such as why it is *isotropic*—or looks similar at locations that are so far apart in time and space. However, it is also speculated that there were lots of tiny fluctuations in the fabric of the universe during inflation, and each of these irregularities also were massively amplified in size. An admittedly lame analogy would be the same way tiny ink dots on the surface of a flaccid balloon grow bigger when the balloon is pumped full of air. These amplified fluctuations ultimately became galaxies, stars, planets and people.[41]

So far, that describes a single universe. However, a more elaborate proposal is that inflation is driven by hypothetical particles called—what else?—*inflatons*.[42] Simplistically, there are countless inflatons permeating the surface of the expanding universe, each possessing their own quantum fluctuations and acting independently of one another. That means they're creating their own new expanding universes[43] at the same time the universe they're *in* expands. That can be visualized as a multidimensional branching tree, with each new twig a new universe that in turn produces more universes, and so on. Not much can be said about these purported universes other than they might or might not be very different in composition from their parent universe(s). If their physical laws do vary, the properties of the particles that reside in them might fundamentally differ from the particles we are familiar with in our universe.[44]

All this is still unconfirmed but very popular cosmological speculation. One aspect that interests physicists is where these hypothetical universes "reside," since they don't have to be considered as anything other than mathematical possibilities. For instance, are they located in very distant regions of conventional space-time, or are they in completely different "epochs of time" in a cyclic universe?[45] None of these universes are believed to be contactable, although if there was a chance of contact it might be through the umbilical cord of their creation—a variety of wormhole only 10^{-33} centimeters in diameter, the size of the original quantum fluctuation.[46]

Alternatively, these different bubble universes (as different branches of the quantum wave function) might be coincident with the very spacetime we reside in; but what happens within each of them has no direct influence over *us* or could ever affect *us*. Indeed, they are so completely disconnected from our reality that they can't really be said to have a location *at all*. There might well be lots of overlapping universes within the overarching multiverse, but they're not quite the recognizably close, parallel, but seemingly contactable realms evidenced by the stories of Lerina García and the Tokyo Taured.

We might redeem the concept by suggesting the universes where Lerina and the Taured allegedly hail from are components of a *quantum wave multiverse*. This treatment of multiple universes also better fits the context of jottles and requires an appreciation of the *indeterminacy* of events at a quantum level. Recall that the wave function of a particle exists as superposition of many probability states.[47] Now imagine there are just two simple states for this particle—"up" or "down." One widely enjoyed idea from quantum physics is that *observation* of this particle will result in one of these states being realized, observation meaning that what is being measured interacts with what does the measuring.[48] The particle becomes *either* up *or* down rather than a superposition of both possibilities. In this case, physicists say the wave function superposition has *collapsed*, but only following observation. This approach is known as the *Copenhagen interpretation* and is controversial because it implies that the nature of reality is determined at the macroscopic level (i.e., observation) rather than the subatomic level.[49]

A famous thought experiment created by physicist Erwin Schrödinger in 1935 is the most popular way of bringing the idea of a collapsing wave function into a scale that's easily understandable. A cat is hidden inside a box alongside a vial of poison and a mechanism consisting of an atom that can take one of two states—it will either decay or it won't. If the atom decays, the vial will break. If it doesn't, the vial will remain intact.[50] However, in the absence of observation there is no collapse of the superposition, so the atom remains in an indeterminate state. By extension, the integrity of the vial is also in a superposition—it is both intact *and* broken. And that means the cat is both dead and alive, at least until someone opens the box and makes the observation. This hypothetical situation is simply a way of expressing how the state of a subatomic particle—for example, its spin—is governed by observation. How (and in what way) this collapse might apply to a *real* cat or a *real* person in a *real* box remains equivocal, which is one reason a novel take on quantum indeterminacy has been proposed.

The "Many Worlds" of Jottles

One question arising from the puzzle of Schrödinger's cat is how an observation selects one probability state (e.g., decay) to the detriment of the other (e.g., non-decay). In 1957, Hugh Everett publically proposed a controversial and as yet untestable solution. This is the *relative state formulation*, later reconfigured as the *many worlds interpretation* by Bryce DeWitt.[51] Although this interpretation has been around for many decades, its popularity—along with its respectability—is a product of the last twenty years. Applied to Schrödinger's cat, the *many worlds interpretation* proposes that the act of observation actually generates both possible outcomes—one where the atom *has* decayed and one where the atom *hasn't* decayed. On the larger scale, this requires the creation of two mutually exclusive realities—one where the cat is alive and one where the cat is dead. That requires accepting the creation of separate universes to accommodate each of those outcomes.[52] These are like the separate bubble universes based on quantum fluctuations I've discussed earlier. Applied to everyday reality, this means that any time we make a probabilistic decision, which is *all the time*, separate universes are generated to accommodate all possible outcomes.[53] That's a lot of universes being continually created, so "infinite" is no misnomer.

Jottles in a Multiverse

Schrödinger's actual cat may be a large organism in a macro-scale system, but it doesn't seem very *realistic*. Is the animal's fate truly determined by the decay of a single atom following observation? Surely real living things aren't in such precarious balance, existing in the same superposition of aliveness and deadness? To avoid this conundrum, the story is simply taken as an elegant thought experiment that people can relate to rather than as a real-life situation. It's easier to conceptualize living and dead cats than it is electrons with an up spin or a down spin.

That still doesn't answer the question of what's happening to an actual cat hidden in the box. If *you* were in the same box, would you be in the same superpositional state, waiting for someone to observe and decide whether you live or die? How would that feel? One widely accepted solution is that big living organisms possess countless quantum states, all constantly interacting with each other and the surrounding environment. As a result, information about all these *individual* superpositional states blends into the background and is lost.[54] This corresponds to large objects indulging in a form of *self-observation* at the quantum level, with the global waveform collapsing into a single, resolved state. Therefore, without the need for anyone from outside the box looking in to observe what's inside, you (or the cat) are either alive (we hope) or dead. This self-observation is termed *decoherence* and allows the classic rules of probability to be met for macroscopic systems, restoring sensibleness to the real world and explaining how big objects aren't prone to quantum uncertainty. Superpositions on the scale of protons and electrons are easier to conceptualize because these particles don't interact with the surrounding environment as much and don't decohere as quickly.

Decoherence keeps alive the prospect of jottles because it is compatible with the many worlds interpretation. For any large object, not simply subatomic particles, interaction between its many superpositional states and the surrounding environment will drive the splitting of countless wave functions, constantly generating alternate universes containing different states of that same object. If you *were* that object, you might remain blissfully unaware that other universes were being formed concurrently because you are an integral part of the splitting process—rather than watching it as some disjointed observer. One state of you joins one universe, while another state joins another universe and so on.

This is where jottles and the many worlds interpretation finally meet. Let's accept that an infinite number of universes are forever being created around us, driven by the infinite number of quantum states of the various objects residing within any one parent universe. That implies one universe should be pretty much identical to another if they've only just "split." However, the further back in time you go, the more these independent universes will differ from one another. Imagine two of these "older" universes. There might be one where Belinda Version A resides, and her reading glasses are protected by a black-colored hard case. In another universe lives Belinda Version B, and she keeps her glasses in a blue-colored case. As these worlds are notionally independent, Belinda A will never know about Belinda B and vice versa.

I've alluded to the idea that people cross between universes, not that objects do. However, before we consider that possibility let's first ponder the idea that objects *can* move, and so we assume that somehow the black hard case passes between these two universes, so that Belinda A finds hers has mysteriously disappeared while Belinda B discovers a strange blue case next to her normal black case. Once more, this connection might be through a wormhole. One supportive argument is that the multiverse is a mathematical concept and hasn't been empirically observed. The mathematical equations don't answer everything about space-time topology, so it is possible that the separate universes within the multiverse are linked by inter-universal wormholes, just are there are speculative intra-universal wormholes.[55] Unfortunately, that returns us to the problem of *functional* wormholes. Even acknowledging they can potentially allow teleportation, with regard to jottles we might expect to see as many stories of objects being duplicated as there are objects disappearing. In other words, for every event where Belinda A *loses* something, Belinda B in another universe *gains* that same item. Or using a real jottle story from the collection, in one universe Greg's knife vanishes for good and in another, slightly different, universe, another version of Greg receives an extra knife. This assumes no one universe is favored for disappearance jottles or duplications, and arguing this makes clear the mind-numbing complexity of trying to explain jottles as objects jumping between parallel universes.

Peripatetic Consciousness

That brings us back to the more sensible view that *people* do the jumping rather than the objects. Not the people themselves, but their *consciousness*. Reconsider how the different universes in a multiverse are allegedly formed, starting with the principle of inflation during the period of the Big Bang. An infinite array of budding universes means all combinations and permutations of the laws of physics will be present, and in some of these universes the variables and constants will be just right to allow the emergence of observers—i.e., *consciousness*. This is an expression of the *anthropic principle*, whereby the advent of life will occur only in the tiniest subset of evolving universes.[56]

For these consciousness-containing universes within the inflating multiverse, quantum splitting, based on the *many worlds interpretation*, will mean there are offspring universes created at each moment with the same initial conditions[57]—including conscious observers—and these branch out as a continuum of small differences. New "consciousnesses" are therefore an implicit aspect of these new worlds—the controversial *many minds interpretation*. So far, that's the same as speculating about a universe containing Belinda A and her black eyeglasses case and another universe containing Belinda B and her blue eyeglasses case. However, there are two ways to consider consciousness in the context of the many worlds interpretation. First, Belinda A's consciousness, and Belinda B's consciousness might remain independent and go their own ways after the split, possessing a shared history with other branches of consciousness only up to the point of separation. Alternatively, each Belinda might still retain a link with all her other "consciousnesses," described as a "universality of consciousness" or "conscious mind."[58] In this latter circumstance, weak interaction among universes might be possible through *connected consciousness*, even when the worlds that all the different Belindas reside in are physically uncontactable.

Confusing? Absolutely! It is also terribly speculative. In no way am I using any *respectable* ideas from the many minds interpretation, and reputable theorists would be aghast that I'd even be arguing this point. Nevertheless, like Fort I can throw around ideas without having to explain them too deeply or bravely take total ownership. I can even divert attention from myself by invoking past theorists who freely speculate that various paranormal phenomena, including witnessing UFOs, "appearing people" and vivid and clairvoyant dreams "could be as a result of [the person] slipping, mentally, into some parallel world (227).[59]

So here's my proposal for jottles based on *peripatetic consciousness*, using Belinda as the example. Perhaps Belinda A's consciousness in Universe A becomes "unglued" and in a disembodied state enters a very close, parallel Universe B. In this sense, "close" might mean the two universes have only recently split. Alternatively, Belinda A's consciousness might be subsumed upwards to "conscious mind" and returned down a different branch to observe another expression of her *many worlds*—one that has slight physical differences that are strange enough to be recognized as jottles. That certainly fits Lerina García's claims, although it remains an unsatisfactory explanation because she cannot prove her mind has travelled from one universe to another (acknowledging that the many minds interpretation is just that, a worthy but unprovable interpretation). It's far easier to blame her story on something that can be demonstrated empirically—mental illness. Taking a more pessimistic stance, we can posit that peripatetic consciousness *doesn't* fit the Tokyo Taured, since this alleged man brought with him actual material from his "home world"—his passport—rather than just inserting his consciousness into an equivalent physical body that was already here. Therefore, despite the lack of supporting evidence, Lerina García's story is perhaps the more authentic.

In summary, the many minds interpretation is marginally less absurd than accepting that jottled objects physically travel among universes. Rather than the object moving, it is consciousness that passes from one of these worlds to another. Belinda A (in Universe A) puts her black glasses case down on the kitchen counter and moments later finds it is no longer there. That's because her consciousness has entered a new parallel world (Universe B) where she *never* owned a black case. Should Belinda A's consciousness end up in the new location permanently, the event will stay a disappearance. If the visitation is only brief, and Consciousness A returns to Universe A, Belinda would rediscover the case where she originally left it. That accounts for an object return. And what about those strange and rare replacements? Easy! Belinda A might shift permanently to Universe B, where her black glasses case never was and a blue one always has been. That's why swapped objects consistently involve the same category of object. Working with another real example, Deborah borrowed a book called *Foul Shot*, but on the bus ride home her consciousness drifted to another highly similar parallel universe where she'd borrowed another book (the name of which is now forgotten), and that's where she stayed from that time on.

This is great "magical" thinking—preposterous and unfalsifiable but intuitively quite satisfying—until you study it more deeply. There are some obvious problems.

Jottles Don't Suit the Multiverse

The value of the database is that it tells us what jottles *are*, hence how well an interpretation fits the evidence. Regrettably, the "alternate universe" theory of jottles simply doesn't match the evidence very well at all. The most obvious problem centers on the question of why jottles happen so often at home and why select types of objects are the focus. Or, re-expressed for the many minds interpretation, why would a person's consciousness unwittingly cross to another universe where the sole objects that differ in the fabric of reality are in the home—things like keys, apples and USB sticks? Surely *any* object or circumstance could potentially, and equally, be subject to a jottle, couldn't it?

Presuming every probability decision at a quantum level creates a new bubble universe, one might expect that the place you're sitting or standing now is matched by an equivalent place in an alternate universe where one thing nearby is missing, and another universe where two things are missing, and so on ad infinitum. If your wristwatch vanishes from the tabletop because your consciousness has drifted into an alternative universe where you'd instead placed it in a drawer, why aren't there more cases of bigger things also vanishing—a chair, a husband, or a garden shed?

And why aren't there more accounts of *collections* of things going missing, or appearing unexpectedly—for instance, a home where the furniture is suddenly a different style or where the kitchen is no longer painted blue but yellow? Apart from the tale of the appearing mound of dirt, I'm unaware of large or multiple objects being jottled, although the Internet contains many stories of trees, cars and houses disappearing, appearing or moving. Nevertheless, these tales are dwarfed in number by our domestic, single, small item jottles.

Maybe this obstacle can be overcome by claiming that jumps in consciousness are a function of interaction. To have recently touched an object somehow facilitates a temporary or permanent "jump" of consciousness to a universe where this object (and this object alone) *isn't*. Occasionally consciousness quickly jumps back to the original universe where the object remains. That might explain why there aren't more stories of chairs, suitcases or pet dogs disappearing. The downside is that appearance jottles are harder to place as interactive events, and some of the stories don't match what one would expect from a nomadic consciousness. Take stories where a coin appears in mid-air before dropping. Has the experient's consciousness crossed to a parallel universe where a hovering coin is ready to fall? Surely this shouldn't occur, as the laws of physics should be the same in the original *and* destination universes.

There's also little room for *intention* in this interpretation of jottles. Take the story of Kate's relocating keys. We can attempt to backward-engineer a many minds interpretation to account for her experience, but the resulting justification becomes so convoluted it's farcical. Kate returns home from work and her keys go missing from the front door. Did her consciousness unsuspectingly slide into an alternative universe where the keys were *never* in the door or in the house or even in the yard, for that matter (recall she tore the house and yard apart and couldn't find them anywhere)? Does that mean in her new universe she never owned those keys? How is that possible? There's still a lock on the front door and a car parked in the driveway. She would never have been able to enter the house or start the car without keys. We could suggest that in this new universe she'd recently lost the keys, perhaps throwing them across the road in a fit of rage after she opened the door and before she answered the phone. Her newly arrived consciousness is oblivious to this sudden, uncharacteristic behavior. Cutting a new set of keys, Kate then happily and unknowingly resides in her new, virtually identical alternative universe. Six months later, she arrives home to a new house and finds her original keys lying on the bed. That can only be explained by Kate's having slipped into yet *another* universe sometime during the day—a universe where she possessed both the original set of keys, which she'd left on her pillow, and the new set of keys.

If that argument is not silly enough, here's another serious problem that further undermines this interpretation. What happens to the *other* consciousness in the new universe? Has Kate A from the original universe swapped with Kate B from the destination universe? Or is it one-way travel, with Kate A's consciousness suppressing Kate B's exiting consciousness? If that's the case, who's occupying Kate's mind back in the original universe?

Just as damning is the occasional but pertinent veridical support from friends and family that something belonging to the experient has gone missing or appeared or reappeared. This doesn't have to involve a mutually witnessed event (which is incredibly rare). All that's needed is an acknowledgement from these outsiders that an object now located on the hall table *is* foreign or that something that's mysteriously disappeared *had* once existed. One would presume that if we found our glasses case missing because we'd transitioned to another universe and mentioned this to a friend or spouse *in that universe* they'd look at us strangely and reply, "But you've never owned a glasses case!" That might suit the reaction of Lerina García's friends and family, but it doesn't apply to anyone associated with a real-life jottle.

Jottles in Other Dimensions?

These arguments make "alternate universes" an unsatisfactory candidate for jottles (alongside teleportation and wormholes). However, there is one final possibility associated with the mechanistic universe. Should your coffee mug be missing from the table where you put it down only five minutes ago, it's not because it's been sucked into a wormhole or your consciousness has traveled from this universe to a parallel one. Rather, it's been transported to *another dimension*. This certainly isn't a novel idea. Charles Fort made reference to the "fourth dimension" back in the 1930s when introducing his theory of teleportation, although he couldn't explicitly state what the fourth dimension *was*: "Oh yes, I have heard of the 'fourth dimension' but I am going to do myself some credit by not lugging in that particular way of showing that I don't know what I'm writing about (567).[60]

Experients often claim their lost objects have been conveyed into "another dimension," but what does this actually mean? The best I can come up with is reference to the same oversimplified physics that helped describe wormholes. Consider the four dimensional space-time continuum. As previously suggested, only three of those dimensions are spatial—the fourth is time. How would four *spatial* dimensions look? That's difficult—nigh impossible—to visualize. Length is at right angles to width, which is at right angles to height. We'd have to go another right angle—somewhere—to imagine the fourth spatial array, although it makes perfect sense mathematically. One intriguing idea is that our familiar universe of three spatial dimensions is embedded in a universe that possesses four, or perhaps more, spatial dimensions. The three-dimensional part is known as a *brane*, and the expanded universe of which it is a part is known as the *bulk*. If we accept that there can be a four-dimensional bulk universe, then this universe comprises four-dimensional galaxies made up of four-dimensional stars, stars which must eventually run out of fuel.

In our three dimensional universe, should a big enough star (much bigger than the sun) run out of fuel it collapses on itself and can form a *singularity*. That's a one-dimensional "point" possessing infinite mass squashed into an infinitely small space. Since this mass is infinite, gravity is also infinite and that means a breakdown in the laws of physics.[61] This singularity is "covered," so to speak, by an event horizon. This barrier has no thickness, so it's two dimensional. Anything close enough to the event horizon becomes trapped by the immense gravitational field of the *black hole* within, so nothing can escape back into space and be observed by us—not even light. That's why black holes are "black."

Returning to the four-dimensional universe: the substance from a collapsing *four*-dimensional star may become a *three*-dimensional event horizon—in other words, *this* universe. That implies we're the product of a black hole formed in a bulk universe! We'll never know, of course, because it's not theoretically possible for three-dimensional, everyday objects trapped in the event horizon to leave and enter the bulk universe or even observe this universe, assuming there *is* a bulk universe at all.

And if there was a way to depart our three-dimensional event horizon home, does that really describe a jottle? For instance, why would a necklace be more prone to entering a higher four-dimensional array compared with an item that doesn't seem jottle prone, like a cell phone? Furthermore, what would the necklace end up looking like—a three-dimensional item in four-dimensional space? In truth, saying something has "gone to another dimension" makes no sense, as a dimension is only an additional *projection* to an existing array. It's about as sensible as claiming an object resides in the first or second dimension or a four-dimensional object now sits happily in three-dimensional space. When hoping to solve the case of an inexplicable jottle, holding the fourth dimension responsible is less helpful than alternative universes. At least objects can be meaningfully envisioned in these (equivalent) universes because they are assumed to be structurally similar. Even the idea of an object travelling through a wormhole to somewhere else in *this* universe makes sense because the characteristics of the universe *here* match the characteristics over *there*. As an explanation for jottles, the "Fourth Dimension" is about as much help now as it was back in Charles Fort's day.

8

External Agents

"A ghost took my perfume."
"A poltergeist moved my coffee mug."
"The fairies stole my underwear."

Before toying with these wacky statements, let's review the good and bad points of jottles as a function of natural processes in a mechanistic universe. Teleportation might not be a viable method of object transportation, at least in the overly simplistic manner I've presented, but at least there's an inherent logic to it, and the process can account—in some as yet unknowable way—for prior *interaction* between an experient and a jottled object. By touching the object an experient, sometimes and somehow, transfers its quantum state elsewhere. The object is destroyed here (a disappearance), then reconstituted in this distance place (an appearance). Should someone else interact with an object at *their* end, maybe it becomes *our* appearance. That might account for disappearance and appearance jottles, but is less appropriate for "rapid returns." Objects would need to reappear using the same quantum processes, and that would require the returned object to be physically different from whatever went missing only moments before. This interpretation seems overly complicated, so an alternative proposal is that the experient's consciousness has flitted between two almost identical universes—one *with* the object and one *without*. Unfortunately, the underlying theory is mind-numbing and stretches credulity to the breaking point.

Then there are the problems making sense of *intentional* jottles. There's little scope in a mechanistic universe or universes to deal with jottles that are something other than a quirky accident. You might recall the story of Martin finding an egg in an otherwise empty egg carton. Here's a similar story, from Trish, which is about as "intentional" as you can imagine:

> Probably the strangest thing that's ever happened to me occurred one day at home when I was alone about 5 years ago (I can't remember what day it was). I just

remember wanting to make a sandwich and there was no bread left in the cupboard (or if there was, they were bunnies or stale). I couldn't be bothered driving out to the shops to get a loaf, and I said out loud, to no-one in particular, "I wish I had bread!" It wasn't a proper wish, I mean, I wasn't asking God for bread, as that's not right. What upset me the most is that a loaf of bread appeared on the kitchen table soon after. About 10 minutes after my request. I didn't see it appear, and I wasn't in the kitchen when it happened. It was a normal fresh loaf in a plastic bag, the same as what you buy in the shops. I didn't eat it, as I believed it was not proper for me to receive the bread as I was being selfish. I believe it was sent from something bad, wanting to tempt me, so I apologized to God and threw it away. I didn't know what else to do, as since then I've been very careful about what I say to myself, and never say anything that could be thought of as self-serving.

It hardly seem reasonable that Fort's "universe as organism" uses teleportation in response to personal appeals for material needs, in the same way it allegedly redistributes natural substances, things like seeds or fish or rocks for the purpose of reestablishing environmental harmony. Then again, why presume that such a universe *is* mindless? Fortean researchers Bob Rickard and John Michell show a keen awareness of the intentionality apparent in rock showers *within* buildings: "Though usually spontaneous and unbidden, in some cases teleportation seems as though it is directed and purposeful.... Apart from the problems of authentication what often makes such stories unpalatable to serious scientists is a sense of mischievous, frequently malicious, intent in the actions (11)."[1]

Let's take Trish at her word and accept her story is true. The unexpected arrival of a branded loaf, fresh and wrapped, surely indicates a powerful sentient force overseeing teleportation. This force is both omniscient and omnipotent and is able to relocate from some other kitchen or perfectly reproduce a sophisticated product that conforms to the precise expectations of the requestor. The same intelligence could also be blamed for mischievous object relocations. When a key or a wallet is lost, the experient frequently makes an explicit plea (to no one in particular) for the lost item to be returned. There are plenty of examples of such appeals, including this story told by parapsychological researcher Michael Thalbourne:

> I had a kitchen spoon, plain not fancy, but unique in its size. I was (perhaps inordinately) fond of this spoon. One night I was doing the washing up; the spoon was on the counter off to the left. I turned around, and it was gone! I brought my eyes to the front and said aloud "Please return the spoon!" I again turned my head to the left, and hey presto, the spoon was back again, to my relief [8].[2]

If we accept that an unseen intelligence actively controls jottles, then there's no reason to assume it can't access unconscious desires (Martin's need for an egg) as well as spoken requests (Trish's demand for a loaf of bread and Michael's wish that his spoon be returned). Still, we're justified in wondering why such an intelligence doesn't respond to *all* our requests *all* the time—and why it seems to do only trivial things, like providing a single egg or bread loaf or stealing keys and relocating them in a petty fashion. There must be something unique about Martin, Trish and Michael—and the time and place—that encourages a jottle. This "something" is spontaneous and unrepeatable, because none of them, as far as I'm aware, were able to—or, in the case of Trish, *wanted* to—conjure this very helpful force at any other time in their lives.

One solution is to hold something more personal than the wider "universe" to account for intentional jottles—namely a tormenting *poltergeist*, haunting *spirit* or mischievous *fairy*. At least, that's who the experient blames. Perhaps these mysterious entities are able to manipulate universal teleportational forces in sophisticated ways that humans cannot. Alternatively, they might use their own peculiar methods to influence the behavior of objects, methods we've yet to consider. Although this all seems faintly ludicrous, external agents at least provide the intentional element missing from ideas of random wormholes or consciousness inadvertently surfing the multiverse.

Poltergeists, Ghosts and Spirits

Of all the attributions for jottles, blaming a poltergeist is by far the most popular. This German word literally means a "noisy spirit" or "knocking spirit," and that's just what experients are referring to—an autonomous, invisible entity causing mischief and mayhem around their homes. There's also a rationale to their conviction. Appearing and disappearing objects are a recognized feature of "authentic" poltergeist infestations. The problem is that these infestations also involve far more than the disappearance of a salt shaker from the pantry or the relocation of a key from the front door to the bedroom. Apart from objects being thrown around, levitating or shaking, there can be movements of doors and windows, luminous phenomena, unusual and unexplained noises such as percussive explosions in mid-air, raps on walls and furniture, disembodied human voices and even physical attacks on the body![3] There are also subjective effects, such as the feeling of intense emotions (by definition, poltergeist cases don't feature *apparitions*, so they are classed differently from traditional hauntings).[4]

Generally speaking, the jottle-like appearance or disappearance of objects usually takes place in the early stages of a poltergeist infestation, and these trivial events are soon forgotten in the melee of subsequent, more impressive, activity. A perfect example of this happened in the early 1940s to Broadway columnist Danton Walker. Walker bought a historic house in Rockland County, New York, and began renovating it. By 1944 he was visiting the house more frequently and that was the start of a gamut of paranormal episodes, including the sound of boots pacing around empty rooms, a sense of oppression in parts of the house, and events resembling jottles—specifically the initial disappearance of objects and their rediscovery after a few days or weeks. These initial events suggested a typical poltergeist disturbance—that is, household paranormal activity with no obvious agent. That changed when the famous psychic Eileen Garrett visited the residence in 1952 and with the help of Unvani, her "spirit control," began channeling through voice and behavior a Polish mercenary named Andreas who had been murdered in one of the rooms during the Revolutionary War. Apparently Andreas felt affinity with Danton Walker because he physically resembled his brother, also killed in the war. This was the trigger for Andreas's haunting escapades.[5] Therefore, what was initially considered the work of a poltergeist, with disappearing and reappearing objects, transitioned into a far more interesting *haunting* even though an apparition of Andreas was never actually seen.

A more recent story is from a friend of mine, Robb Tilley, who has experience "clearing" houses of spirits. In 1996 he travelled to a ranch in outback New South Wales, Australia, because the owners were disturbed by poltergeist activity. Like the Walker case, these events featured disappearing, appearing and reappearing objects. For example, the property owner, Peter, noticed the disappearance of "two pairs of scissors, a bottle of Worcester sauce, video tapes, spanners, fencing pliers, salt and pepper, peanut butter, honey, half a bottle of scotch and cigarettes (152)."[6] Soon Peter would begin to hear commotion in the house not attributable to living people, such as the sound of two grown men fighting in the attic when no one was present. An investigation was conducted, and the equivocal poltergeist activity transitioned into a classical haunting. Through mediumship it was determined that a long-dead worker of Yugoslavian origin called Boxer Tops still resided on the property, along with an even earlier inhabitant of that part of the country—an escaped convict called George who'd lived with the local aboriginal tribe. Apparently, the fighting in the attic were these two pugilists! George was responsible for the stealing—he was the jottle culprit—and Boxer Tops was annoyed that such thievery had been performed in his former, respectable workplace. As part of the spirit clearing process[7] a request was made for the return of the stolen goods. A little over a month later, Peter phoned Robb to say that the missing items had indeed reappeared—and some unexpected ones at that. There were three pairs of scissors found in a cupboard, $1,100 in a filing cabinet, and a gardening book and a full set of Tupperware in the kitchen— a windfall that no one in the house recognized or owned.

As we have seen, the jottle-like activity in both Danton Walker's house and Peter's outback ranch were purportedly the work of deceased individuals rather than a nameless poltergeist. This situation is very different from "real" jottles, where additional paranormal activity is not reported. That's the reason why Mary-Rose Barrington named them *"just one of those things"* and why Nicola Holt uses the term *discontinuities* when reviewing the 2003 jottle study day. They are singular incidents independent of any wider ongoing paranormal occurrence or syndrome like a haunting.

Plates flying around the room and smashing against furniture, goo oozing from the walls and even the presence of a spirit divined through mediumship simply don't occur in conjunction with any of our stock-standard jottle stories. That's not to say the two circumstances aren't somehow causally connected (as I'll shortly discuss); it's just that *traditional* poltergeists and ghosts don't seem to be responsible for the jottles we're interested in. However, I'm not finished with ghosts just yet. Correctly speaking, Frederick Myer's classical definition of a ghost is as a *veridical afterimage*, meaning it isn't an active participant in this realm: "[T]here is strong evidence for the recurrence of the same hallucinatory figures in the same localities, but weak evidence to indicate any purpose in most of these figures, or any connection with bygone individuals, or with such tragedies as are popularly supposed to start a ghost on its career. In some of these cases of frequent, meaningless recurrence of a figure in a given spot, we are driven to wonder whether it can be some deceased person's past frequentation of that spot, rather than any fresh action of his after death—which has generated what I have termed the veridical afterimage—veridical in the sense that it communicates information, previously unknown to the percipient, as to a former inhabitant of the haunted locality (215–216)."[8] From this description, ghosts can't really be held responsible for moving things around the house. Rather, it must be the work of a more active *spirit presence* such as those assumed responsible for haunting Danton Walker and Peter's respective residences. When it comes to these types of spirits, paranormal researcher Gary Schwartz writes, "the term spirit is used to refer to the hypothesized continued existence of the consciousness and information (and associated energy) after physical death (also termed an entity); the term presence is used to refer to the potential hypothesized localization of the consciousness, information, and energy/spirit of the deceased person (166)."[9]

That means a spirit *can* be a dynamic participant in the haunting. However, not everyone lives in a house where the active spirits of revolutionary war soldiers or kleptomaniac convicts still reside. Strictly speaking, most houses aren't haunted at all, so it is more reasonable to attribute jottles to the actions of a *revenant*.[10] That's the term for a recently deceased relative or friend who has briefly returned from "the other side" to make contact with the experient, to let them know they are just fine. For some unaccountable reason, their presence is felt through unusual object movements rather than as a witnessed apparition. This would account for both the isolation of the jottle as a single or intermittent event and the intentionality underlying object movements. Eleanor's experience suggests the actions of a revenant, as does this similar short story from Ruth: "One of mum's little ornaments disappeared from the bookshelf at exactly the time we found out dad had died. It turned up again on the carpet at the front door a week or two later. I'm not sure whether mum or dad did it, but it was one of them letting us know they were still around."[11]

Spirit Construction and Jottles

Admittedly I don't know what spirits are made from, but then again no one *really* knows, despite what "experts" might claim. It's common knowledge that people report seeing active spirits in the form of apparitions, but since these spirits don't consist of everyday matter they must instead exist as free-floating bundles of energy that emit photons detectable to human eyes and camera equipment. The question is, what is the nature of this energy and where did it originate? It's surprisingly hard to find an answer. About the most sophisticated, publishable idea anyone can come up with (as opposed to a thought-bubble on the Internet) is that spirits are somehow "organized energy and information that presumably comprises the history and essence of a person [that] continues in some form in the 'vacuum' of space after physical death."[12]

The energy most paranormal investigators hold responsible is *electromagnetic energy*.[13] Consequently, these investigators use devices to measure the electromagnetic fields in haunted locations as evidence of a spirit presence. What weakens this assumption is that electromagnetic energy is produced by the acceleration of atomic particles in ordinary matter, which means a spirit's presence must be grounded in an existing reality. To avoid this awkward fact, it might instead be posited that spirits comprise an *alternative*, and more subtle, energy source able to excite electrons in everyday atoms at the location of the haunting, which in turn allow electromagnetic waves to be propagated. Perhaps these secondary fields, and not the spirits themselves, are what investigators measure through electromagnetic meters—and also what witnesses *see*, if the energy is in the form of visible light.[14]

If you're happy to accept that spirits are directly or indirectly represented by electromagnetic energy, the next problem you face is pinpointing exactly where in the electromagnetic spectrum they reside. Are they lurking in the infrared or the ultraviolet? That tends to get brushed over in popular ghost-hunting discussions, although you hear a lot of talk from enthusiasts of spirits as "low energy beings." They operate somewhere in or below the *extremely low-frequency* range. The premise is that spirits haunt a location in this unperceivable state but sporadically draw on ambient energy from the environment and the people in it to enter a "higher" or more energetic existence. That way they can manifest as a dark fleeting shape or be heard as a raspy voice without a physical source. That's why ghost hunters also measure temperature as well as electromagnetic field fluctuations in haunted spaces. Lowered temperatures indicate a source of energy being drained. From personal experience, I'll admit this idea is a quite attractive one. I once participated in an investigation of an old hospital (now a hotel) and paranormal activity did seem to be taking place in the stone cellar beneath the building. At one stage the air became "charged" and I distinctly heard disembodied speech coming from midair. It felt as though the available energy in this cramped space was being diverted to allow these scratchy words to form. I'm not saying that's what actually happened, but it did allow me to appreciate this low-energy theory of spirits.

That's all very well for spirit consistency, but it doesn't account for how they move small objects around the house—like Eleanor's photograph and Ruth's ornament. If a spirit possesses such low energy that it is barely able to be seen or heard, then surely it hasn't the capability of relocating heavy objects, has it? And even if personal spirits could somehow access enough energy to initiate a domestic jottle, apart from Eleanor and Ruth (and the occasional tale found on the Internet), there simply aren't *that* many stories of a deceased relative or friend behaving with this benign explicit intention. It's far more likely an intentional jottle is implicit and downright annoying—typically the time-delayed relocations of house keys and credit cards or in Mark's case the recurrent stealing of a TV remote control. In this light, experients rarely consider a revenant responsible for their jottles, and they don't blame obscure former resident ghosts either. Instead, they may conjure a *paraphysical* entity that *isn't* human.

Daemons, Fairies and Jottles

"Paraphysical" is an old parapsychological word describing the *physical* aspects of *psychical* events generated by mediums and their spirit guides in the séance room.[15] Applied to entities, it simply means they are neither purely spirit nor purely physical but display the characteristics of both states. Belief in nonhuman paraphysical entities has been popular for thousands of years. For instance, the ancient Greeks conjured both good and bad *daemons*—*eudaemons* and *cocodemons* respectively—entities they believed to be somewhere in-between humans and the gods.[16] This definition fits the modern concept of a demon (from which the word derives) as well as various other nonhuman entities that aren't necessarily *evil* but don't always act in the best interests of people either. These include aliens, who for some investigators and their supporters aren't extraterrestrial creatures from elsewhere in the galaxy but simply another variety of paraphysical being. That was the belief of author and professional diplomat Gordon Creighton, who linked flying saucer occupants to *jinn*—a class of entity found in pre–Islamic and Muslim teaching that resides halfway between humans and angels. They also have a recognized habit of moving people around in this world! For instance, "the Jinns are wont to snatch up humans and teleport or transport them, setting them down again—if indeed they ever do set them down again—miles away from where they were picked up, and all this in the 'twinkling of an eye' (6)."[17] Creighton attributed the relocation of Gil Pérez to the work of the jinn.

In Western culture, various paraphysical beings have traditionally interacted with people, such as the vampiric *incubi* and *succubi*. However, the entities most strongly associated with making people and objects disappear and reappear are *fairies*. And when it comes to jottles, a fairy is the second most popular agent held responsible, after poltergeists. That's because the stories in this book mostly derive from the Anglosphere, where fairies are the primary cultural expression of a paraphysical entity. Writers contemporary with widespread belief in fairies implicitly understood their ethereal nature. A description by Scottish minister Robert Kirk in the very first chapter of his 1691 book *Secret Commonwealth* showed fairies to be "of a midle Nature betuixt Man and Angel, as were Daemons thought to be of old; of intelligent fluidious Spirits, and light changeable Bodies, (lyke those called Astral), somewhat of the Nature of a condensed Cloud, and best seen in Twilight. Thes Bodies be so plyable thorough the Subtilty of the Spirits that agitate them, they can make them appear or disappear att Pleasure (60)."[18] Kirk was an expert in fairy matters and very aware of the different origins attributed to fairies *at that time in history*. They might be souls of the dead or fallen angels or even a long-dead race of underground pygmy people.[19]

More recently, psychosocial rationalizations have become popular, and fairies are now considered nothing more than a means by which primitive societies accounted for natural phenomena or they were folk memories of the magic practices of the Druids (or some earlier peoples). They might even be the old gods of the pre–Christian era in another guise.[20] However, one influential commentator of Irish fairy lore from the turn of the 20th century, Walter Evans Wentz, was far more enamored with the idea that fairies *actually* exist and take the form of Reverend Kirk's "subtilty of spirit."[21] That's an approach also favored by many modern paranormal investigators who view fairies as autonomous beings with a quasi-physical nature. Usually fairies are visible only to children or adults immersed in an altered state of consciousness—perhaps a dream, trance, ecstatic state or state of relaxation such as that felt by Mrs. Celia Alleyne in the 1920s:

> I was on the Downs near here in the morning and it was very still and quiet and no one about, and as I sat in the grass I felt the conditions change—I became aware of faculties which normally I have not at all. I could hear each little blade of grass vibrating and there was harmony in every note, I could see an aura to every flower and the fairies were there in colours like the auras. I seemed to be conscious of being in quite a new world of colour, music and scent, and perfect peace and happiness [64].[22]

On other occasions the spectators are sensible adults in a *normal* state of consciousness going about their daily business. In this situation, fairies exert their presence in *our* realm:

> Mr. Lonsdale, in the company of Mr. Turvey, was sitting perfectly still in the garden of the latter's estate in Bournemouth, England, one warm summer day, when "Suddenly I was conscious of a movement on the edge of the lawn.... In a few seconds a dozen or more small people, about two feet in height, in bright clothes and with radiant faces, ran on to the lawn, dancing hither and thither." He whispered to Mr. Turvey, "Do you see them?"; his companion nodded. For four or five minutes these fairies danced about "in sheer joy." One of them grabbed a croquet hoop like a horizontal bar and gaily tumbled round and round. They remained until they were frightened off by a servant bringing tea [47].[23]

8: External Agents

Once they are visible, or at least physically present in the environment, fairies are wont to indulge in jottles, since one of their most widely accepted behaviors is the stealing or gifting of everyday items. It's been suggested this interest in human property might be related to the interdependency of fairies and people, because human observers like Mr. Lonsdale and Mr. Turvey are necessary for fairy materialization[24]—a claim that closely resembles quantum indeterminacy!

Things get more interesting when we consider that fairy lore stems from antiquity, and the relevant objects that vanish, appear or reappear tend to be very simple things like food items and basic crockery and cutlery. They can also be small useful objects of a domestic nature:

> The elves are also blamed for lifting with them articles mislaid. These are generally restored as mysteriously and unaccountably as they were taken away. Thus, a woman blamed the elves for taking her thimble. It was placed bedside her, and when looked for could not be found. Some time after she was sitting alone on the hillside and found the thimble in her lap. This confirmed her belief in its being the fairies that took it away. In a like mysterious manner a person's bonnet might be whipped off his head, or the pot for supper be lifted off the fire, and left by invisible hands on the middle of the floor [18].[25]

Who could deny these events match the flavor of a jottle? I've heard a similar story from a contemporary source, although unfortunately it's "second hand" so I can't completely trust its veracity. Nevertheless, it is worth telling, so I've taken the liberty to write it from the perspective of the experient: "I put a sewing kit on the chair, and when I came back it was gone. I presumed a fairy had taken it, so I asked for it back in a firm voice and left the room because that's how these things work with me. That afternoon, the sewing kit was returned. This kind of thing happens all the time."

According to fairy lore, items permanently vanish because fairies like taking things that are small enough for them to carry away or they look nice or they are edible or useful to people (so the loss will be lamented). That corresponds to food items, jewelry, articles of clothing, household goods and utensils—the most frequently disappearing objects in the collection. For this reason, when fairies are blamed for object disappearances it would be fair to say that experients are very close to the mark. It's the same explanation as that held by the 18th century Gaelic peasant who lost her thimble.

I can see the attraction of blaming fairies for jottles, but of course there are plenty of problems to overcome. First, a modern story might resemble a tale from three hundred years ago, but that is not necessary evidence for an invisible paraphysical being known as a fairy. After all, hardly anyone ever *sees* fairies around the house taking things or putting them back where they belong. It's simply evidence that jottles are a historical phenomenon. Second, fairies are capable of gifting much more than small objects. In times past they presented people with sheep, cattle and sometimes real children who had been stolen from *other* people. And when it comes to stealing things, it was not always inanimate objects but also the vital essence of living possessions like a farmer's crops or livestock, causing them to wither and die. Third, folklore contains plenty of information about the things that *Celtic* fairies don't like, such as oatmeal and iron—and anything made from iron, such as steel. That means they avoid stealing swords, iron bars, knives, scissors, rings, needles, nails, gun barrels and fishhooks.[26] This doesn't augur well for modern jottle stories. I'm not sure about swords and gun barrels, but knives, scissors, nails and rings feature in the collection as disappearing objects, as do keys, although these are generally made out of brass, which is a mixture of copper and zinc. Are we perhaps dealing with nontraditional fairies? Wouldn't *real* fairies avoid jottling such articles?

Jottles Are Elemental

The most effective way to salvage a fairy explanation for jottles is to divorce them from the restrictions of Gaelic tradition and consider them as a cultural expression of a more basic paraphysical entity—the *elemental*. Although experients seldom, if ever, blame their jottles on an elemental, these are certainly more versatile beings. They display the intentionality of a fairy but also possess greater flexibility as initiators of modern-day jottles.

For thousands of years the composition of elementals has been debated, leading to theories of how these beings interact with people and even make objects appear and disappear. I'll start with the writings of Paracelsus (Philippus Theophrastus, Bombast von Hohenheim), the 16th-century Swiss Renaissance physician. Borrowing from, and adapting, earlier traditions—e.g., Aristotle's four basic elements of classical matter: earth, air, fire and water—he puzzled over the nature of the invisible entities that share this world with us. Apparently they are as transparent as air, but on occasion they are dense enough for us to perceive, in the same way we feel a breeze on our cheek.[27] They also come in countless varieties, both good and bad. There are personal familiars called *Flagae* and a class called the *Saganae* or the *elemental spirits of nature*—the *Nymphae* of water, the *Sylphes* in the air, *Pigmies* in the earth and *Salamanders* in fire.[28] These elementals aren't derived from Adam, so they're not material beings in the manner of humans. If descendants of Adam (i.e., us) want to pass through a solid wall they need to make a hole first, whereas beings *not* descended from Adam will slide right through the wall! However, these elementals are technically *not* spirits. Rather, they occupy a place between men and spirits, and as a consequence they live, eat, talk, sleep and have offspring, although their flesh, blood and bones are more subtle than a human's. And unlike humans, elementals possess an animal intellect and hence are incapable of spiritual development: "Man is made after the image of God, and they may be said to be made after the image of man; but man is not God, and the elemental spirits of nature are not human beings, although they resemble man (151–152).[29]

Since they are made in the image of man, perhaps that explains their interest in human possessions. The barrier is that elementals tend to cling to their respective substrates, e.g., water, and avoid mixing with people, let alone their cousins. If there were one type of elemental that *might* fraternize it would be the *Sylphes,* or *Sylvestres*, since they are the closest to humans in terms of where they reside (in the air). They also enjoy a good disposition and may become attached to nearby people out of sheer interest. Beyond these main features there's not much detail about specific elemental behaviors regarding something like jottles because Paracelsus wasn't terribly concerned with lowly folktales.

Belief in elementals was once quite fashionable, with plenty of discussion even in mainstream theology. However by the mid–19th century elementals lost credibility, even with *spiritualists*, since the focus of occult investigation was to document the presence and activities of deceased humans rather than ponder the possibility of invisible *non*humans. Then along came Helene Blavatsky, the founder of the *Theosophical movement.* In her many books and those of her Theosophical followers, she helped reinstate the place of elementals in the modern world. She did this with copious helpings of Near Eastern mysticism, and her ideas strongly influence modern occult (i.e., New Age) teachings—although it is apparent that many contemporary paranormal adherents are completely oblivious to the debt they owe Theosophy—and Blavatsky in particular.

Blavatsky took the traditional view that elementals were "the spirits of the elements" and the same entities variously identified as fairies, jinn, elves, dwarves, pixies and brownies. These elementals don't possess a physical form and are better thought of as centers of force.[30] Like Paracelsus's elementals they are simple and irresponsible creatures who possess instinctive desires but lack more advanced consciousness, in the human sense of being *self-aware*. Consequently, elementals are neither good nor bad; it is the behaviors they exhibit in the world that are morally interpreted by those on the receiving end of their actions. Because they lack consciousness, elementals are merely servants of "general law." That is, they assist nature to operate efficiently—a rather vague concept that sounds similar to Fort's ideas of a redistributive universe. The corollary is that, as irresponsible tools of nature, elementals can be diverted from their normal tasks when recruited by magicians and sorcerers for selfish reasons, such as the casting of spells. They might even be engaged by *elementaries* (the *souls* and *shells* of dead people, according to Blavatsky) for lowly purposes that are variously good, bad or indifferent.[31] That's because in Blavatsky's opinion deceased humans cannot directly influence the physical world, an idea that differs from the more popular low-energy theory of spirits. Therefore, paranormal activity taking place in a séance room or a haunted house is directly attributable to elementals rather than active spirits. To butcher Blavatsky's careful argument, *spirits exploit elementals in order to be seen, heard, and perhaps even move things around*. Fascinating as that may be, it's not terribly helpful for solving jottles because it only complicates matters by adding an intermediary agent to the phenomenon—the elementary. Luckily, Blavatsky and her followers also developed ideas about what elementals are made of, and this has relevance to the magical nature of jottles.

Good Vibrations

Blavatsky believed that elementals reside in the *ether*.[32] Ether is the invisible material that fills up all the empty space of the universe and exerts its influence through the propagation of *etheric waves*. The idea is that elementals either *consist* of these waves, or *use* these waves to affect actions in the real world. For instance, they can manipulate ether to make themselves visible, although their appearance simply takes on the psychic form of whatever a witness is thinking about at that moment. That's why you can't trust a ghostly apparition to be what you *assume* it to be, such as a deceased relative. It might simply transpire that an elemental has drawn on etheric ingredients to take physical form, and if that form happens to resemble Great-aunt Gertrude, then that's simply because the blueprint for Gertrude is readily available from your unconscious psychic library (assuming you've *had* a Great-aunt Gertrude).

Regarding jottles, it turns out that elementals also *manipulate* objects using ether. A good analogy is the way air or water can be compressed by "pneumatic and hydraulic apparatus"[33] to create motion. Therefore, if prompted by elementaries or sorcerers, elementals might compress ether to create force and initiate the movements typical of an old-fashioned séance, like turning tables or levitating the trumpets used to amplify the disembodied voices of spirits.[34] Ether hasn't been an acceptable scientific concept since the late 1800s, so it's not surprising that later Theosophists and current New Age proponents distance themselves from the etheric model of elementals and embrace the more scientific-sounding notion that elementals are entities possessing a different *vibrational state* from the normal, visible world. As far back as 1894, Theosophist C.W. Leadbeater discussed how elementals and the objects they interact with can become invisible and move around using the process of *altered vibration* rather than ether: "The phenomenon of disintegration ... may be brought about by the actions of extremely rapid vibrations, which overcome the cohesion of the molecules of the object operated upon. A higher rate of vibrations of a somewhat different type will separate these molecules into their constituent atoms. A body reduced by these means to the etheric condition can be moved by an astral current from one place to another with very great rapidity; and the moment that the force which has been exerted to put it into that condition is withdrawn it will be forced by the etheric pressure to resume its original form (36)."[35] This has implications for appearing and relocating objects. Leadbeater continues. "It is in this way that objects are sometimes brought almost instantaneously from great distances at spiritualistic séances, and it is obvious that when disintegrated they could be passed with perfect ease through any solid substance, such, for example, as the wall of a house or the side of a locked box, so that what is commonly called 'the passage of matter through matter' is seen, when properly understood, to be as simple as the passage of water through a sieve, or of a gas through a liquid in some chemical experiment (36)."[36]

How easy is that! When it comes to explaining jottles there's no need to stress over complicated things like wormholes or multiverses or even substances called "ether." Objects disappear, appear and reappear (and are sometimes replaced) following an alteration in the vibrational frequency of their constituent molecules and atoms, which is initiated by elementals *also* vibrating at this higher frequency. These entities manipulate matter in a way that corresponds to their *own* state of being, perhaps at the behest of some even greater intelligence. All in all, if an invisible elemental wants to steal or relocate something as it floats by you, it simply reaches out and synchronizes the "vibration rate" of atoms in the selected object with its own vibrational frequency, lifting the object to a higher state and causing it to disappear. Transitioning the vibration back to a normal frequency will allow the object to reappear—in five minutes or perhaps six months later.

There's a certain charm to ascribing jottles to high-energy beings. After all, low-energy spirits surely don't possess the necessary power to affect changes in the environment, other than being seen out of the corner of the eye as an ephemeral shadow or as an ambiguous spoken phrase captured on a digital recorder. And since high-energy beings are such versatile and powerful creatures, we find allusions to them in other fields of the paranormal—fields that also involve appearing and disappearing objects. Most famously, John Keel argues that flying saucers "are not stable machines requiring fuel, maintenance, and logistical support. They are, in all probability, transmogrifications of energy and do not exist in the same way this book exists. They are not permanent constructions of matter (182)."[37] Instead, flying saucers are made from extremely short wavelength electromagnetic energy and are visible to humans only when they drop down the electromagnetic spectrum. Keel also ponders an issue reminiscent of intentional jottles: whether the behavior is directed by intelligence: "The UFO phenomenon does seem to be controlled. It does follow intelligent patterns. If the objects themselves are manifestations of higher energies, then something has to manipulate those energies somehow and reduce them to the visible frequencies. Not only do they enter the visible frequencies, but they take forms which seem physical and real to us, and they carry out actions which seem intelligent.... The source has to be a form of *intelligent energy* operating at the very highest possible point of the frequency spectrum (191.)"[38]

That's not to say jottles are *caused* by the Keel's flying saucer *ultraterrestrials*, his word for an elemental-like entity. It simply shows how theories of etheric planes and their high-energy inhabitants are solutions to a variety of paranormal phenomena sharing characteristics with our jottles.

Bad Vibes

As you might expect, sentient beings making merry at super-high vibrational frequencies have no scientific credibility. The word "vibration" has been appropriated from physics and used to describe these paranormal entities without much thought of what the word actually *refers* to. For instance, there are conflicting perspectives on what is actually doing the vibrating. Keel's ultraterrestrials are the very opposite of low-energy spirits. They're composed of high-energy, high-frequency electromagnetic waves. That's very different from Leadbeater's elementals, who seem to be made from actual *substance*, the components of which are vibrating at abnormally high rates. Regarding the latter, conventional physics tells us that the atoms and molecules comprising matter *do* vibrate, but this is a very complicated and multifaceted type of vibration. For example, a solid object is made up of molecules that vibrate relative to one another. Within these molecules are atoms, and the bonds connecting these atoms also vibrate in many different ways. For this reason it's not appropriate to spout the opinion that some everyday objects vibrate "normally," while others vibrate at abnormally high frequency and that's the distinguishing feature separating everyday people from elementals. In fact, at normal temperature *all* molecules in *all* objects vibrate at an incredibly high frequency simply because they're so small. And this vibration is measured an *average*, because not every atom or molecule is doing the same thing at the same time.

Another problem with the notion of high-vibrational beings is that molecules might be bonded together in a solid object, but when energy is added to the system (such as heat) these bonds are weakened and can break, hence the object melts. If energy continues to be added the fluid material transitions to a gas, and at even greater energies the gas progresses to a *plasma* or some other nonclassical high-energy state. There's no room in this orthodox treatment of matter to accept that increasing or decreasing the energy in an object creates anything other than this standard *phase change*. It certainly doesn't correspond to a drastic alteration in the vibrational behavior of the component atoms, resulting in the object magically becoming invisible and unmeasurable in the "astral plane," yet maintaining enough integrity that it can be "brought back to reality" by the removal of energy. Matter can be highly energetic, as can electromagnetic waves, but these states are measurable and don't resemble anything like an autonomous elemental or ultraterrestrial. That means we're back to square one with jottles.

To rescue the concept, I'd argue that the terms "high vibration" and "high energy" don't refer to the *classical* vibrations and energies measureable in everyday objects using laboratory equipment but something entirely different—states far beyond anything currently conceivable. In other words, elementals don't vibrate at a frequency of ten trillion hertz (typical of atoms) but at a tremilliatrecendotrigintillion hertz (that's actually a real number, although it's not one that accurately represents atomic vibration). A more pessimistic approach would be to accede that high-vibration and high-energy are nothing more than metaphors for how matter can either *be* seen or *not be* seen by people. That avoids any collision with established scientific paradigms and removes the need to think too deeply about how this state of invisibility might be scientifically possible. However, in both cases we're still no closer to explaining how or why non-human entities cause jottles.

Assessing the External Agent Theory of Jottles

In summary, spirits of the dead have a long association with jottle-like occurrences. In many poltergeist and haunting cases, objects are said to disappear from one place and reappear in another. However, these movements aren't isolated events; they're accompanied by all sorts of paranormal activity, like bumps and thumps and occasionally the appearance of apparitions. There's also the strongly held view that spirits are energetically weak, so it's unlikely they possess the energy to transport things around the house. That's why elementals seem a better prospect for jottles, despite their "vibrational" impossibility. However, apart from a remnant tradition of fairies and their peculiar interest in human possessions, there's no strong justification as to why specific *modern* items (like keys) are targeted by elementals. Intention is only *implicit*, since the experient is unlikely to find a satisfactory reason for why an object appears or relocates around the house. If elementals are to blame, it seems they are indulging in nothing more than trite attention-seeking. In those few jottle cases where intention is *explicit* we might take a theosophical perspective and propose that elementals are simply the conduit for a powerless revenant to communicate, but that's an even more tortuous argument to make.

I recommend a third solution, one that not only accounts for explicit and implicit intention but also makes sense of interaction. To find it, we need go no further than the experients themselves.

9
Human-Centered Causes

Experients often complain that their jottle was caused by a powerful but invisible external agent—good, evil or indifferent. However, I've just argued that such agents aren't a satisfactory explanation for jottles. How exactly do they make objects appear and disappear? What is their motivation? Do they even exist in the first place? It's actually far simpler (and more elegant) to propose that the experient is unwittingly responsible for the phenomenon, but in a paranormal way rather than a physical way.

Revisiting Teleportation

The methods used by the experient may be nothing other than the conscious or unconscious manipulation of putative natural physical processes—like teleportation. A crude analogy would be kicking a soft drink vending machine just to see what happens. You don't expect an outcome, but you hear the surprising thud of a soda falling through the slot. There's no reason for the soda to be delivered, since you didn't pay for it, and you can kick the machine a hundred times more in a hundred different points front, back and rear without receiving the satisfaction of another free soda. Yet for some reason your first kick bypassed the machine's engineered restraints and provided a free gift.[1] In the same way, our "penniless" experient accidently "kicks" a (super)natural transportatory mechanism, bypasses *its* restraints, and a jottle is the unexpected outcome.

Fort himself hinted that the universe's blind teleportatory mechanisms could be coerced in this very manner:

> Sometimes, in what I call "teleportations," there seems to be "agency" and sometimes not. That the "agency" is not exclusively human, and has nothing to do with "spirits of the departed" ... My suggestion as to the frequently reported "agency" of children is that "occult forces" were, in earlier times of human affairs, far more prevalent, and far more necessary to the help and maintenance of human communi-

ties than they are now, with political and economic mechanisms somewhat well-established, or working, after a fashion; and that, wherein children are atavistic, they may be in rapport with forces that mostly human beings have outgrown.[2]

Following this reasoning, there may be very little difference between a Fortean rain of fish and a jottle, after all. Fort suggested that teleportation was a force responding to the desires present in nature. Since people are part of nature, they can potentially harness energy but infuse it with conscious or unconscious personal intention—perhaps accounting for Martin and Trish's unexpected gifts. At a higher spiritual level, the same process might be employed by holy people who levitate and even teleport themselves from one location to another as a result of their devotional practices.[3]

More recently, individuals considered "gifted" might also be able to draw upon the universe's teleportatory mechanisms. For example, Alex Imich reports that an Egyptian "healer" named Safwat El Amin could teleport himself around the place, albeit in an uncontrolled fashion. In one instance, El Amin left Imich's apartment and entered a lift on the thirteenth floor. Shortly thereafter, the Egyptian landed forcefully behind Imich, inside his apartment, closely followed by the man's suitcase. And it wasn't simply personal teleportation that allegedly occurred. Apparently, when placed in a controlled environment, El Amin was able to materialize objects such as "leafs, twigs, flowers, tree bark, soil, stones, mussels, crystals, old and contemporary coins, dollars, Euros and pound sterling bills, pieces of fabric, a small gold cylinder, old match boxes with matches and a variety of jewels."[4] The appearance of these small and trivial items mimics the behavior of jottles, although in the context of a person who displays various "special" talents. That's very different from unsuspecting, everyday people such as Trish, Martin and Kate. Nevertheless, if El Amin's alleged powers have the side-effect of causing unexpected and unwanted things to appear in his presence, perhaps the same is happening, albeit in a less ostentatious way, to jottle experients.

The appearance of *unowned familiar* objects might not be the only possible outcome of tapping into the machinery of teleportation. Although I have yet to hear of a specific case where a conscious request was made for an object to *vanish*, one is easy to imagine. An individual might be busy in his workshop and, instead of hammering the head of a nail, he bangs his thumb instead. Furious, he mutters a few expletives about "never wanting to see the hammer again," and successfully accesses natural teleportatory forces that allow the tool to be "wished" out of existence. That results in a *disappearance*. Taking this dubious prediction even further, perhaps the same individual could "wish it back"—leading to a *reappearance*. And why stop there? Perhaps some, or all, of our exceedingly rare *replacements* are unconscious desires for alternative objects! This was an idea Fort was happy to consider, although with some reservation. He was aware that showers of nonorganic objects such as coins had been recorded over the years—outdoors at places as populated as Trafalgar Square but also inside houses such as the Robinson's in Battersea, London, in 1928.[5] Fort then asked whether coin showers might be a result of adepts mastering the teleportation of precious objects for their own satisfaction: "Maybe there are experimenters who have learned to do such things, teleportatively. I'd see some sport in it myself, if it wouldn't cost too much."[6]

The Vibrations Just Won't Go Away

Rather than psychic control over a natural but as yet unknown teleportatory process, an equally popular, old-fashioned, view is that people can occasionally influence the vibrational state of matter, and *this* is the force behind paranormal object movements. Harking back to the beliefs of Theosophists, an alteration in the frequency of solid matter lifts the constituent particles to an etheric state and perhaps back again. This doesn't have to be a skill exclusive to elemental beings but is something that can be mastered by a human adept. That's one explanation for *apporting* objects in séances (assuming the material isn't cheesecloth or objects discretely positioned in the medium's gown). C.W. Leadbeater even explains object duplications in this manner. Replications are "produced by simply forming in the astral light a perfect mental image of the object to be copied, and then gathering about that mould the necessary astral and physical matter. For this purpose it is necessary that every particle, interior as well as exterior, of the object to be duplicated should be held accurately in view simultaneously, and consequently the phenomenon is one which requires considerable power of concentration to perform (37)."[7]

To claim that *every* particle must be viewed and acknowledged bears similarity to the conditions required for physical teleportation—knowledge of the quantum state of an object's components. We've already seen the logical barriers to this idea and the general problem with suggesting that physical matter can be altered as a function of its vibrational state. And to put the nail in the coffin, *real* jottles simply don't coincide with periods of "considerable concentration." Using Trish's loaf of bread as a case in point, her verbal request was not coupled to an intense period of mental effort. Trish was uncompromising in her belief she wasn't tired, uncomfortable or emotional before, during or after the loaf's appearance. It's easier for Trish to accept that some external entity did the concentrating for her.

Despite these obstacles, it's worth persisting with an agent-centered solution to jottles because of its implicit association with a much-studied phenomenon—psychic ability, or *psi ability*. In psi, we find a long and thoughtful framework matching the jottle phenomenon.

Jottles as an Expression of PSI

There are many documented, and controversial, examples of individuals who display anomalous perceptual abilities such as clairvoyance or who generate anomalous *forces*, in the sense that they can produce kinetic energy through atypical means. The latter is best identified as *psychokinesis* (PK), and demonstrations range from "spoon bending" and the ability to move objects without touching them to less impressive, but more statistically sound, displays taking place within the strict confines of parapsychological laboratories, such as influencing the output of a computer-controlled random number generator.[8] There are also examples of spontaneous and apparently accidental psychokinesis, such as *streetlight interference*.[9] Then there's the most celebrated application of psychokinesis, the proposition that certain people—not spirits—are responsible for poltergeist activity.

Agent-Centered Poltergeists

Despite Hollywood's fixation with poltergeists as evil spirits and the historical connection between poltergeist-like activity and the early stages of a haunting (e.g., the Danton Walker case), it's widely accepted that authentic poltergeist events are just as likely to be caused by the human mind.[10] That's no new idea. At the turn of the century, scientist and parapsychologist Sir William Barrett was of the opinion that poltergeist activity was human-centered, since activity in an affected location ceased when the responsible agents were no longer present. Charles Fort also acknowledged the role of human agents in poltergeist cases, although his view was that adults often accuse children of causing mischief around the home to avoid attributing the activity to a spirit. However, Fort was well aware of another potential origin: "I do not know that poltergeists can be considered spirits.... It may be that many [cases] relate not to occult beings, as independent creatures, but to projected mentalities of living human beings (694)."[11] That said, Fort still preferred his idea that anomalous events such as stone-throwing were less to do with mischievous indivisible entities or psychically-gifted people and more to do with *extra-telluric* (i.e., out-of-earth) forces. When stones fall from the sky, it's redistributive teleportation. When stones fall from the ceiling of a house, it's *still* a form of redistributive teleportation, but it is wrongly labelled a poltergeist event: "Water falls on a tree, in Oklahoma. It is told of in an entomological magazine. Water falls in a house in Eccleston. I read that in a spiritualists' periodical.... These are the isolations, or the specializations, of conventional treatments. I tell of water falling upon a tree, in Oklahoma, and of water falling in a house in Eccleston, and think that both phenomena are manifestations of one force (572)."[12]

Fort's views have never been popular with mainstream parapsychology, the *living agent hypothesis* becoming the preferred explanation for poltergeists from the 1940s onwards.[13] The psychokinetic agent is not only young but also emotionally disturbed, frequently as a result of a domestic upheaval. As a consequence, her household is plagued with unexplained noises and object movements. Hungarian psychoanalyst Nandor Fodor was a leading proponent of this theory,[14] since it blends nicely with Freudian notions of the unconscious. The adolescent's *repressed thoughts* are no longer able to be "bottled up." But instead of the content of these thoughts being consciously actualized by the adolescent, thus relieving the symptoms in a safe fashion, she *unconsciously* projects them onto the material world using the energy associated with puberty. An analogy is the way a physical vessel under intense pressure requires venting or otherwise it will explode. Parapsychologist Michaeleen Maher provides the context for this human-centered approach to poltergeists: "With the advent of psychoanalytic theory and its seminal constructs of unconscious motivation and covert sexual drives, a prepubescent, person-centered theory of poltergeists was formulated. The new theory of ghosts was in step with the zeitgeist; the afterlife was out of favor but neurosis was very much in vogue (365)."[15]

One important aspect of human-centered poltergeist activity is that the physical effects don't have to be random and undirected. Often the adolescent agent is seeking attention—perhaps they're being ignored by their parents and siblings—and reward the novel interest of family members and investigators with the noises and object movements typical of poltergeist cases.

Where in the Brain?

To shore up the psychological origins of psychokinesis, modern researchers have sought a theory of the brain that might explain *how* physical movements can be generated from a distance. The most respectable contemporary method is to study the cerebral activity of a psychokinetic individual and compare it with the activity exhibited by "normal" people. Of course, any relationship between a particular brain state and simultaneous displays of psychokinesis is merely correlational. Unique brain processes don't necessarily *cause* anomalous object movements. Indeed, it might be the other way around—the ability to psychokinetically move objects might in turn affect brain activity. There's also a third option: the possibility that an external force moves objects and *concurrently* alters baseline cortical recordings. Nevertheless, the last two ideas aren't popular, as they complicate our understanding of the origins of psychokinesis. It's far easier to assume that a uniquely functioning brain influences matter *directly* using unconventional mechanisms. Psychokinesis is rare, so it can hardly be deemed a normal neurological condition. That's why theorists speculate that subtle brain dysfunction is responsible, derived from childhood illness or unusually heightened emotion.[16] There's even evidence that psychokinetic agents show signs of epilepsy focused in the right temporal lobes.[17]

That still doesn't explain how perfectly normal individuals are allegedly able to generate object movements in parapsychological laboratories. To maintain the "brain dysfunction" theory of psychokinesis, it's held that healthy people can occasionally produce psychokinesis when there's an accidental and transient reversal of the brain's hemispheric dominance. The normally quiescent right hemisphere temporarily takes charge of the *rational* left hemisphere,[18] and one consequence is an *irrational* display of psychokinesis that resembles poltergeist activity. The resulting movement is unrefined; objects are roughly flung around a room or clumsily tipped over because the right hemisphere lacks control of left-hemispheric brain circuits in charge of fine motor movement.

Having spent many decades quantifying the paranormal movement of objects in homes and scientific laboratories, parapsychologist and professor of psychology William Roll coined the expression *recurrent spontaneous psychokinesis* (RSPK) to describe agent-centered poltergeist activity.[19] *Spontaneous* refers to a form of psychokinesis that is uncontrolled, hence surprising to the agent and anyone else in the vicinity. This surprise deflects attention away from the agent as the source of events and leads to the false assumption that "spirits" are responsible. In the best studied cases, psychokinetic displays are also *recurrent* and therefore potentially measurable should investigators be present at the location. Unfortunately, the time course of the events is usually of short duration, meaning in situ investigation can be unrewarding.[20]

RSPK Poltergeists and Jottles: The Similarities

On the surface, jottles have much in common with RSPK poltergeist activity. For instance, RSPK poltergeists routinely affect a household living space, and the objects involved tend to be small and domestic in origin—things like cutlery, plates and bowls. For instance, in the Seaford, Long Island, case of 1958, medicine and shampoo bottles relocated around the Herrmann family's bathroom and porcelain figurines were displaced in their living room.[21] In 1920s Poona (Pune), India, the poltergeist was centered on an 8-year-old boy and in one situation a missing tub of shoe polish owned by the boy's teacher landed at her feet, seemingly from nowhere, when she requested it be returned.[22]

In terms of psychokinetic theory, small objects are targeted because the forces available to initiate movement, as well as disembodied sounds and electrical disturbances typical of traditional poltergeists, are presumed to be weak—no more than that required for regular muscle activity. The implication is that RSPK is not supernatural, because the law of conservation of energy has not been violated. In some unknown way, the kinetic energy concomitant with basic skeletomuscular movements has been transduced into a force that's just strong enough to permit a small plate to smash on the kitchen floor or a light switch in the living room to be toggled without human intervention. Likewise, if RSPK is responsible for jottles then those jottled objects will also be small because the available energy requirements do not allow larger objects like chairs and tables to be displaced. That may be why such objects are rarely claimed to disappear, appear or reappear.

A second feature linking jottles and RSPK poltergeists is the composition of the affected objects. RSPK-initiated motion is most suited to nonconductive (dielectric) materials—articles like plastic cups, glass tumblers, ceramic plates and bowls. Metal items are conductors and therefore act as an energy sink, so they warm up before they have the energy to move. My analysis shows that jottled objects are frequently made from nonconductive materials (e.g., food),[23] although when metal items *are* jottled (e.g., jewelry and keys) they are never reported as being warm or hot to touch.

A third common feature involves the distance the agent is from the object that is moved. The smaller this distance the greater the available energy. Close objects will therefore behave more energetically than remote objects. Depending on the available energy, an agent *might* be able to influence objects a few feet away, although a dinner plate at this location will not be flung around as much as one a few inches from the agent's fingers. According to William Roll, this is an expression of the *inverse square of distance rule*, meaning the farther away an agent is from an object the less influence he has and this occurs at an exponential—not steady or linear—rate. Compare this with jottles and the finding that disappearing and returning objects are affected by recent *interaction*. Experiments must be very near to the object for it to jottle, which complements Rolls's inverse square rule.

The fourth shared feature is *focusing*, expressed as either *object focusing* or *area focusing*. Object focusing refers to the way certain types of objects are targeted by RSPK poltergeists, an attribute also found with jottles. In the Seaford poltergeist case these objects happened to be bottles. As well as moving around the house, the tops of the bottles were sporadically blown off with a load bang, to the point where the (presumed) spirit was given the nickname "Popper." It's been suggested that in poltergeist cases specific objects are targeted because they are displaced representations of the *real* object of tension,[24] most commonly a mother or father if the agent is a child.

In *area focusing*, the poltergeist-driven movement of objects occurs in particular rooms of the house. Again, that's similar to the way jottles favor kitchens and bedrooms. Turning to the Seaford case once again, the master bedroom, kitchen, bathroom, and cellar were the sites of activity—probably because that's where the household's bottles were located. In other poltergeist infestations, such as the case from Enfield, England, in the late 1970s, the agent's bedroom features prominently. Chairs, dressers and toys were thrown around this room, and the dramatic levitation of 11-year-old Janet Hodgson was recorded on camera.[25]

A fifth and final feature that RSPK poltergeists and jottles have in common is that the motion of objects is *rarely ever witnessed directly by onlookers*, although a century of investigation into poltergeists has found no systematic evidence of hoaxing.[26] For instance, an RSPK agent and an investigator might be standing together in a living room. The investigator briefly turns his back to a sideboard holding an ornamental cup, and moments later the item is found lying in pieces on the floor across the room. In the opinion of the investigator, the physical position of the RSPK agent precludes the agent reaching out, grabbing the article and throwing it across the room without being detected, although that's often an untrained assumption rather than an expert observation. This gives RSPK the reputation of a *jealous phenomenon* in the fashion of hauntings—where investigators can spend hours in the affected room of a "haunted house," only to find the activity ceases when they are present but starts in another room, or on another, floor or returns when they leave.[27]

RSPK Poltergeists and Jottles: Are There Differences?

Recapping, there are features of orthodox RSPK poltergeist cases—*place, object, energy (object size), distance, composition, focus* and *motion*—that are also characteristics of jottles. However, it is most common for objects in RSPK poltergeist cases to levitate or move rapidly through space (or both) rather than materialize and dematerialize. For example, in a case from Olive Hill, Kentucky, in 1968 a plastic bowl and the doily on which it sat mysteriously fell from the top of a television set to the floor of the living room. What makes this incident particularly interesting is that the bowl held a bunch of plastic flowers, and these hovered in the air momentarily before they also disappeared behind the television. All three objects were then found in their original arrangement, the flowers neatly in the bowl, and the bowl sitting on the doily.[28] In the Poona case, the reappearance of the shoe polish was an exception. It was more typical for objects in this house (e.g., an ink bottle, a glass paper weight and toys) to be thrown around rather than disappear, appear or reappear.

A poltergeist affected a family in Nicklheim, Germany, also in 1968. Household objects would disappear from inside their house and reappear outside the house. Hearing of this, an investigator called Mr. Adam conducted a small experiment. He placed a bottle of perfume and a bottle of tablets on the kitchen table, then positioned the affected family outside the house (a 13-year-old girl, Brigitte, was the identified agent). Mr. Adam then closed and locked all the windows and doors and stationed himself next to the family. A short time later, the perfume appeared in mid-air at roof height and tumbled to the ground, followed by the tablet bottle, which fell with a zig-zag motion.[29] Once again, that's very different to how jottled objects behave.

There's also the issue of age. Children and adolescents are overwhelmingly the focus of poltergeist activity, whereas the current analysis shows that jottles are very much an adult phenomenon. Self-selection might play a role in distorting this age preference, since children's stories weren't included in the collection (admittedly I didn't have any to start with), and many childhood jottles are likely to have been forgotten by adulthood. Then again, the propensity of adults to suffer jottles doesn't necessarily negate an RSPK explanation. Using some liberal theorizing, it might be proposed that children have access to a repository of developmental energy and use this to indulge in juvenile attention-seeking. The outcome? Flamboyant displays of poltergeist activity. Furthermore, the concerns of parents and other family members mean the event is publicized and a formal investigation ensues. Compare this to lone adults with less available energy and no interest in drawing attention to themselves. Their (unconscious) expression of RSPK will possess the subtlety of a jottle rather than a public demonstration of object levitation or motion. Furthermore, they are likely to keep the experience to themselves, perhaps even dismissing it as unseemly or not worthy of further attention. This corresponds to David Rousseau's description of jottles as "the everyman's psychokinesis."[30]

Theories of RSPK

Since RSPK seems such a valid, albeit paranormal, solution to jottles, I'll briefly mention some of the underlying ideas about *how* a person's brain could directly affect matter. Sober theorizing about psychokinesis is scarce, since the field is not exactly popular in the hallowed halls of academia. That's what makes the thoughts of William Roll worth repeating, as they provide a schema for psychokinetically generated jottles.

Back in the 1960s, Roll suggested that *all* objects, living and inanimate, possess an invisible radiating field—a *psi-field*—that is intimately connected to the object's physical state and is in contact with the psi-fields of all surrounding objects, at any distance. Therefore, with the necessary *intention*, a person will be able to influence environmental objects without explicit macro-contact, although based on the inverse-distance law the farther away the object is from that person the weaker the influence will be. As yet, psi-fields haven't actually been detected, so this is all pure speculation.

More recently, a development of psi-field theory has been proposed by Harold Puthoff and concerns the space *separating* objects. Rather than thinking of this space as empty, let's assume that it is populated with a fundamental type of energy linked to gravitation and inertia called *zero point energy* (ZPE).[31] ZPE matches in many ways the "ether" beloved of Theosophists and earlier classical thinkers and is active even when the temperature of space is absolute zero and particles are no longer in motion. In Puthoff's opinion, the psychokinetic agent doesn't *literally* send large amounts of "brain energy" into space to move an object, since the quantity required would be considerable and surely measurable. Instead, the agent merely projects an imperceptible *psi-signal* that is able to harness an immense source of untapped ZPE near, or associated with, the target object. It's the ZPE that forces movement, not the original psi-signal! This removes the question of how much energy is available to adolescents (allowing poltergeist activity) and how much is available to adults (only enough to allow mere jottles).

If the psi-signal isn't a form of measurable energy, what is it? Consider the idea that any individual's observation of the external world possesses the characteristics of that individual. People interpret objects and events through the prism of past knowledge, beliefs and emotions. They are adding personal qualities to the observation, so a perceived object has a dimension of meaningfulness *beyond* its three-dimensional spatial properties and one-dimensional temporal property, i.e., space-time. To steal from our earlier discussion of quantum physics, the object has become *entangled* with the observer's psyche.

It is this subtle entanglement, rather than an energetic psi-signal, that harnesses ZPE and disturbs an object's quantum state. That causes the effects of gravity and inertia to be weakened or removed from the object, so its behavior will be anything *but* normal. In addition, the more meaningful the object the greater the degree of entanglement, hence the greater the probability of movement. If enough ZPE were harnessed, then it wouldn't simply be cups and saucers taking flight but potentially much heavier items—even pieces of furniture. Furthermore, should the disruption of an object's quantum state be large enough, the object could dematerialize as it is no longer restricted to four-dimensional space-time. Once the fundamental forces associated with the object are realigned, the object will be redeposited in the same place—a return jottle—or elsewhere—a relocation jottle.

Although this contemporary theory of RSPK might sound like a dressed-up version of the claim that disappearing objects "vibrate to the astral plane," there's good reason to suspect that human-centered RSPK is the best solution, so far, for jottles. Even though RSPK is primarily associated with troubled adolescents and the events performed by these adolescents are more spectacular than "run of the mill" disappearing and reappearing objects, perhaps the intense and short-lived adolescent RSPK referred to as a "poltergeist infestation" is expressed, even for the first time, during adulthood in a much more limited, less dramatic and atrophied guise.

For everyday adults, a comfortable home environment and the accompanying relaxation leads to an altered state of consciousness where the mind becomes delicately enmeshed with the quantum state of nearby familiar items. Experients "zone out" and the TV remote goes missing from their lap or they discover the salt shaker has disappeared from their fingertips while they are engrossed in a cookbook recipe. This accounts for *interaction*. Divorced of the attention-seeking behavior and repressed frustrations of adolescent RSPK, adult jottles won't manifest as hovering plates and smashing teacups but as personal items that simply disappear in rather dull ways. Despite the differences between jottles and RSPK poltergeists, the mechanisms of action—close proximity (interaction) and unconscious quantum entanglement—are identical.

The relevance of an agent's "tense" relationship with an object would also account for why specific objects are targeted and why many jottle cases possess intentionality. Unfortunately, I don't have any direct evidence of persistent stress, unconscious or even overt, between the experient and a jottled object—whether it happened to be Kate's set of car keys or Mark's TV remote control. However, we could venture that robust entanglement is derived through something other than emotional attachment. Take Dave's story of the appearing cricket bat. That day, he certainly had a strained relationship with cricket bats *in general*, so why not theorize that the ongoing entanglement he shared with a dormant bat hidden deep in the garage was stimulated and the bat somehow reconstituted itself in the living room—a place where this tension could be observed and comprehended? It is irrelevant that the bat was larger than regular jottled objects, as the important variable is significance not size. The garage and house walls are no impediments to its voyage through higher space. The beauty of the theory is that it accounts for jottles occurring as the result of very personal and routine thought processes—avoiding the convoluted proposal that random teleportation or elementals dwelling in the astral plane are responsible. Of course, Dave might have completely forgotten he had performed this (uncharacteristic) relocation; or someone unknown had sneaked into the garage—knew where to find the bat, grabbed it, broke into the house and left it in a visible place, for no good reason. In light of these unlikely solutions, RSPK actually seems more sensible, despite its enigmatic nature.

Jottles and Synchronicity

While we're considering a case like Dave's, it's worth noting his experience bears similarity to the concept of *synchronicity*. Most famously attributed to Carl Jung, synchronicity refers to coincidental situations that possess implicit meaningfulness. That's what makes these *meaningful coincidences* different from mere chance. An example would be two worldly events coming together in a seemingly purposeful way, or more notably a worldly event coinciding with a psychological event. For instance, one time I had a vivid dream of a seagull, and the next day I saw a seagull—plain as day—on the footpath in my small town miles from the sea and high up in the mountains. Suffice it to say, I'd never seen a seagull there before, and I haven't seen one since. Realistically, this isn't a genuine episode of synchronicity, as the coincidence should feel *numinous* (ethereal) and accompanied by a profound insight or glimmer of transcendental knowledge.[32] Maybe it's just me, but I simply couldn't find any explicit meaning in these two obviously connected but acausal incidents (the dream and the seagull), which probably means I've missed its purpose entirely!

If I do accept this event to be an example of synchronicity, I'd theorize that the physical event (the seagull) and the psychical event (the dream of a seagull) are separate in this reality but are intimately connected in a more fundamental realm (the *Unus mundus,* or "latent unity of the world").[33] Their essences are entangled in the form of an *archetype,* or universal idea lying dormant deep in the unconscious. Should, for whatever reason, this archetype be activated, two intimately but impossibly related events transpire—the dream and the seagull. Unfortunately, I have no idea what the archetype represents and why it was triggered.

Returning to Dave's jottle, were his private concerns, and the physical appearance of the bat linked synchronistically? Perhaps they were, although the coincidence does seem rather prosaic. Concern over personal performance in a third-grade cricket final with three spectators in tow is hardly a profound Jungian insight, although some archetypal significance might be discerned—perhaps the resulting synchronicity is a subtle expression of *the mentor* or *the trickster.* Dave's jottle also has the added aspect of being physically impossible. The bat moved from its location anomalously.

If Dave's were a textbook display of synchronicity, it might instead involve him thinking nervously about batting and then stumbling over a bat that had been left in the hallway by someone else—two separate everyday events coming together in a meaningful way. Indeed, even my seagull wasn't completely inconceivable—maybe it had simply gotten lost on its flight from the coast sixty miles away. That makes Dave's jottle an *atypical* expression of synchronicity. Here's another example of a synchronistic jottle (a relocation) that's paranormal, from Michael Thalbourne:

> On Wednesday September 4th, 2002, I was waiting for the bus, having put my multitrip ticket into one of my coat pockets. The bus arrived and I got on, but had to get off at the next stop because my ticket was nowhere to be found! I thought at first that I had dropped it, but I had not. Feeling around inside the coat I felt something the correct size but *next* to the pocket *on the inside of the lining.* You will say there was a hole in my pocket. There was no such thing. I checked thoroughly and found no means of entry into the lining, so I took it home and reluctantly used scissors to cut open the part of the lining nearest the card. And there it was! So back to the bus-stop half an hour later! It might be worth mentioning that at the time I was putting some additions into my second-edition Glossary, and teleportation of matter through matter was one of the entries.[34]

Michael (who died in 2010) was a repeater and experienced various jottle-like events he termed *macro-psi*, meaning they were the demonstration of psi (e.g., psychokinesis) on a real-world scale. These included the appearance of a small button-like item on his coffee table through no apparent cause (he lived alone) and the rediscovery of a medicine capsule on the kitchen floor four months after it had vanished while falling to the carpet. He saw these afflictions as a side-effect of *transhumanation*—a process leading to "mental evolution." One of the many outcomes of transhumanation is the realization that no material object is ultimately owned, which might explain Michael's reaction following the reappearance of his favorite (missing) spoon: "I promised not to show it so much favouritism in future. But in fact I did fail to be democratic with all my spoons, and focused on this one."[35] On account of Michael's failure to be so democratic the spoon disappeared once more, for good. A little later and relaxing on a couch with Plato's *Republic*, he read that the loss of property to a good man is of little significance, as he will mourn it less and stay more calm than other men!

When it comes to the intentional quality of jottles, some explicit cases, like Dave's and Michael's, might indeed be expressions of a *truly* uncommon paranormal variant of synchronicity. However, I'll leave that for the transpersonal psychologists to accept or dismiss at their leisure.

A Return to an Entity-Focused View of Jottles

Despite the many similarities shared by jottles and RSPK, there is still one troublesome question yet to be answered. *Why* would the experient psychokinetically—and unintentionally—generate poltergeist-like activity in adulthood that results in objects disappearing, appearing or reappearing? Most experients simply *do not* exhibit a conspicuous relationship with their jottled objects (should they own them). This lack of intent leaves the door open for *discarnate entities* to be held responsible for jottles and at least *some* poltergeist-like events. At least, that's the argument made by Paul Burgess, a neurophysiologist at the University of Utah's School of Medicine. Burgess has written extensively about mysterious poltergeist-like events that have affected him in his home and laboratory. However, he is hesitant to identify himself as an RSPK agent because that requires his accepting that undesired, unintended and unanticipated *unconscious* processes act in place of a traditional discarnate.[36] These forces emerge effortlessly and involuntarily and are disassociated from current mood states and thoughts. In Burgess's view, this is simply shifting the blame from an invisible and unmeasurable *external* cause—a spirit or poltergeist—to an invisible and unmeasurable *internal* cause—unconscious RSPK.

To explore this idea further, imagine a situation where a gifted individual is able to demonstrate legitimate psychokinesis in a controlled laboratory setting. For example, she might successfully nudge a paper clip along a tabletop without touching it. Now bring to that same laboratory another individual who's experienced domestic poltergeist activity (or an everyday jottle). This individual would be hard-pressed to show the same extraordinary talents, even though he generates gross object movements in his own home (or disappearance, appearance and reappearance jottles). The assumption is that this person is unable to *consciously* perform psychokinesis, but can initiate similar latent talents when he is *not* consciously trying.

This in turn implies the person's unconscious mind can influence the material world even when they dismiss the legitimacy of psychokinesis, poltergeists, jottles, or indeed anything paranormal. Taking this argument to its logical conclusion, the unconscious mind must be independent of the constraints placed on it by consciousness. It holds separate beliefs about what *can* and *can't* be enacted physically that are at odds with what the conscious mind holds as true. Take Deborah's library book replacement as an example of hidden psychokinesis. Her unconscious mind desired a different library book to that which was purposefully borrowed, and using psychokinesis it magically replaced this book with a different one *it* wanted to read. Michael Thalbourne pondered this very notion of hidden unconscious desires with regard to the disappearance and reappearance of his favorite spoon. Was his unconscious mind eager to provide convincing evidence of its existence? It is a claim he simply couldn't answer.

Even if we accept that powerful and autonomous unconscious processes are responsible for jottles, how could those processes produce the required psychokinesis without practice? Paul Burgess's home was plagued by many insignificant anomalous events, such as a light switch flicking to the off position without human interaction. If his unconscious mind was responsible for psychokinetically manipulating the switch, how could it succeed despite never having attempted it before? Or had his unconscious secretly been practicing for many years, studying conscious learning processes and performing private rehearsals in preparation for that one moment it could achieve the greatest impact and let off a little steam in the process? Granted Paul Burgess's unconscious mind—by raiding existing learned motor skills—*might* be able to manipulate a light switch through psychokinesis. Yet why, he asks, should this wondrous facility go missing after only a brief manifestation? That's at odds with how people normally acquire and retain learned skills. Applied to jottled objects this argument is even more potent, as we can't even depend on borrowed skills and abilities. No one is consciously able—or even *believe it is possible*—to teleport objects in the manner described throughout this book. And where do these objects go, and where do they come from? Is the unconscious privy to information about other realms, leaving the conscious mind in the dark?

Even from a mainstream scientific perspective, personal unconsciousness is surmised as a distributed process across the higher cortex rather than an autonomous "thing" sitting somewhere inside the skull. That's because it can't be *directly* observed or measured. The further away from credible science we get the hazier the location of consciousness becomes. This untraceable unconsciousness, secretly able to enforce its will in unpracticed ways on the outside world, is analogous to an external, autonomous entity. Despite my initial enthusiasm for RSPK as a solution to jottles, on further consideration we might simply have gone "full circle" and returned to the realm of spirits and elementals!

10

What Are Jottles?
(In My Opinion, at Least)

Personally, I've very happy to accept that jottles are objectively real. They're the only unambiguous "paranormal" event I've experienced, and they occur at reasonably close intervals—perhaps every six months on average. That's one of the motivations for writing this book and the reason why the story collection is so large. I've been amassing jottle tales for years! Out of principle I haven't included any of my experiences in the database, although I'll admit that apart from the tale of the reappearing key in the paddock, three other narratives are mine—the stories of Dave's cricket bat and Robert's wallet and tap fitting. I didn't want to give that away until now.

Here's another jottle I recently experienced. Early one Saturday morning I was fixing a fence—replacing a section of the existing rusted wire with new netting. The previous day I'd bought all the necessary bits and pieces, including two rolls of straining wire. I was aware that an old roll of wire was stored away in the garage, left over from a previous fencing task. However, the garage was a mess and I couldn't be bothered sifting through all the clutter to find it.

The two new rolls rested on the ground near my feet as I worked, and I remember using each one intermittently. After a short while a neighbor pulled up and I walked over to the neighbor's car for a quick conversation, although I was only ever about ten steps from, and in direct sight of, all my tools and equipment—including the wire. When I returned to the work area about fifteen minutes later I discovered to my surprise *three* rolls of wire sitting side by side on the ground. The two shiny new ones were where I had left them, but now they were joined by a half-used roll of tarnished wire suspiciously similar to the roll stowed somewhere in the garage. I was in full view of other people during the entire episode, so I can't have trance-walked to the garage to fetch it (presuming I knew where it was hidden). I also *know* I hadn't bothered searching for any left-over wire. Since this type of event occurs frequently to me it was of no great concern—I was just relieved the outcome wasn't mischievous or, even worse, malicious. On this particular occasion the "appearance" was actually helpful. As it turned out, two rolls weren't enough to finish the job, and I needed the third. It took me a long time—a number of years—to recognize these personal jottles. Otherwise, I probably would have shaken my head with puzzlement then quickly forgotten it ever happened (despite happily using the third roll for the job). That's why I'd argue that jottles are more prevalent than we care to realize.

So what *really* causes a jottle? Let's reconsider Jacques Vallée's quote that opened this book: "Whenever a set of unusual circumstances is presented it is in the nature of the human mind to analyze it until a rational pattern is encountered at some level (164)."[1] To some extent, a pattern for jottles *has been* found, although it's not entirely rational. We've discovered there are four types: disappearances, appearances, reappearances and replacements, each of which involve the anomalous behavior of small objects in a home environment. Interaction between the experient and the object seems to initiate a permanent disappearance or a disappearance *then* a return to the same location after a short interval. Situations where an object disappears, then relocates at some later time to a place different from where it was lost is often suggestive of intention. Various explanatory frameworks help experients make sense of these patterns, and I've systematically explored the most popular ones, ideas such as teleportation, multiverses, spirits, fairies and psychic power. Unfortunately, these "explanations" are all theoretically weak and only accommodate small fragments of the mystery.

One solution is to explain each jottle on a case-by-case basis using independent theories, whereby a feature such as *interaction* has one cause (e.g., quantum teleportation) and *intention* another (e.g., troublesome elementals). For some stories, both interaction and intention can be accounted for (as in personal RSPK). Hence Cameron's fast-returning keys were a function of his conscious mind temporarily slipping into a parallel universe, while Kate's relocating keys and Trish's windfall of bread were, respectively, the actions of the unconscious mind performing psychokinesis and a mysterious paraphysical entity.[2] Despite these vastly different causes, the symptom is identical—the personal experience of a jottle. This is the best way to accommodate my suggestion that whatever causes an object to disappear is different from what makes an object reappear. It is also suits the four basic points of jottles gleaned from the analysis.

Another possibility is that there is a unified theory that jottles does exist; however, the current analysis of the jottle collection, while sincere, is able to uncover only a fraction of what these stories represent. The variables of interaction and intention may only be two emergent "tips" of a vastly bigger phenomenon that resembles a huge, hidden iceberg floating beneath the ocean surface, the form of which is inconceivable through standard scientific investigation. Simplistic models of multiverses and other-dimensional reality simply cannot provide an adequate level of understanding, making Vallée's sentence that follows very pertinent: "[I]t is quite conceivable that nature should present us with circumstances so deeply organized that our observational and logical errors would entirely mask the pattern to be identified (164)."[3] Multiverses and other dimensions are certainly "deeply organized" perspectives on reality; however, our understanding of what they represent is too coarse to assist with deciphering everyday jottles. In the basic form presented here, ideas of teleportation, or peripatetic consciousness, are also unwieldy. The same can be said for agent-centered RSPK or invisible elemental entities lingering around the kitchen in high vibrational states waiting to steal your banana.

Unfortunately, Vallée's pessimistic conclusion may best fit the phenomenon of jottles. But all is not lost. Embracing his idea of a deeply organized reality leads to another, very interesting, possibility.

Jottles Are Seamless

I'm not saying what follows is *the* unified solution for jottles, but it does accord with a great many of the cases in the collection. Here's how it works. For the moment, ignore what type of object is jottled and which room of the house it is jottled from. Ignore whether the object has been recently touched and whether it was returned soon after it was lost or was relocated many months later to another room of the house. Even ignore the purposefulness inherent to many jottle stories. These are all variables in the saga of jottles, as they diverge significantly across the story collection. However, there's one feature of jottles that does appear to be *constant* in all cases—and that is the *seamlessness* associated with an object's disappearance, appearance, reappearance or replacement. The variable of "seamlessness" wasn't explicitly measured in the story collection because I didn't even *think* to measure it until the analysis was complete. In hindsight, it is inherent to just about all jottle stories and is a feature I've offhandedly referred to throughout the book, e.g., with regard to content-specific delusions.

Here's what I mean by the seamlessness of jottles. Should a slice of cheese go missing from the kitchen counter right under your nose, it is as though it was *never* there. On the other hand, should a strange fountain pen be discovered on the dining room table for no apparent reason, it's as though it has *always* been there. The keys that reappeared on Kate's pillow were the same keys she'd lost six months previously. They were *not* hot to the touch or weathered or changed in any way. They also rested quite naturally where they were found. There was no evidence of other paranormal events occurring in the vicinity, either—no hovering teacups or clicking light switches, no sense of presence or visual sightings of shadowy spirits.[4] That's why jottles are dismissed so easily by so many experients. Despite what they might represent (teleporting, psychokinesis, fairies, or whatever), they are so ordinary—so comfortable a part of everyday reality—that they are quickly forgotten.

I've pondered the topic of jottles carefully, having thought long and hard about how objects disappear, appear, reappear and are occasionally replaced. If I was forced to favor an answer I'd choose one best able to deal with the seamlessness of the jottle experience while at the same time acknowledging that jottles *aren't* a function of mere hallucination (i.e., content-specific delusions). That requires accepting the notion that everyday reality is derived from conscious observation and jottles just happen to be an uncommon but perfectly sensible by-product of this process. Such an interpretation is compatible with previous discussion of the way consciousness and physical reality are entangled, but the implications are more profound.

Observation and Reality

Conventional wisdom sees consciousness as merely observing objects in a passive way, as though these objects are entirely independent of whom or what is observing them. In this treatment of reality, consciousness is simply a side-effect of physical reality[5]; and the brain is no more than a group of cells made up of molecules, which in turn are made up of atoms, atoms being in turn made up of subatomic particles, and those in turn being made up of a collection of points existing in space-time, and so on.[6]

However, you'll recall that the collapse of a wave function involves what is *observed* (e.g., an electron) and what does the *measuring* (e.g., a piece of laboratory equipment), and consciousness is a potential measuring device—as we've noted in the context of Schrödinger's cat. Indeed, there exists a view that measurement of quantum states is progressive, with the different measuring devices connected in series like links in a chain, referred to as a *Von Neumann chain*. At any arbitrary point on this chain the quantum wave may collapse,[7] although conscious observation is ultimately the last link—the final arbitrator of the quantum state and more important than any preceding measuring instrument. That implies consciousness is an active determinant of reality. In other words, matter doesn't really *exist* in an objective sense—other than in its essential quantum state. What we call matter is formed by the actions of consciousness: "[I]f we decide to break off the chain [of conscious observation] ... it follows that, according to one of our definitions of reality, matter cannot be regarded as real.... [I]f consciousness is required to turn ghostly probability waves into things that are more or less like the objects we meet in everyday life, we will not be able to say that matter is what would be there anyway, whether or not human minds were around (at least if we assume that humans minds are all the minds there are (46)."[8]

That might sound a lot like *subjective idealism*—the notion that we can really only ever know our own mental state and nothing else. An external, material world is ultimately "unknowable." However, what I'm trying to convey here, strictly speaking, isn't idealism. The static attributes of matter—for example, mass and charge—*do* exist independently of the observer, although the dynamic attributes of those particles—position, momentum, spin and orientation—are "mind-dependent." Without these dynamic attributes, a universe of static properties wouldn't really resemble a real, sensible place. Consciousness gives rise to this "sensibleness." Therefore, observers do not create matter from nothing[9] but rather imagine the *conformation* of matter from a quantum soup of vital ingredients—a *prephysical substrate*.[10] Perhaps some deeply fundamental process has determined what the world *should* look like from these ingredients, and observers are merely carrying out the final act of realization, an analogy of this being the way a radio receiver transmutes existing information-rich radio waves into coherent sound.

Interacting Conscious States

This view of reality opens up all sorts of problems in terms of how such a physical world is held together—particularly if it's *not* being directly observed by somebody. I have a simple solution. There's no need to rely on constant observation to hold an object in its resolved, material configuration. You might be at a restaurant having dinner with friends and briefly take your eyes off the menu you are holding, but that doesn't mean the menu will pop out of existence until you look back and re-create it. Rather, your menu is held in place by your own observation *and* everyone in the vicinity. Generally speaking, there are many, many individual and interacting conscious minds each observing the pre-physical substrate[11] and together they sustain the animated multisensory landscape that is consensus reality.[12] A simple representation of this idea, constrained to two dimensions, is the adaptation of a Venn diagram shown in Figure 3.

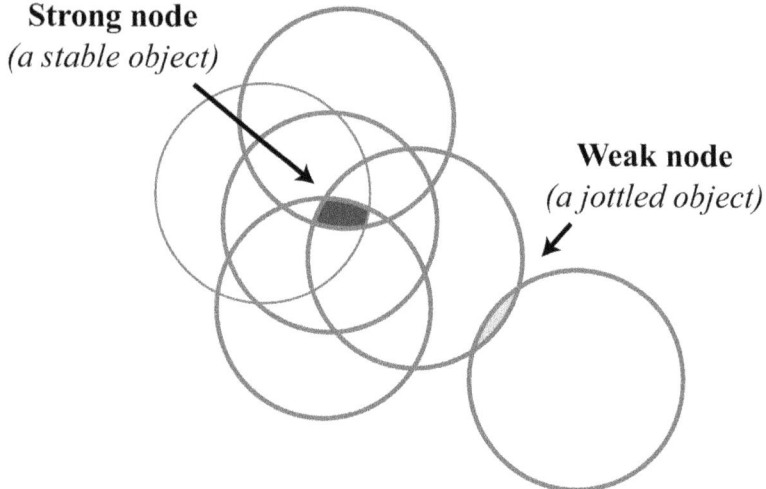

Figure 3: Interpreting jottles as reality creation through interacting consciousness.

Each circle corresponds to a separate person, or *conscious observer*. When the circles overlap, "nodes of reality" are created that allow everyday objects and events to be conceived. The observers' existing beliefs and assumptions allow the node-dependent objects to persist even when there is no direct observation by any one individual. Some nodes are very strong because they are constituted from many separate observers (e.g., the dark grey shading in Figure 3). Alternatively, some nodes are weak, as they are maintained by only a few observers—or in some cases only a *single* observer. That situation is represented by the light grey shading in the figure.

While the overall result is a stable and seemingly material reality, an anomaly in the configuration of a weak node could force the associated object *out* of existence and return it to the pre-physical substrate or bring additional, unrealized, objects *into* existence. An analogy would be the way the content of a single frame can be inserted into, or removed from, an animated cartoon to give the appearance of materialization and dematerialization. I suggest here that jottles are situations where objects are immediately "drawn" (for want of a better word) *into* and *out of* subjective reality by the actions of consciousness on the pre-physical substrate. That's not merely the object's visual presence but also its full physical presence—its *reality*. Again I'll admit I'm no pioneer when it comes to this proposal. A similar idea has been tendered by Mary-Rose Barrington, who suggests that reality is produced by many "consciousnesses" that are local elements of a greater "mind."[13] Jottles are therefore a failure of any one of these conscious states to hallucinate reality.

This idea of *reality creation through interacting consciousness* captures the most endearing aspect of jottles: why small personal items are so frequently targeted and why they overwhelmingly occur at home. These domestic objects are less stable than public objects because fewer conscious minds are "aware" of them or at least contemplated them at some time in the past. They might be fully dependent on one person (the owner) for their permanency. Roads and buildings and cars are constituents of reality maintained by many minds, and these are *very* rarely the focus of a disappearance or appearance. You might be unwittingly jealous of a friend's car and unconsciously wish it would disappear, but it *won't* disappear, because its solidity is determined by the powerful actions of multiple individual conscious states. On the other hand, hidden around the home are smaller private items such as keys and wallets that are primarily maintained by a single consciousness … the owner's. Unsurprisingly, they're the objects that are jottled, and that is why jottles are the bane of people who live alone. Michael Thalbourne is a perfect example, and a repeater to boot.

In this framework of jottles, object disappearances are random quirks following close personal interaction. For unidentified reasons, physical contact or motion or a combination of the two weakens the glue of conscious observation, removing the support that keeps an object in its particular conformation. The wave state of the object dissipates into the substrate and the object is instantly scrubbed from reality. It never comes back. Whether the object rematerializes in someone else's house as an appearance jottle is something I can hardly answer with any confidence.

However, I could suggest that if the disruption to the observation process is only short, then it might be easier for the object to return to its original, realized state when the experient goes to look for it. That's a fast return, and they are very common in the collection.

To account for intentional jottles, I must rely once more on the unfalsifiable notion of an autonomous, personal unconscious. This subconscious has its own hidden reasons for deleting "tense" items from reality, and if it is naturally powerful (or encouraged by the experient to *be* powerful, e.g., through meditation) then we have justification for why some individuals exhibit a disappearing trait. Indeed, if a person's unconscious mind possesses such capability then there's no reason why the same objects can't be reestablished at a later time in the same or a different place. That "solves" the problem of *implicit* intention and might explain why certain individuals also display the characteristics of a universal repeater—their unconscious processes have free rein over the manifestation of any type of jottle! An object's reappearance may possess apparent meaningfulness, but the conscious individual cannot crack the code of *why* it occurred. Even *explicit* intention might be generated by a freewheeling subconscious. Reversing Paul Burgess's argument, a relocation jottle with unequivocal purpose might not be caused by a recently deceased relative as in the cases of Eleanor and Ruth's revenants, but by the clandestine workings of the unconscious mind expressing sorrow for the relative's departing!

Alternatively, and taking a personal example, my unconscious has effortlessly actualized, on my front lawn, a half-used and tarnished roll of wire while the *original* roll, located in the garage in a parlous state of being, is simultaneously snuffed out of existence (or might remain as a *duplication*[14]). This entire process does *not* involve moving the roll from one place to another but instead imagining it in one place, so by default "unimagining" it in another. This neatly removes all the problems we've encountered with messy physical models of teleportation and wormholes, to name just two. Furthermore, it's not a problem that my subconscious has never practiced or performed the jottling of a wire roll, because this very subconscious is integral in producing everyday reality in the first place. My subconscious might not have much scope to alter consensus reality, but it can easily play around with private reality when the circumstances permit.

On those occasions where multiple individuals have witnessed a jottle, there is a primary agent and one or more secondary bystanders. The story of my rediscovered wallet is a perfect example of this. Neither I nor my wife actually saw the wallet appear in the cupboard. My wife just happened to be in the immediate vicinity when I found it, and the circumstances of the disappearance and relocation were entirely my concern. The presence of my wife simply confirms that jottles are objectively real and not a subjective hallucination. However, for my wife and any peripheral witnesses there's nothing overtly paranormal about the event, because what's happened isn't paranormal in the popular sense of the word (for instance, apparitions of the dead or levitating coffee cups). It's much deeper than that. My wife was merely privy to the actions of a single conscious state that had collapsed private reality in an unusual way. For some obscure reason my mind caused my wallet to be removed *from*, then returned *to*, existence, and these actions simply rippled out to become a wider consensual experience.

I can't claim this eccentric interpretation suits all jottles, since it doesn't account for the many idiosyncrasies found across the story collection.[15] For instance, why are the objects targeted for permanent disappearance so different from those that reappear, whether three minutes or three months later? Of course, ad hoc reasons can always be invented to account for such disparities, using a little imagination and a pinch of psychobabble. Here are some examples:

> Sam's deep unconscious doesn't want her scrubbing in the sink any longer, so it got rid of the scrubbing brush for good, by collapsing it back into quantum soup;

or

> Kate's unconscious stayed strong for many months but eventually regretted dematerializing "her" keys, so it reimagined them on her pillow many months later as a personal apology to her outward, conscious self;

or even

> Because of its sophisticated knowledge of the process of physical decay, the unconscious has an understandable aversion to relocating fresh food items over long periods of time. That's why preserved foods are targeted in long-delayed relocations.

It's also difficult for my interpretation of jottles to justify the great number of foreign things that appear, best represented by the propensity of coins to drop from mid-air. Does an accidental or purposeful alteration of reality favor these unique events? If a conniving subconscious is a dubious explanation for unowned appearing objects, we could instead hold the underlying essence from which individual consciousness emerges responsible. In other words, these impressive jottles are manifestations of *deep consciousness* rather than the personal unconscious. Depending on your bent, this deep consciousness manipulates reality for noble, nefarious or insane reasons. I have no answer to which one is most appropriate.

Despite this being the end of the book, an understanding of jottles has really only commenced. I cannot provide an absolute conclusion about what jottles are and how or why they occur. However, I do offer the suggestion that they are subtle indicators—and important evidence—of a mutually created reality.

Chapter Notes

Introduction

1. Kate and Mark's stories are both real; however, I've paraphrased the loss and subsequent search for their respective lost objects.

2. M.R. Barrington (1991), "JOTT—Just one of those things," *Psi Researcher* 3, pp. 5–6.

3. Examples of more easily accessible internet sources include http://paranormal.about.com/od/poltergeists/a/Disappearing-Object-Phenomenon.html; http://www.visionaryliving.com/2008/09/05/have-you-been-jottled; and http://amasci.com/weird/unusual/objs.html.

4. M.A. Thalbourne (2003), *A Glossary of Terms Used in Parapsychology*, 2nd ed. (Charlottesville, VA: Puente).

5. In this book, I'll refer to people who experience jottles as "experients" because "experient" is not as dramatic or judgmental as "victim" or "sufferer."

6. N. Holt (2004), Study Day No. 45: "Discontinuities: Things That Come, Go and Relocate," *Paranormal Review* 30, pp. 31–33.

7. For example, http://www.dailymail.co.uk/news/article-2675583/Dog-coughs-owners-missing-wedding-ring-SIX-YEARS-disappeared.html.

8. H.J. Irwin and C.A. Watt (2007), *An Introduction to Parapsychology*, 5th ed. (Jefferson, NC: McFarland).

Chapter 1

1. For most stories in this book I've changed the names of the storytellers, simply to protect their privacy.

2. James McDonald and certain other high-quality writers are the exceptions to this rule.

3. J.A. Hynek (1974), *The UFO Experience* (London: Corgi) (original work published 1972).

4. *Ibid.*

5. Tedford was 68 years old in some sources.

6. T. Lewis (2014), *Haunted Inns and Ghostly Getaways of Vermont* (Charleston, SC: Haunted America).

7. Anonymous (12 December 1950), "Girl vanishes, police baffled; sixth to disappear in five years," *Pittsburgh Press*, p. 24.

Chapter 2

1. S. Cardeña, S.J. Lynn and S. Krippner (2000), "Introduction: Anomalous Experiences in Perspective," in *Varieties of Anomalous Experience: Examining the Scientific Evidence* (pp. 3–23), ed. E. Cardena and S. Lynn (Washington, D.C.: American Psychological Association).

2. Paraphrased from an Internet tale, with the name of the experient changed. Internet tales have *not* been included in the broader story collection, although I will occasionally include them because some, like Lucy's, possess unusual attributes, e.g., object type or behavior.

3. Gleaned from the Internet.

4. N. Holt (2004), Study Day No. 45: "Discontinuities: Things That Come, Go and Relocate," *Paranormal Review* 30, pp. 31–33.

5. I've yet to come across a trustworthy story where a jottled object has been scientifically analyzed and shown to be "not-of-this-world," so this interpretation is complete conjecture.

6. Gleaned from the Internet.

7. Although it's perfectly reasonable to interpret the event as a meaningful coincidence—something I'll touch on later in this book.

Chapter 3

1. As opposed to *everyday* mysterious circumstances, such as, "It's a mystery who stole my car."
2. C.D. Bader (2003), "Supernatural Support Groups: Who Are the UFO Abductees and Ritual-Abuse Survivors?," *Journal for the Scientific Study of Religion* 42(4): 669–678.
3. P.J. Klass (1997), "FAA Data Sheds New Light on JAL Pilot's UFO Report," in *The UFO Invasion: The Roswell Incident, Alien Abductions, and Government Coverups*, ed. K. Frazier, B. Karr and J. Nickell (pp. 171–177) (New York: Prometheus).
4. T. Rabeyron and C. Watt (2010), "Paranormal Experiences, Mental Health and Mental Boundaries, and Psi," *Personality and Individual Differences* 48(4), 487–492.

Chapter 4

1. Thanks must go to (in alphabetical order) Mitchell Day, Kirsty Jacobs, Ayesha Jilani and Monika Magar, who conducted this research as part of their postgraduate diploma of psychology at the University of Western Sydney. The data was included in the collection for analysis.
2. Participants were to choose the most memorable story if they self-identified as a repeater.
3. Lucy's story wasn't included in the database. There are also plenty of examples in the paranormal literature where the same object is targeted by anomalous forces (e.g., movement or some other strange behavior). However, these events frequently occur in a wider paranormal context that bears little resemblance to Mark or Lucy's jottle—something I'll discuss in part 3.
4. Based on personal experience. I have very little interest in what clothes I own, and if I lost an item in mysterious circumstances or an item appeared or reappeared (socks in particular), it's likely I'd remain completely oblivious to the jottle.
5. Overwhelmingly, cell phones (rather than stationary telephones).
6. J.A. Marusich, T.W. Lefever, K.R. Antonazzo, R.M. Craft, and J.L. Wiley (2014), "Evaluation of Sex Differences in Cannabinoid Dependence," *Drug and Alcohol Dependence* 137, pp. 20–28.
7. There are no dependable stories of *appearing* drinks or liquids in the collection, although a few degraded examples can be found on obscure Internet sites.
8. C. Fort (1974), *The Complete Books of Charles Fort* (New York: Dover).
9. Although not represented in my collection, stories can be found on the Internet of appearing *unowned unfamiliar* objects; however, again these are low-information stories, so it is difficult to judge their legitimacy.
10. Although few in number, toy appearances also possess gift-status, as they are most likely *unowned*.
11. There might be an exception for jewelry, as I'll mention shortly.
12. Kate's story is therefore unrepresentative of most key reappearance stories. The last seen delay was short, but the loss delay was a year and the reappearance delay a single day. I've included her case because it's one of the most highly detailed I possess and worth retelling in full.
13. Of course, this is not an invariant rule, as there can be examples where the keys were last seen hours previously but only recently were noticed as missing, then turned up within minutes in the original location.
14. A. Jinks (2011), *An Introduction to the Psychology of Paranormal Belief and Experience* (Jefferson, NC: McFarland).
15. That's not to say the keys haven't travelled *somewhere* during the interim. Rather, there appears to have been little distance travelled from *our* frame of reference.
16. Although not for human consumption, cat food is still a food, and the container was kept in the kitchen.
17. Cell phones and eyeglasses are the target objects in a majority of the 15 percent of cases involving the loss or reappearance phase occurring at locations *other* than the home.

Chapter 6

1. Like most ideas in this book, these criticisms of jottles are not novel. Barrington herself notes that to dismiss jottles we have to accept that all cases involve carelessness, absent-mindedness, hallucination and lies. However, in this book I'm examining these skeptical arguments in significant detail.
2. That doesn't mean everyday spontaneous events are not studied, and acted on, using subjective evidence—for example, a traffic accident black spot (at least in the days before cameras could be set up to monitor the location). Detailed information about each accident can be collected after it happens, then collated and used to make decisions about causes and potential solutions.
3. S.Y. Rim, K.E. Min, J.S. Uleman, T.L.

Chartrand, D.E. and Carlston (2013), "Seeing Others Through Rose-Colored Glasses: An Affiliation Goal and Positivity Bias in Implicit Trait Impressions," *Journal of Experimental Social Psychology* 49(6), 1204–1209.
  4. L. Festinger (1985), *A Theory of Cognitive Dissonance* (Stanford, CA: Stanford University Press [original work published 1957]).
  5. N. Holt, "Discontinuities," *Paranormal Review*, 31–33.
  6. Ibid.
  7. P.J. Bauer and M. Larkina (2014), "The Onset of Childhood Amnesia in Childhood: A Prospective Investigation of the Course and Determinants of Forgetting of Early-Life Events," *Memory* 22(8), 907–924.
  8. D. Strange and H. Hayne (2013), "The Devil Is in the Detail: Children's Recollection of Details About Their Prior Experiences," *Memory* 21(4), 431–443.
  9. Although this is not a fixed age, since mild memory deficits have been reported for 11–12-year-olds (e.g., Bauer and Larkina, "Childhood Amnesia in the Making," 597–611).
  10. D.L. Schacter, J.Y. Chiao and J.P. Mitchell (2003), "The Seven Sins of Memory: Implications for Self," *Annals of the New York Academy of Sciences* 1001: 226–39.
  11. V.G. Morwitz (1997), "It Seems Like Only Yesterday: The Nature and Consequences of Telescoping Errors in Marketing Research," *Journal of Consumer Psychology* 6(1), 1–29.
  12. T. Lanciano and A. Curci (2011), "Memory for Emotional Events: The Accuracy of Central and Peripheral Details," *Europe's Journal of Psychology* 7(2), 323–336. Of course, meticulous historical recollections involving unexpected and emotional events should be viewed with caution, as the details they possess aren't necessarily accurate—they're simply more vivid and more confidently recalled than other, "everyday," memories. There's no evidence that stories with greater detail are more precise. Detailed stories are persuasive, but they shouldn't be accepted as correct on that basis alone (e.g., J.M. Talarico, and D.C. Rubin (2007), "Flashbulb Memories Are Special After All, in Phenomenology, Not Accuracy," *Applied Cognitive Psychology* 21(5): 557–578.
  13. J.A. Cheyne, J.S.A. Carriere, and D. Smilek (2006), "Absent-Mindedness: Lapses of Conscious Awareness and Everyday Cognitive Failures," *Consciousness and Cognition* 15(3): 578–592.
  14. Michael was aware of Mary Rose Barrington's work.
  15. E.F. Loftus (2003), "Make-Believe Memories," *American Psychologist* 58(11): 867–873.
  16. S.J. Read and M.B. Rosson (1982), "Rewriting History: The Biasing Effects of Attitudes on Memory," *Social Cognition* 1(3): 240–255.
  17. Schacter, Chiao and Mitchell (2003), "The Seven Sins of Memory," 226–39.
  18. Similarly termed the misinformation effect (e.g., Mazzoni, G. and Vannucci, M. (2007), "Hindsight Bias: The Misinformation Effect, and False Autobiographical Memories," *Social Cognition* 25(1): 203–220.
  19. H. Otgaar, A. Scoboria, and T. Smeets (2013), "Experimentally Evoking Nonbelieved Memories for Childhood Events," *Journal of Experimental Psychology: Learning, Memory, and Cognition* 39(3): 717–730.
  20. Read and Rosson (1982), "Rewriting History," 240–255.
  21. A.K. Taylor (2013), "Leveling and Sharpening," in *Encyclopedia of Human Memory*, vol. 1 (pp. 618), ed., A.K. Taylor (Santa Barbara, CA: ABC-CLIO).
  22. P. Rogerson (29 July 2010), "Slide Rules," *Magonia Blog*, retrieved November 8, 2014, http://pelicanist.blogspot.com.au/2010/07/slide-rules.html.
  23. S.B. Most, B.J. Scholl, E.R. Clifford, and D.J. Simons (2005), "What You See Is What You Set: Sustained Inattentional Blindness and the Capture of Awareness," *Psychological Review* 112(1): 217–242.
  24. K. Weir (2014), "Your Cheating Brain, *New Scientist* 221(2961): 35–37.
  25. I.E. Hyman Jr., S.M. Boss, B.M. Wise, K.E. McKenzie, and J.M. Caggiano (2010), "Did You See the Unicycling Clown? Inattentional Blindness While Walking and Talking on a Cell Phone," *Applied Cognitive Psychology* 24(5): 597–607.
  26. A. Richards, M.G. Hellgren, and C.C. French (2014), "Inattentional Blindness, Absorption, Working Memory Capacity, and Paranormal Belief," *Psychology of Consciousness: Theory, Research, and Practice* 1(1): 60–69
  27. V. Beanland and K. Pammer (2010), "Looking Without Seeing or Seeing Without Looking?: Eye Movements in Sustained Inattentional Blindness," *Vision Research* 50(10): 977–988.
  28. G.M. Slavich and P.G. Zimbardo (2013), "Out of Mind, Out of Sight: Unexpected Scene Elements Frequently Go Unnoticed Until Primed," *Current Psychology* 32(4): 301–317.
  29. V.S. Ramachandran (1992), "Filling in Gaps in Perception: Part 1," *Current Directions in Psychological Science* 1(6): 199–205.

30. Patients with this disorder hallucinate complex visual scenes, such as abstract geometric patterns, animals and people. These hallucinations are released as the visual system deteriorates, for instance as a consequence of macular degeneration, cataracts, glaucoma or damage to the visual cortex (e.g., D.F. Hughes (2013), "Charles Bonnet Syndrome: A Literature Review into Diagnostic Criteria, Treatment and Implications for Nursing Practice," *Journal of Psychiatric and Mental Health Nursing* 20(2): 169–175).

31. Alternatively, the object might be incongruent ("aschematic") with personal expectations and isn't noticed because it is so different to these expectations.

32. M. Grissinger (2012), "'Inattentional Blindness'": What Captures Your Attention?," *P and T: A Peer-Reviewed Journal for Formulary Management* 37(10): 542–545.

33. There are exceptions, such as seizures and vegetative states, where patients appear to be awake but are not self-aware. However, such definitional distinctions are beyond the scope of this book.

34. A. Revonsuo, S. Kallio, and P. Sikka (2009), "What Is an Altered State of Consciousness?," *Philosophical Psychology* 22(2): 187–204.

35. H. Evans (1984), *Visions, Apparitions, Alien Visitors* (London: Book Club).

36. *Ibid*.

37. P.F. Malloy and E.D. Richardson (1994), "The Frontal Lobes and Content-Specific Delusions," *Journal of Neuropsychiatry and Clinical Neurosciences* 6(4): 455–466.

38. H.D. Tawney and B. Benson (1956), "Self-Hypnosis and Autosuggestion," in *Hypnosis and You* (pp. 131–147), ed. H.D. Tawney and B. Benson (New York: Fawcett).

Chapter 7

1. M. Kaku (2008), "The Impossible Made Possible," *Prospect* 145, pp. 20–21.

2. C. Fort (1974), *The Complete Books of Charles Fort* (New York: Dover).

3. *Ibid*.

4. *Ibid*.

5. *Ibid*.

6. I interpret Fort to mean that what we call "consciousness" stands outside this functional, reconstitutive activity.

7. Fort, *Complete Books*.

8. *Ibid*.

9. *Ibid*.

10. *Ibid*.

11. Imich died in 2014 at the ripe old age of 111, officially the world's oldest man at the time.

12. A. Imich (1996), "The Variety of Poltergeist Phenomena," *Journal of Religion and Psychical Research* 19(1): 40–41.

13. F. Podmore (2010), *The Naturalisation of the Supernatural* (Whitefish, MT: Kessinger Legacy Reprints [original work published 1908]).

14. R.S. Gordon (2000), *The Paranormal: An Illustrated Encyclopedia* (London: Caxton [original work published 1992]).

15. Fort wrote at a time when many people still wore long white nightgowns.

16. Fort, *Complete Books*.

17. Although (as previously suggested) this might be an expression of an unrecognized relocation rather than an appearance jottle.

18. D.S. Rogo (1979), *The Poltergeist Experience: Investigations into Ghostly Phenomena* (New York: Penguin).

19. Fort, *Complete Books*.

20. M. Brooks (2012), "Does Consciousness Create Reality?," *New Scientist* 215 (2884): 42–43.

21. Anonymous (2005), "Teleportation Is a Reality," *Forest Products Journal* 55(9): 12.

22. Kaku, "The Impossible Made Possible," 20–21.

23. J. Mullins (2011), "A Multiverse of Parallel Worlds," *New Scientist* 210 (2815): 8–9.

24. Kaku, "The Impossible Made Possible," 20–21.

25. J. Bennett (2014), *What Is Relativity?: An Intuitive Introduction to Einstein's Ideas, and Why They Matter* (New York: Columbia University Press).

26. K. Moskvitch (2014), "Thar She Blows," *New Scientist* 223(2978), 2.

27. A. Everett and T. Roman (2012), *Time Travel and Warp Drives: A Scientific Guide to Shortcuts Through Time and Space* (Chicago: University of Chicago Press).

28. *Ibid*.

29. T. Hayden (2008 February 21), "Wormholes Could Be the Way to Go," *USA Today*, retrieved 15 February 2015, http://web.a.ebscohost.com.ezproxy.uws.edu.au /ehost/detail/detail?vid=57andsid=4d7a3b77-29e9-4ebf-b3d8-666b9c8cd2e2%40sessionmgr4001andhid=4214andbdata=JnNpdGU9ZWhvc3QtbGl2ZSZzY29wZT1zaXRl#db=ulhandAN=J0E118880081308.

30. V.M. Neppe and E.R. Close (2011), "Applying Consciousness, Infinity and Dimensionality Creating a Paradigm Shift: Introducing the Triadic Dimensional Distinction Vortical Paradigm," *Neuroquantology* 9(3): 375–392.

31. J. Bergier (1975), *The Secret Doors of the Earth* (Chicago: Henry Regnery).
32. P. Begg (1982) "Appearing People," in *The Directory of Possibilities* (pp. 93–94), ed. C. Wilson and J. Grant (1982) (London: Corgi [original work published 1981]).
33. T. Aym (n.d.), "Terrified Woman from Another Universe Wakes Up Here," retrieved 4 April 2015, http://www.mindpowernews.com/WomanFromAnotherUniverse.html.
34. P. Begg (1982), "Vanishing People," in *The Directory of Possibilities* (pp. 109–112), ed. C. Wilson and J. Grant (1982) (London: Corgi [original work published 1981]).
35. This was also discussed at the *Society of Psychical Research* study day on jottles (2003).
36. The word "moral" was added to the 1896 text and wasn't included in the original 1895 address. The talk was titled, "Is Life Worth Living?," and if you're interested, the answer from James is, "Yes, it is."
37. W. James (1896), "Is Life Worth Living?," in *The Will to Believe: And Other Essays in Popular Philosophy* (pp. 32–62), ed. W. James (London: Longmans, Green).
38. M. Buchanan (2014), "No End to Multiverses," *New Scientist* 221(2952): 45–46.
39. Alan Guth was the physicist who came up with inflation theory in 1980. Of course, inflation is a lot more complicated than the way I'm presenting it here.
40. L. Krauss (2014), "A Beacon from the Big Bang," *Scientific American* 311(4): 58–67.
41. N. Afshordi, R.B. Mann, and R. Pourhasan (2014), "The Black Hole at the Beginning of Time," *Scientific American* 311(2): 36–43.
42. L. Grossman (2014), "Cosmic Ripples Put Inflation to the Test," *New Scientist* 221(2962): 10–11.
43. L. Grossman (2014), "Ripples of the Multiverse," *New Scientist* 221(2961): 8–10.
44. G.F.R. Ellis (2011), "Does the Multiverse Really Exist?," *Scientific American* 305(2): 38–43.
45. Ibid.
46. M.M. Waldrop (1988), "The Quantum Wave Function of the Universe," *Science* 242 (4883): 1248–1250.
47. M. Brooks (2012), "Does Consciousness Create Reality?," *New Scientist* 215 (2884): 42–43.
48. J. Westerhoff (2012), "Is Matter Real?," *New Scientist* 215(2884): 37–44.
49. H.P. Stapp (2009), *Mind, Matter and Quantum Mechanics*, 3rd ed. (Heidelberg: Springer).
50. J. Mullins (2011), "A Multiverse of Parallel Worlds," *New Scientist* 210(2815): 8–9.
51. B.S. DeWitt (1973), "The Many-Universes Interpretation of Quantum Mechanics," in *The Many Worlds Interpretation of Quantum Mechanics* (pp. 167–218), ed. B.S. DeWitt and N. Graham (Princeton, NJ: Princeton University Press).
52. M.D. Jones and L. Flaxman (2012), *This Book Is from the Future: A Journey Through Portals, Relativity, Worm Holes, and Other Adventures in Time Travel* (Pompton Plains, NJ: New Page).
53. R. Hooper (2014), "Life in the Multiverse," *New Scientist* 223(2988): 32–37.
54. J. Mullins (2011), "A Multiverse of Parallel Worlds," *New Scientist* 210(2815): 8–9
55. S. Goforth (2005), "Forget Rocket Ships. Teleport!," *Popular Science* 266(2), 87–88.
56. B. Carr and G. Ellis (2008), "Universe or Multiverse?," *Astronomy and Geophysics: Journal of the Royal Astronomical Society* 49(2): 2.29–2.33.
57. L. Grossman (2014), "Quantum Twist Kills the Multiverse," *New Scientist* 222 (2969): 8–9.
58. E.J. Squires (1991), "One Mind or Many: A Note on the Everett Interpretation of Quantum Theory," *Synthese* 89(2), 283–286.
59. G. Grant (1982), "Parallel Worlds," in *The Directory of Possibilities* (pp. 226–227), ed. C. Wilson and J. Grant, J. (London: Corgi [Original work published 1981]).
60. Fort, *Complete Books*.
61. B. Schutz (2003), *Gravity from the Ground Up: An Introductory Guide to Gravity and General Relativity* (Cambridge: Cambridge University Press).

Chapter 8

1. B. Rickard and J. Michell (2007), *The Rough Guide to Unexplained Phenomena*, 2nd ed. (London: Rough Guides).
2. M.A. Thalbourne (n.d.), "The Transhumanation Hypothesis," *Journal of the American Society for Psychical Research*, retrieved 22 December 2014, http://www.psychognosis.net/cgi-bin/default.pl?page=viewdocanddoc=thalb1andgroup=3.
3. J. Bynum (1993), "Poltergeists: A Phenomenon Worthy of Serious Study," *ETC: A Review of General Semantics* 50(2): 221–226.
4. L. Auerbach (2004), *Hauntings and Poltergeists: A Ghost Hunter's Guide* (Oakland, CA: Ronin).
5. D. Cohen (1984), *The Encyclopedia of Ghosts* (London: Guild).
6. L. Storm and R. Tilley (2002), "Expe-

riences: Precognitive Dreams, Poltergeist Disturbances and Hauntings," *Australian Journal of Parapsychology* 2(2): 125–160.

7. This "clearing" was successful, as the two spirits apparently "moved on."

8. F.W.H. Myers (2013), *Human Personality and Its Survival of Bodily Death* (London: Forgotten Books [original work published 1907]).

9. G.E. Schwartz (2010), "Possible Application of Silicon Photomultiplier Technology to Detect the Presence of Spirit and Intention: Three Proof-of-Concept Experiments," *Explore* 6(3): 166–171.

10. Used in the correct Latin sense of a soul returning to this realm after death (without any nefarious connotations).

11. I couldn't use this story in the collection because details were lacking (the actual object and time delays), although it is still a good example of a jottle associated with a revenant.

12. G. Schwartz (2011), "Photonic Measurement of Apparent Presence of Spirit Using a Computer Automated System," *Explore* 7 (2): 100–109.

13. From a radically different perspective, it might be that that spirits aren't energy at all but are seen "telepathically," bypassing the normal senses entirely (as proposed by physicist George Tyrrell). That is beyond the scope of this argument.

14. For many decades the energy-carrying particles called neutrinos have been termed ghost particles by physicists because they are "elusive, weakly interacting [and] putatively massless" (see D.E. Thomsen (1975), "Odd Particles Out," *Science News* 108 (8/9): 140–140). Not surprisingly, decades later we're told that ghosts are comprised of neutrinos!

15. T. Besterman and O. Gatty (1934), "Investigation of Paraphysical Phenomena," *Nature* 133(3363): 569–57.

16. R.P. Flaherty (2010), "'These Are They': ET-Human Hybridization and the New Daemonology," *Nova Religio: Journal of Alternative and Emergent Religion* 14(2): 84–105.

17. G. Creighton (1983), "A Brief Account of the True Nature of the 'UFO Entities,'" *Flying Saucer Review* 29(5), 1–9, retrieved 8 November 2014, http://www.sacred-texts.com/ufo/jinns.htm.

18. R. Kirk and A. Lang (2003), *The Secret Commonwealth of Elves, Fauns and Fairies* (New York: Cosimo [originally published 1691/1893]).

19. R. Black (2005), "Introduction," in *The Gaelic Otherworld: Rev. John Gregorson Campbell's Superstitions of the Highlands and Islands and Witchcraft and Second Sight in the Highlands and Islands of Scotland*, ed. R. Black (Edinburgh, UK: Birlinn).

20. H. Evans (1984), *Visions, Apparitions, Alien Visitors* (London: Book Club).

21. Ibid.

22. O. Lodge (1921), "Testimony to a Child's Impression of Fairies," *Journal of the Society for Psychical Research* 20: 63–70.

23. R. Shaeffer (1977), "Do Fairies Exist?," *Zetetic* 2(1), 45–52.

24. Evans, *Visions, Apparitions, Alien Visitors*.

25. Campbell, "The Fairies," in *The Gaelic Otherworld*.

26. Ibid.

27. F. Hartmann (1992), *The Life and the Doctrines of Philippus Theophrastus, Bombast of Hohenheim, Known by the Name of Paracelsus* (Whitefish MT: Kessinger [original work published 1891]).

28. Paracelsus contributed a lot more to human knowledge than this obscure categorization of elementals, so he shouldn't be remembered just for this.

29. Hartmann, *The Life and the Doctrines of Philippus Theophrastus*.

30. H.P. Blavatsky (1966), *Collected Writings*, vol. 6 (Wheaton, IL: Quest Books [original work published 1954]).

31. Ibid.

32. Theosophists used "fourth dimension" to describe the astral plane where noncorporeal elementals reside.

33. H.P. Blavatsky (2012), *Isis Unveiled: A Master-Key to the Mysteries of Ancient and Modern Science and Theology*, vol. 1, Science (New York: Cambridge University Press [original Work published 1877]).

34. R. Bainton (2013), *The Mammoth Book of Unexplained Phenomena* (London: Constable and Robinson).

35. R.B. Durham (2015), *Charles Webster Leadbeater: The Astral Plane, the Devachanic Plane, Clairvoyance, the Inner Life*, vols. 1, 2 (Morrisville, NC: Lulu).

36. Ibid.

37. J.A. Keel (1973), *Operation Trojan Horse* (London: Sphere).

38. Ibid.

Chapter 9

1. The assumption is that something intelligent built the vending machine in the first place, just as it must be considered that the purposeful process of teleportation—while "blind"—was developed with original intention.

2. Fort, *Complete Books*.

3. Fort saw ostensibly religious events, such as blood flows from holy objects, as expressions of teleportation (he felt there was no necessary difference between fluid emanating from the walls of a house and fluid from a "holy image"). This is a purely secular approach. While it might assume an omnipotent natural force, it doesn't consider, for example, the material provenance of the Christian God.
4. A. Imich (2007), "Report about Teleportation of a Living Person," *Journal of Spirituality and Paranormal Studies* 30(4): 230–231.
5. Fort, *Complete Books*.
6. *Ibid*.
7. Durham, *Charles Webster Leadbeater*.
8. A. Iqbal (2013), "A Replication of the Slight Effect of Human Thought on a Pseudorandom Number Generator," *Neuroquantology* 11(4): 519–526.
9. H. Evans (2010), *Sliders: The Enigma of Streetlight Interference* (San Antonio: Anomalist).
10. D.S. Rogo (1979), *The Poltergeist Experience: Investigations into Ghostly Phenomena* (New York: Penguin).
11. Fort, *Complete Books*.
12. *Ibid*.
13. P.R. Burgess (2012), "Recurrent Spontaneous Anomalous Physical Events Suggestive of Poltergeist Activity: Evidence for Discarnate Agency?; Clinical, Evolutionary and Learning Perspectives," *Journal of the Society for Psychical Research* 76(906): 1–16.
14. N. Fodor (1948), "The Poltergeist—Psychoanalysed," *Psychiatric Quarterly* 22: 195–203.
15. M.C. Maher (2000), "Quantitative Investigation of the General Wayne Inn," *Journal of Parapsychology* 64(4): 365–390.
16. W.G. Roll and M.A. Persinger (2001), "Investigations of Poltergeists and Haunts: A Review and Interpretation," in *Hauntings and Poltergeists: Multidisciplinary Perspectives* (pp. 123–163), ed. J. Houran and R. Lange (Jefferson, NC: McFarland).
17. W.G. Roll, K.S. Saroka, B.P. Mulligan, M.D. Hunter, B.T. Dotta, N. Gang, M.A. Scott, L.S. St-Pierre and M.A. Persinger (2012), "Case Report: A Prototypical Experience of 'Poltergeist' Activity, Conspicuous Quantitative Electroencephalographic Patterns, and sLORETA Profiles; Suggestions for Intervention," *NeuroCase* 18(6): 527–36.
18. J. Ehrenwald (1979), "Psi Phenomena, Hemispheric Dominance and the Existential Shift," *Parapsychology Review* 9(5): 1–3.
19. Roll argued that RSPK can also describe the forces utilized by discarnate entities, which I believe is confusing the issue. Whatever energies discarnates might use to effect object displacements, let's not call it RSPK.
20. J. Bynum (1993), "Poltergeists: A Phenomenon Worthy of Serious Study," *ETC: A Review of General Semantics* 50(2): 221–226.
21. B. Ingliss (1986), *The Paranormal: An Encyclopedia of Psychic Phenomena* (London: Grafton).
22. W.G. Roll (1972), *The Poltergeist* (New York: Nelson Doubleday).
23. Admittedly, many poltergeist cases refer to levitating metal objects. In 1966, the Pritchard family of Pontefract, Yorkshire, was afflicted by a poltergeist that caused metal pots and candlesticks to levitate. Some wondered whether the ghost of a monk executed at the site of the house in the 16th century was to blame, although author Colin Wilson took the more prosaic stance that 15-year-old Philip Pritchard's puberty and his tension with his father, Joe, were the cause of the events.
24. Roll and Persinger, "Investigations of Poltergeists and Haunts," 123–163.
25. The supporting consensus is that a deceased spirit, or even a demon, caused the activity rather than its being a display of adolescent RSPK from Janice Hodgson. The skeptical view is that Janet and her older sister Margaret were responsible for the mischief.
26. A claim that will always be rejected by skeptics.
27. A. Green (1976), *Ghost Hunting. A Practical Guide* (St. Albans: Mayflower [original work published 1973]).
28. S. Krippner (1982), *Advances in Parapsychological Research*, vol. 3 (New York: Plenum).
29. A. Gauld and A.D. Cornell (1979), *Poltergeists* (London: Routledge & Kegan Paul).
30. Holt, "Things That Come, Go and Relocate," 31–33.
31. W.G. Roll and W.T. Joines (2013), "RSPK and Consciousness," *Journal of Parapsychology* 77(2): 192–211.
32. L. Browne (in press), "Some Difficulties in Coincidence Analysis," *Australian Journal of Parapsychology*.
33. *Ibid*.
34. M.A. Thalbourne (n.d.), "The Transhumanation Hypothesis," *Journal of the American Society for Psychical Research*, retrieved 22 December 2014, http://www.psychognosis.net/cgi-bin/default.pl?page=viewdocanddoc=thalb1andgroup=3.
35. *Ibid*.
36. P.R. Burgess (2012), "Recurrent Spon-

taneous Anomalous Physical Events Suggestive of Poltergeist Activity: Evidence for Discarnate Agency?: Clinical, Evolutionary and Learning Perspectives," *Journal of the Society for Psychical Research* 76(906): 1–16.

Chapter 10

1. J. Vallee (1988), *Dimensions: A Casebook of Alien Contact* (London: Souvenir).
2. Just as I was finishing this book, I heard a firsthand story from a gentleman who claimed he'd experienced a jottle and at around the same time observed what could only be described as a small elemental entity in his bedroom. That's surely an "elemental jottle."
3. Vallee, *Dimensions*.
4. My elemental-observing gentleman is a rare exception.
5. V.M. Neppe and E.R. Close (2011), "Applying Consciousness, Infinity and Dimensionality Creating a Paradigm Shift: Introducing the Triadic Dimensional Distinction Vortical Paradigm," *Neuroquantology* 9(3): 375–392.
6. Westerhoff, "Is Matter Real?," 37–44.
7. P. Byrne (2010), *The Many Worlds of Hugh Everett: Multiple Universes, Mutual Assured Destruction, and the Meltdown of a Nuclear Family* (Oxford: Oxford University Press).
8. J. Westerhoff (2011), *Reality: A Very Short Introduction* (Oxford: Oxford University Press).
9. Thankfully avoiding the doctrine of *continuous creation*.
10. Resembling physicist David Bohm's *implicate order*.
11. I. Baruss (2006), "Quantum Theories of Consciousness," *Baltic Journal of Psychology* 7(1): 39–45.
12. Transpersonal theorists might argue these are derived from extended or "deep" consciousness (a collective unconscious perhaps) which resides outside of space-time.
13. Holt, "Things That Come, Go and Relocate," 31–33.
14. I haven't bothered to check, but I don't think I'll ever find the original roll of wire in the garage.
15. And there's no accounting for events discussed in chapter 7 that are outwardly similar to jottles but are also distinct from them—such as showers of rocks or seeds or questionable stories of disappearing and appearing people.

Bibliography

Afshordi, N., R.B. Mann, and R. Pourhasan (2014). "The Black Hole at the Beginning of Time." *Scientific American* 311, no. 2.

Anonymous (2005). "Teleportation Is a Reality." *Forest Products Journal* 55, no. 9.

Auerbach, L. (2004). *Hauntings and Poltergeists: A Ghost Hunter's Guide*. Oakland, CA: Ronin.

Aym, T. (n.d.). "Terrified Woman from Another Universe Wakes Up Here." Retrieved April 4, 2015. http://www.mindpowernews.com/WomanFromAnotherUniverse.html.

Bader, C.D. (2003). "Supernatural Support Groups: Who Are the UFO Abductees and Ritual-Abuse Survivors?" *Journal for the Scientific Study of Religion* 42, no. 4.

Bainton, R. (2013). *The Mammoth Book of Unexplained Phenomena*. London: Constable and Robinson.

Barrington, M.R. (1991). "JOTT—Just One of Those Things." *Psi Researcher* 3.

Barušs, I. (2006). "Quantum Theories of Consciousness." *Baltic Journal of Psychology* 7, no. 1.

Bauer, O.P.J, and M. Larkina. (2014). "Childhood Amnesia in the Making: Different Distributions of Autobiographical Memories in Children and Adults." *Journal of Experimental Psychology: General* 143, no. 2.

_____. (2014). "The Onset of Childhood Amnesia in Childhood: A Prospective Investigation of the Course and Determinants of Forgetting of Early-life Events." *Memory* 22, no. 8.

Beanland, V., and K. Pammer. (2010). "Looking Without Seeing or Seeing Without Looking?: Eye Movements in Sustained Inattentional Blindness." *Vision Research* 50, no. 10.

Begg, P. (1982). "Appearing People." In *The Directory of Possibilities*. Edited by C. Wilson and J. Grant. London: Corgi (original work published in 1981).

_____. (1982). "Vanishing People." (1982). In *The Directory of Possibilities*. Edited by C. Wilson and J. Grant. London: Corgi (original work published in 1981).

Bennett, J. (2014). *What Is Relativity? An Intuitive Introduction to Einstein's Ideas, and Why They Matter*. New York: Columbia University Press.

Bergier, J. (1975). *The Secret Doors of the Earth*. Chicago: Henry Regnery.

Besterman, T., and O. Gatty. (1934). "Investigation of Paraphysical Phenomena." *Nature* 133, no. 3363.

Black, R. (2005). Introduction. In *The Gaelic Otherworld: Rev. John Gregorson Campbell's Superstitions of the Highlands and Islands and Witchcraft and Second Sight in the Highlands and Islands of Scotland*. Edited by R. Black. Edinburgh: Birlinn.

Blavatsky, H.P. (1966). *Collected Writings*. Vol. 6. Wheaton, IL: Quest (original work published in 1954).

_____. (2012). *Isis Unveiled: A Master-Key to the Mysteries of Ancient and Modern Science and Theology*. Vol. 1, *Science*. New York: Cambridge University Press (original work published in 1877).

Brooks, M. (2012). "Does Consciousness

Create Reality?" *New Scientist* 215, no. 2884.
Browne, L. (in press). "Some Difficulties in Coincidence Analysis." *Australian Journal of Parapsychology.*
Buchanan, M. (2014). "No End to Multiverses." *New Scientist* 221, no. 2952.
Burgess, P.R. (2012). "Recurrent Spontaneous Anomalous Physical Events Suggestive of Poltergeist Activity: Evidence for Discarnate Agency?; Clinical, Evolutionary and Learning Perspectives." *Journal of the Society for Psychical Research* 76, no. 906.
Bynum, J. (1993). "Poltergeists: A Phenomenon Worthy of Serious Study." *ETC: A Review of General Semantics* 50, no. 2.
Byrne, P. (2010). *The Many Worlds of Hugh Everett: Multiple Universes, Mutual Assured Destruction, and the Meltdown of a Nuclear Family.* Oxford: Oxford University Press.
Campbell, J.G. (2005). "The Fairies." In *The Gaelic Otherworld: Rev. John Gregorson Campbell's Superstitions of the Highlands and Islands and Witchcraft and Second Sight in the Highlands and Islands of Scotland.* Edited by R. Black. Edinburgh: Birlinn.
Cardeña, S., S.J. Lynn, and S. Krippner. (2000). "Introduction: Anomalous Experiences in Perspective." In *Varieties of Anomalous Experience: Examining the Scientific Evidence.* Edited by E. Cardena and S. Lynn. Washington, D.C.: American Psychological Association.
Carr, B., and G. Ellis. (2008). "Universe or Multiverse?" *Astronomy and Geophysics: Journal of the Royal Astronomical Society* 49, no. 2.
Cheyne, J.A., J.S.A. Carriere, and D. Smilek. (2006). "Absent-Mindedness: Lapses of Conscious Awareness and Everyday Cognitive Failures." *Consciousness and Cognition* 15, no. 3.
Cohen, D. (1984). *The Encyclopedia of Ghosts.* London: Guild.
Creighton, G. (1983). "A Brief Account of the True Nature of the 'UFO Entities.'" *Flying Saucer Review* 29, no. 5. Retrieved November 8, 2014. http://www.sacred-texts.com/ufo/jinns.htm.
DeWitt, B.S. (1973). "The Many-Universes Interpretation of Quantum Mechanics." In *The Many Worlds Interpretation of Quantum Mechanics.* Edited by B.S. DeWitt and N. Graham. Princeton, NJ: Princeton University Press.
Durham, R.B. (2015). *Charles Webster Leadbeater: The Astral Plane, the Devachanic Plane, Clairvoyance, the Inner Life.* Vol. 1 and 2. Morrisville, NC: Lulu.
Ehrenwald, J. (1979). "Psi Phenomena, Hemispheric Dominance and the Existential Shift." *Parapsychology Review* 9, no. 5.
Ellis, G.F.R. (2011). "Does the Multiverse Really Exist?" *Scientific American* 305, no. 2.
Evans, H. (2010). *Sliders: The Enigma of Streetlight Interference.* San Antonio: Anomalist.
_____. (1984). *Visions, Apparitions, Alien Visitors.* London: Book Club.
Everett, A., and T. Roman. (2012). *Time Travel and Warp Drives: A Scientific Guide to Shortcuts Through Time and Space.* Chicago: University of Chicago Press.
Festinger, L. (1985). *A Theory of Cognitive Dissonance.* Stanford, CA: Stanford University Press (original work published in 1957).
Flaherty, R.P. (2010). "'These Are They': ET-Human Hybridization and the New Daemonology." *Nova Religio: Journal of Alternative and Emergent Religion* 14, no. 2.
Fodor, N. (1948). "The Poltergeist—Psychoanalysed." *Psychiatric Quarterly* 22.
Fort, C. (1974). *The Complete Books of Charles Fort.* New York: Dover.
Gauld, A., and A.D. Cornell. (1979). *Poltergeists.* London: Routledge and Kegan Paul.
Goforth, S. (2005). "Forget Rocket Ships: Teleport!" *Popular Science* 266, no. 2.
Gordon, R.S. (2000). *The Paranormal: An Illustrated Encyclopedia.* London: Caxton (original work published in 1992).
Grant, G. (1982). "Parallel Worlds." In *Directory of Possibilities.* Edited by C. Wilson and J. Grant. London: Corgi (original work published in 1981).
Green, A. (1976). "Ghost Hunting: A Prac-

tical Guide." St Albans: Mayflower (original work published in 1973).

Grissinger, M. (2012). "'Inattentional Blindness': What Captures Your Attention?" *P and T: A Peer-Reviewed Journal for Formulary Management* 37, no. 10.

Grossman, L. (2014). "Cosmic Ripples Put Inflation to the Test." *New Scientist* 221, no. 2962.

____. (2014). "Quantum Twist Kills the Multiverse." *New Scientist* 222, no. 2969.

____. (2014). "Ripples of the Multiverse." *New Scientist* 221, no. 2961.

Hartmann, F. (1992). *The Life and the Doctrines of Philippus Theophrastus, Bombast of Hohenheim, Known by the Name of Paracelsus.* Whitefish, MT: Kessinger (original work published 1891).

Hayden, T. (21 February 2008). "Wormholes Could Be the Way to Go." *USA Today*. Retrieved February 11, 201. http://web.a.ebscohost.com.ezproxy.uws.edu.au/ehost/detail/detail?vid=57&sid=4d7a3b77-29e9-4ebf-b3d8-666b9c8cd2e2%40sessionmgr4001&hid=4214&bdata=JnNpdGU9ZWhvc3QtbGl2ZSZzY29wZT1zaXRl#db=ulh&AN=J0E118880081308.

Holt, N. (2004). "Study Day No. 45: Discontinuities: Things That Come, Go and Relocate." *Paranormal Review* 30.

Hooper, R. (2014). "Life in the Multiverse." *New Scientist* 223, no. 2988.

Hughes, D.F. (2013). "Charles Bonnet Syndrome: A Literature Review into Diagnostic Criteria, Treatment and Implications for Nursing Practice." *Journal of Psychiatric and Mental Health Nursing* 20, no. 2.

Hyman, Jr., I.E., S.M. Boss, B.M. Wise, K.E. McKenzie, and J.M. Caggiano. (2010). "Did You See the Unicycling Clown? Inattentional Blindness While Walking and Talking on a Cell Phone." *Applied Cognitive Psychology* 24, no. 5.

Hynek, J.A. (1974). *The UFO Experience*. London: Corgi (original work published in 1972).

Imich, A. (2007). "Report About Teleportation of a Living Person." *Journal of Spirituality and Paranormal Studies* 30, no. 4.

____. (1996). "The Variety of Poltergeist Phenomena." *Journal of Religion and Psychical Research* 19, no. 1.

Ingliss, B. (1986). *The Paranormal: An Encyclopedia of Psychic Phenomena*. London: Grafton.

Iqbal, A. (2013). "A Replication of the Slight Effect of Human Thought on a Pseudorandom Number Generator." *Neuroquantology* 11, no. 4.

Irwin, H.J., and C.A. Watt. (2007). *An Introduction to Parapsychology.* 5th ed. Jefferson, NC: McFarland.

James, W. (1896). "Is Life Worth Living?" In *The Will to Believe and Other Essays in Popular Philosophy*. Edited by W. James. London: Longmans, Green.

Jinks, A. (2011). *An Introduction to the Psychology of Paranormal Belief and Experience*. Jefferson, NC: McFarland.

Jones, M.D., and L. Flaxman. (2012). *This Book Is from the Future: A Journey Through Portals, Relativity, Worm Holes, and Other Adventures in Time Travel*. Pompton Plains, NJ: New Page.

Kaku, M. (2008). "The Impossible Made Possible." *Prospect* 145.

Keel, J.A. (1973). *Operation Trojan Horse*. London: Sphere.

Kirk, R., and A. Lang. (2003). *The Secret Commonwealth of Elves, Fauns and Fairies*. New York: Cosimo (originally published in 1691/1893).

Klass, P.J. (1997). "FAA Data Sheds New Light on JAL Pilot's UFO Report." In *The UFO Invasion: The Roswell Incident, Alien Abductions, and Government Coverups.* Edited by K. Frazier, B. Karr and J. Nickell. New York: Prometheus.

Krauss, L. (2014). "A Beacon from the Big Bang." *Scientific American* 311, no. 4.

Krippner, S. (1982). *Advances in Parapsychological Research*. Vol. 3. New York: Plenum.

Lanciano, T., and A. Curci. (2011). "Memory for Emotional Events: The Accuracy of Central and Peripheral Details." *Europe's Journal of Psychology* 7, no. 2.

Lewis, T. (2014). *Haunted Inns and Ghostly Getaways of Vermont*. Charleston, SC: Haunted America.

Lodge, O. (1921). "Testimony to a Child's Impression of Fairies." *Journal of the Society for Psychical Research* 20.

Loftus, E.F. (2003). "Make-believe Memories." *American Psychologist* 58, no. 11.

Maher, M.C. (2000). "Quantitative Investigation of the General Wayne Inn." *Journal of Parapsychology* 64, no. 4.

Malloy, P.F., and E.D. Richardson. (1994). "The Frontal Lobes and Content-Specific Delusions." *Journal of Neuropsychiatry and Clinical Neurosciences* 6, no. 4.

Marusich, J.A., T.W. Lefever, K.R. Antonazzo, R.M. Craft, and J.L. Wiley. (2014). "Evaluation of Sex Differences in Cannabinoid Dependence." *Drug and Alcohol Dependence* 137.

Mazzoni, G., and M. Vannucci. (2007). "Hindsight Bias, the Misinformation Effect, and False Autobiographical Memories." *Social Cognition* 25, no. 1.

Morwitz, V.G. (1997). "It Seems Like Only Yesterday: The Nature and Consequences of Telescoping Errors in Marketing Research." *Journal of Consumer Psychology* 6, no. 1.

Moskvitch, K. (2014). "Thar She Blows." *New Scientist* 223, no. 2978.

Most, S.B., B.J. Scholl, E.R. Clifford, and D.J. Simons. (2005). "What You See Is What You Set: Sustained Inattentional Blindness and the Capture of Awareness." *Psychological Review* 112, no. 1.

Mullins, J. (2011). "A Multiverse of Parallel Worlds." *New Scientist* 210, no. 2815.

Myers, F.W.H. (2013). *Human Personality and Its Survival of Bodily Death.* London: Forgotten (original work published in 1907).

Neppe, V.M., and E.R. Close. (2011). "Applying Consciousness, Infinity and Dimensionality Creating a Paradigm Shift: Introducing the Triadic Dimensional Distinction Vortical Paradigm." *Neuroquantology* 9, no. 3.

Otgaar, H., A. Scoboria, and T. Smeets. (2013). "Experimentally Evoking Nonbelieved Memories for Childhood Events." *Journal of Experimental Psychology: Learning, Memory, and Cognition* 39, no. 3.

Podmore, F. (2010). *The Naturalisation of the Supernatural.* Whitefish, MT: Kessinger Legacy Reprints (original work published in 1908).

Rabeyron, T., and C. Watt. (2010). "Paranormal Experiences, Mental Health and Mental Boundaries, and Psi." *Personality and Individual Differences* 48, no. 4.

Ramachandran, V.S. (1992). "Filling in Gaps in Perception: Part 1." *Current Directions in Psychological Science* 1, no. 6.

Read, S.J., and M.B. Rosson. (1982). "Rewriting History: The Biasing Effects of Attitudes on Memory." *Social Cognition* 1, no. 3.

Revonsuo, A., S. Kallio and P. Sikka. (2009). "What Is an Altered State of Consciousness?" *Philosophical Psychology* 22, no. 2.

Richards, A., M.G. Hellgren, and C.C. French. (2014). "Inattentional Blindness, Absorption, Working Memory Capacity, and Paranormal Belief." *Psychology of Consciousness: Theory, Research, and Practice* 1, no. 1.

Rickard, B., and J. Michell. (2007). *The Rough Guide to Unexplained Phenomena.* 2nd ed. London: Rough Guides.

Rim, S.Y., K.E. Min, J.S. Uleman, T.L. Chartrand, and D.E. Carlston. (2013). "Seeing Others Through Rose-Colored Glasses: An Affiliation Goal and Positivity Bias in Implicit Trait Impressions." *Journal of Experimental Social Psychology* 49, no. 6.

Rogerson, P. (2010, July 29). "Slide Rules." *Magonia Blog.* Retrieved November 8, 2014. http://pelicanist.blogspot.com.au/2010/07/slide-rules.html.

Rogo, D.S. (1979). *The Poltergeist Experience: Investigations into Ghostly Phenomena.* New York: Penguin.

Roll, W.G., K.S. Saroka, B.P. Mulligan, M.D. Hunter, B.T. Dotta, N. Gang, M.A. Scott, L.S. St-Pierre, and M.A. Persinger. (2012). "Case Report: A Prototypical Experience of 'Poltergeist' Activity, Conspicuous Quantitative Electroencephalographic Patterns, and sLORETA Profiles—Suggestions for Intervention." *Neurocase* 18, no. 6.

Roll, W.G. (1972). *The Poltergeist*. New York: Nelson Doubleday.

Roll, W.G., and M.A. Persinger. (2001). "Investigations of Poltergeists and Haunts: A Review and Interpretation." In *Hauntings and Poltergeists: Multidisciplinary Perspectives*. Edited by J. Houran and R. Lange. Jefferson, NC: McFarland.

Roll, W.G., and W.T. Joines. (2013). "RSPK and Consciousness." *Journal of Parapsychology* 77, no. 2.

Schacter, D.L., J.Y. Chiao, and J.P. Mitchell. (2003). "The Seven Sins of Memory: Implications for Self." *Annals of the New York Academy of Sciences* 1001.

Schutz, B. (2003). *Gravity from the Ground Up: An Introductory Guide to Gravity and General Relativity*. Cambridge: Cambridge University Press.

Schwartz, G. (2011). "Photonic Measurement of Apparent Presence of Spirit Using a Computer Automated System." *Explore* 7, no. 2.

Schwartz, G.E. (2010). "Possible Application of Silicon Photomultiplier Technology to Detect the Presence of Spirit and Intention: Three Proof-of-Concept Experiments." *Explore* 6, no. 3.

Shaeffer, R. (1977). "Do Fairies Exist?" *Zetetic* 2, no. 1.

Slavich, G.M., and P.G. Zimbardo. (2013). "Out of Mind, Out of Sight: Unexpected Scene Elements Frequently Go Unnoticed Until Primed." *Current Psychology* 32, no. 4.

Squires, E.J. (1991). "One Mind or Many: A Note on the Everett Interpretation of Quantum Theory." *Synthese* 89, no. 2.

Stapp, H.P. (2009). *Mind, Matter and Quantum Mechanics*. 3rd ed. Heidelberg: Springer.

Storm, L., and R. Tilley. (2002). "Experiences: Precognitive Dreams, Poltergeist Disturbances and Hauntings." *Australian Journal of Parapsychology* 2, no. 2.

Strange, D., and H. Hayne. (2013). "The Devil Is in the Detail: Children's Recollection of Details About Their Prior Experiences." *Memory* 21, no. 4.

Talarico, J.M., D.C. Rubin. (2007). "Flashbulb Memories Are Special After All: In Phenomenology, Not Accuracy." *Applied Cognitive Psychology* 21, no. 5.

Tawney, H.D., and B. Benson. (1956). "Self-Hypnosis and Autosuggestion." In *Hypnosis and You*. Edited by H.D. Tawney and B. Benson. New York: Fawcett.

Taylor, A.K. (2013). "Leveling and Sharpening." In *Encyclopedia of Human Memory* Vol. 1. Edited by A.K. Taylor. Santa Barbara, CA: ABC-CLIO.

Thalbourne, M.A. (2003). *A Glossary of Terms Used in Parapsychology*. 2nd ed. Charlottesville, VA: Puente.

_____. (n.d.). "The Transhumanation Hypothesis." *Journal of the American Society for Psychical Research*. Retrieved December 22, 2014. http://www.psychognosis.net/cgi-bin/default.pl?page=viewdocanddoc=thalb1&group=3.

Thomsen, D.E. (1975). "Odd Particles Out." *Science News* 108, no. 8/9.

Vallee, J. (1988). *Dimensions: A Casebook of Alien Contact*. London: Souvenir.

Waldrop, M.M. (1988). "The Quantum Wave Function of the Universe." *Science* 242, no. 4883.

Weir, K. (2014). "Your Cheating Brain." *New Scientist* 221, no. 2961.

Westerhoff, J. (2011). *Reality: A Very Short Introduction*. Oxford: Oxford University Press.

Westerhoff, J. (2012). "Is Matter Real?" *New Scientist* 215, no. 2884.

Index

absent-mindedness 82–84, 86, 90, 95
alien abduction 30
Alleyne, Celia 132
altered states of consciousness 89, 91–92, 95, 104, 132, 152
alternative universes 109
Andy's story 63
anthropic principle 117
autobiographical memories 82

Barrett, William 144
Barrington, Mary-Rose 2, 14, 21, 24, 128, 163
Belinda's story 87–89
Bergier, Jacques 109
Big Bang theory 109, 112, 117
Bigfoot 79
black holes 122
Blavatsky, Helen 135–136
Burgess, Paul 155–156, 164

Cameron's story 24, 26, 158
Charles Bonet syndrome 89
Christian's story 57, 58
Chris' story 21
clairvoyance 144
cognitive dissonance 79, 80
Colin's story 27, 28, 70
confirmation bias 85–86, 95
consciousness 91
content-specific delusions 92–94, 160
Copenhagen interpretation 114
Creighton, Gordon 131

daemons 131–132
Danton Walker case 127–128, 144
Dave's story 54, 74, 152–154, 157
Deborah's story 15, 27–28, 69, 119, 156
decoherence 116
déjà vu 104
DeWitt, Bryce 115
druids 132
duplicated objects 22–23

Ed's story 46
El Amin case 142
Eleanor's story 32, 54, 129–130, 164
electromagnetic radiation 99, 129–130, 138
elementals 134–140, 158–160
Enfield case 148
entanglement 106, 151
ether 136–137
Evans, Hilary 92, 94
Everett, Hugh 115
exotic matter 108

fairies 126, 131–134, 140
fast loss/fast return theory 58, 64, 67, 74
Festinger, Leo 79
Fodor, Nandor 145
Fort, Charles 51, 100–105, 118, 121, 123, 125, 136, 141–145; *Lo!* 101; *The Book of the Damned* 100–101
fugue states 91, 95, 104

Garrett, Eileen 127
gravitational waves 113
Greg's story 22, 117
Greta's story 51
Grosse, Maurice 20

hallucinations 92, 95
Heisenberg's uncertainty principle 106
hemispheric dominance 146
Holt, Nicola 128
Hynek, J. Allen 10–11
hypnosis 94–95

idealism 161
Imich, Alexander 103, 142
inattentional blindness 95, 87–90
inflatons 113
intention theory 54, 61, 66, 70, 72–74, 98, 120, 124, 126, 140, 150, 152, 158–159, 164
interaction theory 40, 42, 51, 53, 70, 74, 98, 120, 124, 152, 158–159, 163

invisibility 97, 98–99
isotopic universe 113

James, William 112
Jeff's story 66
Jemma's story 33
Jessica's story 22–24, 32
jinn 131
jottles: age of experient 30; behavior of object 43; categories of object 37–38; frequency 37–42; imaginary stories 43–44; location 18–19; object significance 16–17, 42–43; occupation of experient 30; seamlessness 159–160; sex differences 37
Jung, Carl 153

Kate's story 1, 3–6, 8, 14–15, 24–26, 108, 120–121, 142, 152, 158, 160, 165,
Katrina's story 50, 52
Keel, John 138–139
Kevin's story 18–19
Kirk, Robert 131–132

Lauren's story 79–80
Leadbeater, C.W. 137, 139, 143
Lerina García case 110–111, 114, 118, 121
Linda's story 61–62
living agent hypothesis 145
long-delay relocation 59, 64, 67, 74

macro-psi 154
Maher, Michlaeleen 145
Malcolm's story 16, 29
Mandy's story 18
many minds interpretation 117
many worlds interpretation 115
Marcus' story 67
Mark's story 2–9, 14–15, 20, 36, 63, 85, 131, 152
Martin's story 10, 14–15, 20, 51, 54, 124–126, 142
meaningfulness 32–33
memory: childhood amnesia 81; episodic memories 82; errors of commission 84; telescoping errors 82; transience 82, 84
Mia's stories 65
Michell, John 125
Michelle's story 48
Mitchell's story 63
multiverses 97, 112–121
Myers, Frederick 128

Naomi's story 20
Nicholas' story 65–66
Nicklheim case 149

Olive Hill case 149
other dimensions 97, 121–123

Paracelsus 134–135
paranormal belief 84
paraphysical entities 97
Pat's story 19, 29, 31
perceptual conspicuity 90
Pérez case 103–105, 131
peripatetic consciousness 117–118
phase change (of matter) 139
plasma 139
Podmore, Frank 103
poltergeists 33, 126–128, 131, 140, 144–150
Poona case 147, 149
positive bias 79–80
psychokinesis 98, 144–153, 155–156, 158–160
Puthoff, Harold 151

quantum teleportation 106–107, 158–160
quantum wave function 105, 114, 160

repeaters 31–32, 36, 84
repression 145
revenants 129
Rickard, Bob 125
Robert's stories 25–26, 31, 66, 157, 165
Robinson case 143
Rogerson, Peter 86
Roll, William 146, 148, 150
Rousseau, David 150
Rowan's story 25
Ruth's story 129–130, 164

Samantha's story 68
Sam's story 17, 165
Schacter, Daniel 81
schemas 89
Schrödinger, Erwin 114–115, 161
Schwartz, Gary 128
scotoma 89
Seaford case 147–148
séances 131, 137, 143
sense of presence 33
Shirley's story 30–31
Sophia's story 31
spacetime 107
Spinoza, Baruch 102
spirit presence 126, 128–129, 140
spontaneous phenomenon 78
standard paradigm of reality 109
Steve's story 62
streetlight interference 86–87, 144
suggestibility 84–85, 95
Sumatra poltergeist case 103, 105
superposition 106
synchronicity 153

Tedford case 12, 104–105, 111
Tegmark, Max 108–109
teleportation 97, 100–107, 124, 141–143
temporal lobe epilepsy 91, 146

Index

Thalbourne, Michael 83, 125–126, 154, 156, 163
Theosophy 135, 137, 140, 143, 151
Tilley, Robb 127
Tokyo Taured 110, 114, 118
transhumanation 154
Trish's story 124–126, 142–144, 158
Tucker the dog story 4

ultraterrestrials 138–139
unidentified flying objects 79, 118, 138

Valdes case 111
Vallée, Jacques 1, 158–159
vibrational state (of molecules) 137–140, 143
von Neumann chain 161

Wentz, Walter Evans 132
West, Donald 81
wormholes 108, 117, 122

zero point energy 151

www.ingramcontent.com/pod-product-compliance
Ingram Content Group UK Ltd.
Pitfield, Milton Keynes, MK11 3LW, UK
UKHW042014140426
5217IPUK00015B/1158